Governing and Governance in France

As a leading European nation with a particular state tradition and historical legacy, France has long fascinated foreign observers. In recent decades, the 'orthodox model' of French politics and policy-making has been challenged by powerful forces of globalisation, Europeanisation, decentralisation, administrative reform and changing patterns of state–society relations. In this compelling examination of French politics since the 1970s, Alistair Cole discusses these key challenges and identifies the key drivers of change. He argues that French-style governance is an untidy affair, rather than a neatly ordered and organised hierarchy, and that, though changes in France are comparable to those in other European Union countries, its governance is mediated by domestic institutions, interests and ideas. The pressures facing France are viewed through nationally specific lenses and mediated in ways that ensure that the French polity retains distinctive characteristics.

ALISTAIR COLE is Professor of European Politics in the Politics Department of the School of European Studies, Cardiff University and one of the UK's leading scholars of French politics.

Governing and Governance in France

ALISTAIR COLE

 CAMBRIDGE
UNIVERSITY PRESS

CAMBRIDGE UNIVERSITY PRESS
Cambridge, New York, Melbourne, Madrid, Cape Town, Singapore, São Paulo, Delhi

Cambridge University Press
The Edinburgh Building, Cambridge CB2 8RU, UK

Published in the United States of America by Cambridge University Press, New York

www.cambridge.org
Information on this title: www.cambridge.org/9780521608312

First published 2008

Printed in the United Kingdom at the University Press, Cambridge

A catalogue record for this publication is available from the British Library

Library of Congress Cataloguing in Publication data

Cole, Alistair, 1959–
Governing and governance in France/Alistair Cole.
p.   cm.
Includes bibliographical references and index.
ISBN 978-0-521-84583-0 (hardback)
ISBN 978-0-521-60831-2 (pbk.)
1. France–Politics and government–1958–.   I. Title.
JN2597.C64   2008
320.944–dc22
2008014965

ISBN 978-0-521-84583-0 hardback
ISBN 978-0-521-60831-2 paperback

Contents

List of tables		*page* vi
Preface		vii
List of abbreviations		x
1	Governing France	1
2	Reforming the state	26
3	Decentralisation and local governance	52
4	Europeanisation	87
5	State capacity and public policy	114
6	State–society relations	138
7	Making sense of the state	168
8	Governing and governance in France	195
Bibliography		214
Index		239

Tables

3.1 Sub-national authorities in mainland France   *page* 57
3.2 The 'Moreno' identity scale in Brittany (n. 1,007)   79
3.3 Institutional preferences in Brittany   80
3.4 Logistic regression estimates for Brittany   82
6.1 Lille's economic policy network: selected centrality
      scores (top 10 by degree)   150
6.2 Rennes' economic policy network: selected centrality
      scores (top 10 by degree)   151

Preface

As a leading European nation with a particular state tradition and historical legacy, France has long fascinated observers. The title of this book is *Governing and Governance in France*. Such a title presupposes that the study of single countries is a legitimate, indeed central dimension of the study of European politics. Some comparativists would contest this claim (Dogan and Pelassy 1990). There are a number of objections levelled against single-country studies. Claims made on the basis of studying a single country are unlikely to be very robust. Single-country studies amass considerable detail, but interpretation of detail is likely to be deficient in the absence of either a comparative perspective or a sound theory, because there is no empirical or theoretical basis on which to draw conclusions. The 'unique' or special character of a particular country can be demonstrated only through comparing one country with others, so as to establish whether it is a deviant case. There is a danger of false universalism, of the drawing of universal generalisations from the single-country case-study. There are also hazards involved with treating countries themselves as coherent units of analysis. Reasoning in terms of overarching political cultures, policy styles or state traditions can overplay state-wide systemic effects and underplay within-country variations between the contrasting dynamics of specific policy sectors and arenas.

This book broadly accepts the logic of such criticisms, particularly the last one. The single-country case-study requires, as a minimum, a set of generically interesting research questions, and preferably a robust theoretical framework as well. There are several ways in which single-country studies can be comparative. They can compare with the past. Understanding a society in relation to its past is the critical variable in many of the new theories in political science, such as historical institutionalism (Pierson 1996, 2000). In-depth analyses of single countries offer their own form of comparisons that are less readily available to cross-national comparisons: across functional sector, or locality, for example. The governance of the welfare policy, education and economic development fields involves different actors, beliefs and sets of internal and external pressures. Most important of all, case-study analysis can form part of a broader enterprise of theoretical development (Guy-Peters 1999; Burnham, Gilland, Grant and Leyton-Henry 2004). Most theoretical innovation in political science has occurred through single case-studies, not large-scale quantitative surveys. The case-study can confirm general trends. Or it can be used to test a particularly difficult theory. This book sets out to 'test' governance in the difficult state context of France. If the central features of governance are verified in this most difficult context, then we can assume that it is robust.

The book reflects my belief in the importance of area-based research that is inductive in its methodological inspiration and assumptions, rigorously empirical and fieldwork based, yet theoretically and conceptually ambitious as well. *Governing and Governance in France* is intended to be the work that draws together the various strands of French politics, policy and society that I have engaged with over the past fifteen years. The book sets out to elucidate the creative tension between the various forces impelling France to change (for example, European integration, changing international trends, decentralisation or the internal contradictions within French society) and the various forces determined to resist change, be they in the form of state-centric institutions, well-organised professional interests, deeply ingrained ideas about society, citizenship, equality and the Republic, or the discursive registers that underpin these structures. Taking as its starting point contemporary debates about governance, the book seeks to confront general statements about the direction of European societies with the difficult case of France, whose key institutions, interests and ideas sometimes appear deeply resistant to change. The book is largely based on empirical research undertaken at various stages since 1993. Around 300 interviews were undertaken during this period across a number of projects. Interviewees are not mentioned by name and no citation can be linked to any living person. Where data are directly drawn from interviews, the organisation is named, as well as the month during which the interview was carried out. Each interview referred to in the text has been taped and transcribed.

I acknowledge the financial and logistical support of various funding agencies and academic partners that have helped to finance my research on contemporary France. I completed writing this book while serving as Vincent Wright Professor at Sciences Po, Paris in 2007. Hopefully, Vincent would have approved and I have fond memories of him. I am grateful to Sciences Po, Paris for logistical and intellectual support over the years, especially to my friend, collaborator, colleague and critic Patrick le Galès. I owe a debt of gratitude to a number of other universities and research institutes: the CRAPE in Rennes and the CERAPS in Lille notably. I thank Cardiff University for facilitating my research over a number of years, as well as my former employers at the universities of Bradford, Keele and Aston.

The Arts and Humanities Research Council generously funded a period of research leave in 2007 to allow the manuscript to be completed (AHRC grant AH/E000134/1). I am deeply indebted to AHRC for this. Most of the interviews carried out from 2004–6 were funded by a British Academy Large Research Grant (LRG-37213). The support of the British Academy was invaluable at a time when travelling to France to carry out interviews had to be very carefully planned and financed. The Economic and Social Research Council provided two grants in 2001–3 and 1994–6 that provided the bedrock for most of the work on local and regional governance (ESRC grants L219252007 and L311253047 (Peter John as principal investigator)). I thank the ESRC very warmly indeed. The Leverhulme Foundation (Rf + G/10711) and the Nuffield Foundation (SGS/LB/0278) provided grants in 1996 and 1999–2000 to allow interviews to continue in the field of educational governance. I thank them. The support of all of funding agencies was absolutely crucial. This type of grounded research can be undertaken only with the support of the Research Councils and charities.

The research has drawn upon a network of contacts in French government, politics, the administration, the media and in cultural and educational circles. I thank all of those individuals over the years who freely gave their time for interviews.

I dedicate this book to the memory of Jacques Coillet, a friend from Lille for twenty-five years who did so much to unpack the intricacies of French politics for me and who sadly died on 5 September 2007.

Abbreviations

AFITF	Agence de Financement des Infrastructures de Transport de France
AFPA	Association nationale pour la Formation Professionnelle des Adultes
AFSSA	Agence Française de Securité Sanitaire des Aliments
AII	Agence d'Innovation Industrielle
ANCS	Agence Nationale pour la Cohésion Sociale
ANR	Agence Nationale pour la Recherche
ANRU	Agence Nationale pour la Rénovation Urbaine
ARF	Association des Regions de France
ARH	Agence Régionale de l'Hospitalisation
ART	Agence de la Régulation des Télécommunications
ATTAC	Association pour la Taxation des Transactions pour l'Aide aux Citoyens
BOP	Budget Opérationnel du Programme
CAC 40	Cotation Assistée en Continu des 40 plus grosses sociétés françaises
CADA	Commission de l'Accès aux Documents Administratifs
CAP	Common Agricultural Policy
CAR	Conférences Administratives Régionales
CEVIPOF	Centre d'Étude de la Vie Politique Française
CFDT	Confédération Française Démocratique du Travail
CFTC	Confédération Française des Travailleurs Chrétiens
CGC	Confédération Générale des Cadres
CGPME	Confédération Générale des Petites et Moyennes Entreprises
CGT	Confédération Générale du Travail
CIACT	Comité Interministériel pour l'Aménagement et la Compétitivité des Territoires
CIVC	Comité Interprofessionnel des Vins de Champagne
CMU	Couverture Maladie Universelle

CNAM	Caisse Nationale Assurance Maladie
CNE	Commission Nationale d'Evaluation
CNE	Contrat Nouvelle Embauche
CNIL	Commission Nationale de l'Informatique et Liberté
CNPF	Conseil National du Patronat Français
CNPT	Chasse, Nature, Pêche, Traditions
COB	Commission des Opérations de Bourse
CPE	Contrat Premier Embauche
CSA	Conseil Supérieur de l'Audiovisuel
CSG	Contribution Sociale Généralisée
CSO	Centre pour la Sociologie des Organisations
DATAR	Délégation à l'Aménagement du Territoire et à l'Action Régionale
DDE	Direction Départementale de l'Équipement
DGCP	Direction Générale de la Comptabilité Publique
DGI	Direction Générale des Impôts
DIACT	Délégation Interministérielle à l'Action et à la Compétitivité du Territoire
DST	Direction de la Sureté du Territoire
EADS	European Aeronautic Defence and Space Company
ECB	European Central Bank
ECHR	European Court of Human Rights
ECJ	European Court of Justice
ECOFIN	Economic and Financial Council
EDF-GDF	Electricité de France – Gaz de France
EMU	Economic and Monetary Union
ENA	École Nationale d'Administration
EPCI	Établissement Public de Coopération Intercommunale
EPIC	Établissement Public Industriel et Commercial
EPR	Établissement Public Régional
EPSC	Établissement Public Scientifique et Culturel
EU	European Union
FCPE	Fédération des Conseils de Parents d'Élèves
FEN	Fédération de l'Éducation Nationale
FN	Front National
FNSEA	Fédération Nationale des Syndicats et Exploitants Agricoles
FO	Force Ouvrière

FTEs	Full-time equivalent jobs
GATT	General Agreement on Trade and Tariffs
GDP	Gross Domestic Product
GIP	Groupement d'Interet Public
GSP	Growth and Stability Pact
IGAEN	Inspection Générale de l'Administration de l'Éducation Nationale
IGAS	Inspection Générale des Affaires Sociales
IGEN	Inspection Générale de l'Éducation Nationale
IGPN	Inspection Générale de la Police Nationale
INAO	Institut National des Appellations d'Origine
JAC	Jeunesse Agricole Chrétienne
LCR	Ligue Communiste Révolutionnaire
LOLF	Loi Organique relative aux Lois de Finance
MBA	Master of Business Administration
MEDEF	Mouvement des Entreprises de France
MPF	Mouvement pour la France
MRC	Mouvement Républicain et Citoyen
NHS	National Health Service
NPM	New Public Management
NUTS	Nomenclature des Unités Territoriales Statistiques
NYSE	New York Stock Exchange
OMC	Open Method of Coordination
OPCA	Organismes Paritaires de Collecte Agrée
PCF	Parti Communiste Français
PEEP	Parents d'Élèves de l'Enseignement Public
PRDF	Plan Régional du Développement et de la Formation des Jeunes
PS	Parti Socialiste
QMV	Qualified Majority Voting
RATP	Régie Autonome des Transports Parisiens
RG	Renseignements Généraux
RMA	Revenu Minimum d'Activité
RMI	Revenu Minimum d'Insertion
RPR	Rassemblement Pour la République
SGAE	Secrétariat Général des Affaires Européennes
SGAR	Secrétariat Général pour l'Action Régionale
SIVOM	Syndicat Intercommunal à Vocation Multiple

SIVU	Syndicat Intercommunal à Vocation Unique
SNCF	Société Nationale des Chemins de fer Français
SNES	Syndicat National des Enseignements de Second degré
STS	Section Technique Spécialisée
SUD	Solidaires, Unitaires et Démocratiques
TOS	Personnels Techniques, Ouvriers et de Service
UDB	Union Démocratique Bretonne
UMP	Union pour une Majorité Populaire
UNICE	Union des Industries de la Communauté Européenne
UNPI	Union Nationale de la Propriété Immobilière
UPA	Union Professionnelle des Artisans
WTO	World Trade Organization
ZEP	Zone d'Éducation Prioritaire

1 | Governing France

The title of this book is *Governing and Governance in France*. If modern day France can be geographically located in a precise manner, there is no easy agreement about the concepts of governing, government or governance. Some basic definitions assist conceptual and empirical clarity. For French political scientist Leca (1996) *governing* 'is a matter of taking decisions, resolving conflicts, producing public goods, coordinating private behaviour, regulating markets, organising elections, distributing resources, determining spending'. Governing is the core business of *government*, which claims to speak with an authoritative voice and to embody a superior legitimacy to other interests or forces in society. For Le Galès (2002: 17) government 'refers to structures, actors, processes and outputs', while *governance* 'relates to all the institutions, networks, directives, regulations, norms, political and social usages, public and private actors that contribute to the stability of a society...'. In this basic framework, governance represents new forms of coordination – or of governing – that go beyond the traditional confines of government. But what is government and how does it exemplify itself in the 'strong state' of France?

Governing as government

In the definition given by Le Galès, the four key features of government were identified as structures, actors, processes and outputs. Though there are semantic difficulties with these terms, a credible definition of government must integrate an understanding of each of them. We would add a fifth variable: namely institutions, a central component that provides meaning between structures and actors.

Structures and institutions

The concept of structure is an essentially contested one. Some research traditions, such as constructivism, reject its existence altogether, or

1

at least challenge the existence of structure as a separate category from agency (Christiansen 2001; Rosamond 2001; Hay and Rosamond 2002). Structure is what actors make of it and portray it to be. Most research traditions accept some form of structuralism, even those such as discourse analysis that are rooted in the power of language and symbols. In its strongest sense, structure signifies deep meta-level variables that determine (or at least strongly influence) the shape of contemporary polities and politics. The most obvious causal variables would include, *inter alia*, the underlying socio-economic system and social class relationships, non-economic cleavages (religion, territory, ethnic identity), the weight of key historical junctures and events and the persistence of competing belief systems. Identifying these macro-structural variables does not necessarily mean predicting any rela-tionship between them or indicating the likely direction of any change. Meta-narratives can provide a rich context for understanding modern French government, but they are expressed at a very high level of generality.[1]

Middle-range institutional analysis allows more scope for empirical investigation than structural meta-narratives. In the rich but rather inconsistent new institutionalist tradition, institutions are understood either as organisations, as beliefs, as history, as human action, as forms of appropriate behaviour, or as some combination of these (Hall and Taylor 1996; Guy-Peters 1999). In the version popularised by March and Olsen (1989), new institutionalism stresses the relative autonomy of political institutions. Institutions are neither a mirror of society (the behavioural critique), nor merely the site for individual strategies (as in the rational actor paradigm). Institutions give meaning to interactions and provide the context within which interactions take place. For the purposes of describing the model of government, we

---

[1] Several competing, credible narratives can account for deep structural features of the French polity. Economic meta-narratives focus on the conformity of the political system with the underlying economic structure. Ideational meta-narratives identify deep ideological cleavages that came to a head at critical junctures, such as the ideological rivalry between the Catholic Church and the Republic throughout the nineteenth century (Hazareesingh 1994). Other meta-narratives have emphasised the importance of spatial and geographical variables. Rokkan and Urwin (1982), for example, identified three types of European state: the strong empire-nations of the Atlantic west; the economically weaker states of the eastern plains; and the states of imperial central Europe, unified only in the nineteenth century (Flora, Kuhnle and Urwin 1999).

interpret institutions as intermediary phenomena between structures and actors. Institutions are understood here in their original form as legal entities vested with formal competencies and a high degree of organisational coherence (implying shared beliefs and understandings of appropriateness). Institutional continuities in France are well exemplified by the importance of constants such as the professional bureaucracy and the system of public law, two examples that are now considered.

The study of the development of the professional bureaucracy is usually linked with the German sociologist Max Weber. For Weber, the development of the bureaucratic state was a general feature of capitalist development, with an impartial state essential to provide legal security for contracts. The role of the bureaucracy is to ensure that rules are respected and that predictability, regularity and conformity to uniform standards are achieved. In the case of France, the bureaucracy came into existence before capitalist take-off. French bureaucracy has its origins in the Napoleonic model of administration carefully crafted at the beginning of the nineteenth century. Under Napoleon, the bureaucracy was viewed as a positive force that would embody the power and legitimacy of the French state and the general interest of the nation as a whole (Stevens 2003). These images have been remarkably persistent. Senior French civil servants view themselves as agents of state power who derive their legitimacy from defending an impartial and legalistic conception of state intervention against particularistic interests (Rouban 1995). Middle-ranking civil servants are, if anything, even more attached to the codes and written procedures that secure their social and professional status (Jones 2003). Though Weber emphasised the superiority of the bureaucratic mode of organisation over those based on tradition and charisma, the influential French organisational sociology school has highlighted the sub-optimal performance of the French bureaucracy as a result of vicious circles (Crozier 1963), loyalty to technical and administrative *corps* (Friedberg 1993) and the existence of zones of uncertainty within organisations (Crozier and Friedberg 1977).

Another middle-level institution is the system of public (administrative) law. Until the 1870s, the French legal system developed in a manner consistent with the overarching liberal economic framework, based on limited state functions, the prevalence of private contracts and detailed legal codification (in the Napoleonic code). A separate branch of administrative law developed from the 1870s, founded upon the legal doctrine of the state as a public servant (Chevallier 2003b). Public law theory emerged to regulate the activities of an increasingly interventionist state in the late nineteenth century. Public law rests on the key principle that the state should be treated differently from private citizens, because it is both vested with public authority and delivers public services. Even the most conservative of public lawyers have had to accept the calling into question of the Weberian model of government, based on authority, hierarchy and a powerful bureaucracy.

Institutions and actors

'Government' signifies the political direction of the state machinery, hence the role of political leadership and the chief political offices. Early observers of the French Fifth Republic emphasised the strength of executive-dominated governments, were fascinated by the office of the presidency, yet worried that there were relatively weak political and judicial counterweights to a powerful executive authority (Williams 1964, 1969; Wright 1978). The hyper-presidentialist narratives of the first two decades of the Fifth Republic gave way during the next two decades to more balanced accounts, the centrality of the presidency having been challenged by repeated episodes of 'cohabitation', variable configurations within the core executive and changing leadership styles in an age of closer European integration (Hayward and Wright 2002). The first few months of Nicolas Sarkozy's presidency appeared to renew earlier presidential traditions and to question the utility of preserving a twin-headed executive, a theme developed in Chapter 7.

Long before political scientists set about theorising the nature of institutionalism, there was a strong tradition of empirical institutionalism in France. Empirical institutionalism focuses upon the role of formal rules in determining outcomes, shaping actor strategies and explaining performance. This trend is perhaps best typified by Maurice Duverger, whose laws about the role of electoral systems in shaping party systems sparked a vigorous debate about the relative importance of institutional and sociological variables in electoral sociology (Duverger 1964, 1986; Benoit 2006). Duverger's subsequent conceptualisation of the Fifth Republic as a semi-presidential system similarly excited a generation of scholars interested in comparative institutional design, and opened new comparative perspectives for measuring institutional influences (Elgie 1999). The focus of such work has been on formal political offices (presidents and prime ministers, legislatures, courts), the rules of the game (electoral systems) or institutional configurations (the semi-presidential model), with a strong methodological belief that institutional arrangements matter. Writers in the empirical institutionalist tradition have performed valuable work by studying key political offices, such as the president (Hayward 1993), the prime minister (Elgie 1993), the parliament (Williams 1969; P. Smith 2006), the Constitutional Council (Stone 1992), the prefects (Machin 1976) or local government (Ashford 1982). While acknowledging this body of work, formal descriptions of political institutions will not be a central feature of this book, except in so far as they directly relate to the arguments underpinning France's governance. Rather than specific political institutions, we reason in terms of the state, statist traditions and challenges to these traditions.

Government is also the product of actors operating in more or less strategically opportune ways. If political leadership has been understudied and specified, the same conclusion is not valid for the elites at the heart of the governmental machine. The French state tradition has been characterised by a close interpenetration of political, administrative and economic actors, encouraged by modes of elite selection. In the orthodox model, the state tradition in France was best exemplified by the role of the *grands corps*. The *corps* are bodies without obvious parallels in the British or American contexts. Rather than designating an institution or a government department as such, the term is used to describe the different state grades to which all civil servants must belong. In traditional representations of French elitism, members of the *grands corps* perform a disproportionately important role. In the orthodox model, the key technical body was the Highways and Bridges *corps* (*Ponts et Chaussés*); Crozier and Friedberg (1977), Friedberg (1974) and Thœnig (1973) all provide detailed accounts of the influence of the role of the *Ponts et Chaussés* in determining technical policy choices. In addition to this technical *corps* there are the three leading administrative *grands corps*, all concerned with controlling and checking the work of other civil servants. The Council of State lies at the apex of France's system of public law. The Financial Inspectorate undertakes financial inspections of government departments and other public administrations. The Court of Accounts publishes annual reports on the uses (and especially abuses) of expenditure by organisations and programmes funded from the public purse.[2] Whether the *corps* have been able to resist exogenous and endogenous pressures is a measure of their ability to adapt strategically to changing circumstances: the Council of State has been much more successful than the Highways and Bridges *corps* in this respect.

Even relatively straightforward descriptions of government usually allow for the delivery, administration and regulation of some public services by non-governmental actors, such as professional associations in the legal and health sectors. More formalised neo-corporatist models include the 'social partners' as co-producers of public policy: organised labour, business and professional interests are fully integrated into the decision-making machinery of most continental European welfare states. Political party actors are sometimes understood as governmental actors, sometimes not. In practice, rigid and strict distinctions between public administration and party politics are unrealistic. The coexistence of party politics and administration is a routine feature of every French government department, where the minister's *cabinet* is in part appointed on partisan grounds, a process that is understood (but resented) by the permanent career civil servants. Moreover, the top 300 or so civil service posts are political appointments, decided in the Council of Ministers.

Bézès (2006) identifies a number of powerful structural characteristics of the French state that make coordination between these actors difficult. These include the strength of departmental traditions, the weakness of the office of prime minister faced with well-entrenched ministers, the delivery of most governmental services either by local authorities or through the complex social security system, the tradition of competition between rival *corps* within the state and the disaggregating effects of party politics. These centrifugal pressures are more than a match for those whose task it is to coordinate the activity of government.

---

[2] Interview, Court of Accounts, July 2004. Though it enjoys great prestige, the finite range of sanctions it possesses limits its effectiveness (as does rivalry with the Financial Inspectorate).

Process: *the case of coordination*

Formal descriptions of governmental actors in terms of their constitutional roles and responsibilities rarely capture the behavioural
complexity at the heart of government. On the other hand, powerful
parts of the governmental machine derive their legitimacy from the
rigorous respecting of formal rules and procedures. Monitoring the
processes of government and their correct implementation provides a
powerful source of legitimacy for key institutions at the heart of
government, the Council of State, the Constitutional Council and the
General Secretariat of the government being the most important.

In a formal sense, political coordination is the province of the
French prime minister and governmental coordination is carried out
by the General Secretariat of the government formally attached to
the prime minister's office (Chenot 1986).[3] But even full mastery of
bureaucratic circuits can provide only a limited form of administrative
coordination. There are several rival claims for the function of *political* coordination. The prime minister is formally charged with political coordination, but the effectiveness of such coordination is highly
contingent, depending upon the actors in question, the prestige of the
premier, the support of public opinion, the strength of other ministers
and, especially, the view of his own role adopted by the president
himself. The Élysée palace (the home of the president) offers a form of
macro-coordination and political leadership, with some presidents
(Giscard d'Estaing, Mitterrand, Sarkozy) reserving for themselves the
arbitration of the most divisive issues and ensuring that their staffs
were present at all key interministerial meetings. The influence of the
presidential staff has been stronger at some times in recent French
history than at others. Under President Sarkozy, the General Secretary
of the Élysée, Claude Guéant, adopted a far more active profile than
any of his predecessors.

Legal and administrative coordination is – in theory – ensured by
the Council of State. More than any other institution, the Council of
State represents the centrality of the law in the French state tradition
(Latour 2004). In textbook descriptions, the Council of State performs
two distinctive, arguably conflicting roles:[4] as a legal advisor to the

---

[3] Interview, General Secretariat of the Government, August 2006.
[4] Interviews, Council of State, January, April and May 2006.

government of the day and as the highest administrative court in the land. These roles are less separate than often described. The Council's legal advice to the government in practice has a binding character which is drawn from its own jurisprudence as the highest administrative court in the land (Del Prete 2004). Before French government bills (and decrees) are considered in the Council of Ministers or the National Assembly, they must be submitted to the Council of State for an appreciation of their legality and administrative feasibility. One key complaint voiced in interviews concerned legislative inflation. There are far too many laws, regulations and directives, and they are poorly drafted.[5]

Through its use of case law, the Council of State has adopted a standard-setting role. Rather like the Constitutional Council, the Council of State edicts 'general principles of law', which go beyond the provisions of any particular legislative act or decree. The effect of this case law is to enshrine a system of judicial review. The Council of State can not only strike down government bills (as in 2004 over a proposed reform to the electoral system for the regional elections), but has also claimed the right to decide the conditions under which a bill will or will not be declared constitutional. Such empire-building is viewed with distaste from within the Constitutional Council,[6] whose own province is that of constitutional conformity (Stone 1992). The Constitutional Council considers all organic laws (those relating to the working of the constitution), as well as those ordinary laws referred to it by the opposition parties. In practice, around one-half of major bills will be referred to the Council. The Council must make known its decisions on a bill within one month of being asked. In the case of the budget, the Council has 'eight days, for over one million documents'.[7] Initially dismissed as an institutional lightweight, the Council has revealed its real political muscle since the early 1980s, constraining governments, among other decisions, to review nationalisation programmes (1982), revise electoral reforms (1986, 2004), to reject far-reaching reforms in Corsica (2002) and to change the constitution to permit ratification of the EU treaties (1992, 1997, 2005). According to one insider, however, there has been a tendency to exaggerate the

[5] Interview, Council of State, January 2006, May 2006.
[6] Interview, Constitutional Council, July 2006.
[7] Interview, Constitutional Council, June 2002.

influence of the Constitutional Council. Governments can change the constitution to get their way.[8] Above all, the Council has suffered from the growing influence of the Council of State in constitutional affairs and the loss of national influence to the European Court of Justice in matters of EU competition policy and to the European Court of Human Rights in issues of citizenship.[9]

Outputs

If 'government' involves ruling or governing something, then France is a heavily governed society. Central government is involved in the direct delivery of some public services. It closely supervises the provision of social security and the operation of local government. It has expanded its remit more in France than in many other countries and has to manage a record level of public debt as a consequence.

The nineteenth century was a period of limited government, state activity being confined for most of the century to the core functions of law and order, security, foreign policy and taxation. By the end of the nineteenth century, the role of government had expanded to include the provision of universal primary education, road-building and postal services in its remit, these public services usually being administered at a local level. The trend to more interventionist governments was due in part to the activism of local councils, strengthened by the 1884 Municipal Reform Act. Communes took over a range of activities from as early as 1905 (slaughter houses) and 1913 (local railways) (Chevallier 2003b). In the interwar period, local councils were charged with delivery of a range of local public services, such as waste management, water, urban transport, heating, funeral parlours and fire-fighting (Lorrain 1991, 1993). In most cases, management of these services was delegated from central to local government and from local government to private service providers (Gaudin 2002). Thus, the French version of the emerging dual state combined considerable local diversity, municipal activism and the delegation of public service delivery to private operators.

---

[8] On 19 February 2007, for example, three constitutional amendments were approved on the same day by the two houses of the French parliament sitting together as Congress at Versailles.

[9] Interview, Constitutional Council, July 2006.

The development of a more uniform mode of service delivery is a feature of the post-war period. After 1945, government became more directly involved in delivering economic public services and expanded its activity into the domain of public services, social protection, public health and housing. Though new public services were introduced by central government, they were often delivered by local government, through the local branches of social partnership agencies or by the field services of central government departments. In the decades preceding decentralisation, local authorities and/or state field services assumed increasing responsibilities for secondary education, social assistance, housing and provision for the handicapped, as well as responsibilities for care of the elderly and child protection. Cultural services also expanded considerably in the post-1945 period (Thuriot 2004). The state takes seriously its responsibility for protecting France's cultural patrimony – museums, libraries, historical monuments and archives – a competence it has jealously safeguarded, notwithstanding a wave of decentralisation reforms. In the post-1945 period, the state also increased its intervention in research and higher education, training, youth and sports, tourism, leisure and environmental protection, the delivery of most of these services involving a multi-organisational operational network. One of the paradoxes of the debates about governance is that the capacity of the state has been challenged at the same time as government, understood in its broadest sense, has never performed so many functions.[10]

In this overview, the concept of government covers an array of different meanings. In the model of governing as government, its traditional defenders consider the state as a moral authority, above specific interests in society. Reduced to its core, government in France rests upon: the legitimate use of force; a tradition of strong central authority which gives direction to other public and private actors; a doctrine of undivided political sovereignty (republicanism); a clearly affirmed territorial hierarchy; established constitutional rules and a hierarchy of legal orders; the development of a powerful bureaucracy, combined with a degree of multi-organisational flexibility in terms of service delivery. The public law approach continues to defend government as providing an overarching normative framework and a monopoly use of force.

---

[10] The proportion of state funding as a proportion of GDP has risen from around 10 per cent in 1914, to 30 per cent in 1939, to around 45–50 per cent today.

Underpinning the model of the sovereign government there is only one source of power and authority. The popularity of governance is that it openly challenges this model. All definitions of governance start from the weakening of older forms of vertical statist regulation. As France is typically portrayed as the ideal type of a European country with an interventionist state tradition, it provides an excellent empirical terrain for testing some of the claims of governance. Understanding the modern French polity also involves comprehending the limits of governance and reaffirming the resistance to governance from embedded institutions, ideas and interests.

Forces and dimensions of governance

Studying governance is one way of exploring the contemporary transformation of the state. The fundamental ambiguity of governance has helped to explain its success, as it can be varied to suit contrasting social and intellectual milieux and academic disciplines. Governance contains within it potentially contradictory causal narratives about the reshaping of the state. It can apply to different levels and scales of analysis (territorial and functional) and across variable temporal and spatial dimensions. It constructs imaginary boundaries between public and private and contains within it implicit theories of the public space. Discussing these controversies is an indispensable preliminary to developing a framework of analysis that is sufficiently robust to withstand the test of operationalisation. First, however, the rise of the theme of governance must be placed in its temporal context.

Since the late 1970s, policy analysts have focused upon the difficulties of governing complex societies (for example Richardson and Jordan 1979). The governance approach developed as a critique of the failings of traditional government, unable to cope with policy overload and economic crisis. Governance has sometimes dressed itself in prescriptive clothing, most notably in relation to the false panacea of 'good governance'.[11] But fundamentally governance became

---

[11] For international financial organisations such as the International Monetary Fund or the World Bank, 'good governance' refers to specific practices of corporate management, accountability and transparency, and to the importance of international benchmarking and standard-setting. 'Governance' has become embraced as a standard to measure performance by developing states, typically in terms of markets and neo-liberal adjustment.

popular in Germany, the Netherlands, the United Kingdom and France as part of a broader reflection on the *governability* of modern complex societies. Why are modern societies so difficult to govern? What problems of coordination do they face? What dynamics underpin their operation and how best can these be understood and compared? There is no fundamental agreement on the answers to these questions. In one account the notion of governability raises the issue of the contradictory nature of the interests in play, the different strategies of social groups and the overloading of the local and national state with demands (Rangeon 1996). Writing in a different tradition, Marin and Mayntz (1991) considered that governance implies agreement among partners.

If modern governments can influence political and policy outcomes, they are less capable than before of engaging in command and control techniques. The metaphor of governance as steering draws obvious inspiration from older, less finite ideas of *pilotage*, or the direction of public affairs (Mayntz 1991; Kickert 1997). Steering can take several forms. In a proactive sense, steering involves attempts to mobilise policy networks and build new partnerships to connect central government, public authorities and civil society. But steering can also take the form of reducing the scope of central government activity, by decentralising difficult decisions, by creating new administrative agencies or policy instruments. In short, governing systems across Europe have tried to reduce the need for governing by deregulation, privatisation and administrative reform (Kooiman 2003). All governments have been confronted with a weakening capacity to steer society by proposing solutions to the problems they have identified. Modern states of very different traditions have felt the need to develop new policy instruments and management philosophies to meet these challenges (Lascoumes and Le Galès 2004).

Causal narratives around the state

Reduced to its core, governance challenges the state-centric construction of political authority that reifies the state as embodying a superior legitimacy to non-state actors. Governance narratives recognise complexity, contingency and diversity far more than traditional politico-administrative models, which insisted upon the uniform application of rules. From a legal perspective, the state has lost its centrality and is now embedded in a complex system of multiple legal orders. The state is no longer an adequate frame for understanding the world; in the opinion of one analyst 'the great narrative of the Sovereign state embodying the general interest is less and less credible' (Caillose 2007: 47). Though the state remains a key player, it has everywhere been undergoing a process of restructuring.

Governance can support contrasting causal narratives around the state. In its strongest interpretation, it is understood as an overarching approach to explaining policy change, with the French case fundamentally no different from that of any other European country (Loughlin 2004). At the heart of the 'strong governance' argument is the claim that there has been a decentring of political power. The state is no longer at the centre of international relations. It is no longer in command of the economy. It is no longer at the centre of public administration and public policy (Gaudin 2002). Contemporary states are called into question in virtually all of their spheres of activity. The state is being fundamentally transformed because it is no longer able to perform its internal (welfare) and external (defence) functions and can no longer manage its own institutions and territorial relationships. In international relations, the new global governance paradigm has steadily gained ground (Rosenau 1992). The international system has escaped the control of states. International organisations such as the United Nations, the World Bank, the International Monetary Fund or the World Trade Organization are assuming a much more important role. Non-governmental organisations and charities are treated as equal stakeholders with governments in various international fora (Kjaer 2004). Within the European context, European integration has removed many competencies from the central state level, even in areas of core sovereignty such as monetary policy and defence. Most accounts now emphasise the loss of functional autonomy for the state. European integration threatens the state because it challenges the mystique of sovereignty (Börzel 2002; Bache and Flinders 2004). European integration also undermines the normative supremacy of states, which can no longer claim a monopoly of the allocation of values. The role of bodies such as the Council of Europe and the European Court of Human Rights is to challenge state-bound values. States no longer occupy the moral high ground, and new actors, such as international organisations, voluntary associations and sub-state authorities, have stepped into the breach (Keating 1998).

The strongest version of the 'hollow state' argument comes from political economists. From a political economy approach, Jessop (2007) identifies a transition from the Keynesian welfare state to the Schumpeterian workfare state as the principal consequence of the shift to a post-Fordist economy since the 1970s. As conceptualised by Jessop, the Keynesian welfare state is an ideal type with the following characteristics: the production of full employment in relatively closed national economies, the promotion of mass consumption, the provision of collective goods to citizens, the intervention of the national state in economic management to compensate for the failures of the market. The Schumpeterian workfare state is of a different nature. Its function is to support the market and to create the conditions for innovation and enterprise in relatively open and competitive economies. The Schumpeterian workfare state sets out to bring down labour costs and to enhance flexibility in the economy. The core decisions in economic policy are no longer taken at a national level, but are international or global in nature. The state is unable to deal effectively with the global or local demands that this new imagined economy requires. Weakened at the core of its capacity, the state is forced to imagine new solutions for governing national societies, most notably through new forms of central steering that involve the state sharing responsibilities with non-state partners in policy networks. Though state capacity has weakened, the national state remains the level of regulation for social policy, hence it has to imagine innovative responses (Levy 2006).

The political economy approach can also be used to describe endogenous changes within capitalist societies. In some accounts the loss of state centrality has been accompanied by a paradigm shift from welfare state to neo-liberalism. The welfare state model is depicted as the final stage of organised modernity by Loughlin (2004: 13), a state based on 'centralisation, standardisation, and bureaucratisation'. During the prolonged post-war period of welfare state hegemony, there was a basic belief about the role of state, the market and civil society and about their relationship to each other. During this period, government was top-down, hierarchical and technocratic, and the state was the dominant actor in mediating social and territorial relationships. In the early 1980s, there was a paradigm shift, with the welfare model replaced by a dominant neo-liberal paradigm. In this neo-liberal governance paradigm, the market is dominant and market approaches have penetrated public administration. These tendencies have been most fully expressed in the UK, US and other Anglo-Saxon countries, such as New Zealand (Schmidt 2002), but all advanced liberal democracies have espoused some form of neo-liberalism. This view is similar to that of Muller (1990b, 1992) or Jobert (1994), for whom the social market economy was replaced by a neo-liberal paradigm in the mid-1980s.

There are comparable trends across European countries. Under the impact of Europeanisation and the challenges of the international political economy, European states have voluntarily pooled sovereignty in international organisations and increasingly converged their rules and institutions to conform to a common standard (Mény 1993). The importance of benchmarking and ideas of best practice is propagated by the EU, as well as national governments. There are various converging forces pushing for change. The economic changes of globalisation have challenged the state in multiple ways. At the international and European levels, new structures of binding rules and institutions have promoted trans-national unity. For all this, it is unlikely that there is a single phenomenon of governance that is producing policy and polity convergence across the developed world. In practice, there is considerable variation between national economic and welfare traditions, captured well by the 'varieties of capitalism' literature, which identifies statist, neo-liberal and corporatist modes of coordination, corresponding to the French, Anglo-Saxon and German traditions (Hall and Soskice 2001; Schmidt 2002).

Actors and agents

At the heart of all governance analyses is a process of negotiation between a plurality of governing actors that go beyond those of the central state or even the public sector. Some national traditions are more explicit than others about this multi-actor dimension of governance. According to the main UK school, governance refers to the role of self-governing networks of public and private actors that steer the main policy sectors (Rhodes 1996, 1997). In the rich Dutch tradition, governance signifies a method of decision-making based on repeated interactions between actors, responding to issues of complexity by cooperation (Kooiman 1993, 2003). This version of governance is inspired by the difficulty that Dutch governments have had in governing a society divided into Catholic, Protestant and secular pillars and marked by a specific urban geography dominated by large cities. Likewise, in the main German tradition, governance signifies the method of macro-coordination between markets (the economy), hierarchies (the state) and networks (civil society), to some extent reformulating the corporatist structures and actors of German society (Mayntz 1991, 1993). The role specifically accorded to economic actors varies in these accounts, which none the less all identify multi-actorness as a core feature of governance. In the specific French context, the public law legal tradition is challenged by the relativity of the notions of public and private. In practice, private actors, vested with no specific legal authority or elective mandate, are involved at all levels in the production of public policies. Moreover, private actors (typically firms or associations) can be vested with a 'public service' mission, and offered the guarantees that public law provides for the delivery of such services.

Governance seeks to understand interactions, as well as to describe an ever-larger number of actors with a stake in policy. Governance poses the question of coordination. It signifies the emergence of new forms of political and policy coordination that stem from the failings of traditional government, from its inability to steer in accordance with overarching goals. Sociological accounts, especially those of Le Galès (1995, 1999, 2002, 2008), emphasise above all the role of governance as coordination ('regulation') and exchange between political, social and economic spheres. Regulation refers to relatively stable relations between actors and social groups, who exchange resources and who are brought together in institutional relationships that are bound by rules and norms (Commaille and Jobert 1999). The French regulation school describes distinct modes of coordination between actors, the five ideal types being the market (competition), the firm (hierarchy), the state (constraint), the community (solidarity) and social partnership (negotiation). To describe a mode of governance of a place or a policy sector, different combinations of these ideal types are used. Governing requires coordination, but modes of coordination vary across sector, space and level.

Levels

In most accounts, there has been a denationalisation of the territorial domination of the state and a relativisation of public power at various levels (Gaudin 2002). State forms and functions have changed. In spite of the European Union's adoption of subsidiarity as an organising principle, state tasks can no longer neatly be attributed to one layer of government above another (John 2001). It is more difficult to perceive of the state as a centre, if decision-making becomes more multi-layered. Multi-level analysis is distinct from governance, though the two approaches were famously unified in the multi-level governance metaphor. As applied to the European Union, multi-level governance describes new forms of interaction between the European Commission and regional governments, specifically in relation to EU structural funds (Hooghe and Marks 2001). Initially developed by Marks, this approach viewed the European policy process as 'a system of continuous negotiation among nested governments at several territorial tiers' (Marks 1993: 392). In so far as this literature focused mainly on interactions between the European Commission and regional authorities (rather than private or associative actors), however, it is more accurate to label it as multi-level government. This limitation notwithstanding, the multi-level governance approach captured new forms of networks that bypassed the member-states, the principles upon which the legitimacy of the Union is theoretically founded. Multi-level governance calls into question the traditional approach towards the study of government. The emphasis is much less on structures or rules, much more on actors, strategy and coalition-building. Beyond its dealings with local and regional authorities, the European Commission has integrated the logic of governance into its own strategic analysis. In its 2001 White Paper on governance, the European Commission embraced the theme of governance enthusiastically as a means of associating non-state players – professional and business actors in particular – with the elaboration of EU policy, as well as providing a coherent cadre for reforming the European civil service.

The multi-level metaphor can also be applied within the confines of the nation-state. This is most obviously the case in a federal state such as Germany, where multi-level negotiation and bargaining between levels of government is essential (Sharpf 1997; Jeffery 2000). The use of the multi-level metaphor is also pertinent in states where there is no federal tradition, as in France. Though citizens continue to focus their attention on the state as guarantor of unity, the French state no longer has the capacity to identify costly and problematic areas of policy delivery alone. At its most strategic, the modern regulatory state coordinates public provision among a variety of service providers and levels of public administration. It no longer directly delivers services. At the meso-level, decentralisation has transformed the state (Chapter 3). At the micro-level, the local official is an interlocutor in the provision of services, rather than an official embodying the authority of the state.

Sectors and beyond sector

Rarely does the ontologically plural nature of governance appear more clearly than in relation to the concept of sector. UK theorists such as Rhodes (1997) link governance to the self-organising networks that govern distinct policy sectors such as education, economic development, health, transport or agriculture. These sectors each contain specific actor constellations and are inhabited by organisations that are dependent upon each other. In this account, governance is closely linked to the operation of policy sectors and to the importance of the professional expertise therein. From this perspective, the dynamics in economic development, welfare or education are contingent upon the structural qualities of the sectors concerned, or, in a weaker definition, upon the structural context within which games are played or prevailing ideas or discursive registers diffused.

The importance of sectoral forms of governance is evidenced in multi-national structures such as the European Union. The European policy process is highly sectoralised, with close linkages between the general directorates of the European Commission, the sectoral meetings of the Council of Ministers and the specialised professional bodies containing recognised expertise in any given field (Beech 2005). The logic of these exchanges is broadly functional. Complex societies produce more autonomy for groups and private interests that can resist attempts to steer from central governors. The EU is, arguably, the only level where functional policies relevant to the operation of the Single Market can be regulated. But the EU lacks the qualities of authoritative coordination and arbitration of a nation-state vested with legitimacy to coordinate complex activities.

Other accounts draw very different conclusions about the pertinence of sector as a guide to contemporary governance. Fine-grained studies of localities and regions, for example, emphasise the cross-sectoral nature of much contemporary governance. The territorial forms of governance uncovered by Pasquier, Simoulin and Weisbein (2007) are characterised by a pooling of expertise across strict professional boundaries, by the democratisation of expertise, by the productive interactions between associations, professional bodies and political authorities.

Participatory governance and the regulatory state

These various governance narratives each challenge the ordered hierarchy represented by state-centric models of politics, administration and society. At the heart of governance are some simple ideas, the loss of centrality of the state and the reconfiguration of the relations between state and civil society being foremost among them. It is easier to identify what governance is against, however, than to conceptualise it as a single framework driving change and imposing convergence. The concept remains essentially contested. From the evidence presented above two main varieties of governance analysis can be identified: we shall label these participatory governance and the regulatory state. These two are not necessarily mutually exclusive, but in practice there is a degree of tension between them that is a recurrent theme throughout this book.

Governance can be constructed in terms of enhancing participation, even reinvigorating democracy. In this sense, governance signifies new forms of participation beyond those of formal representative channels, broadening the community of stakeholders with an interest in the public sphere and vesting responsibilities in non-public actors as part of a broad policy community. Participatory governance involves a more direct dialogue with stakeholders and citizens than formal representative democracy. Modern governance involves the increasing use of partnerships and contractual forms of agreement between stakeholders, rather than the assumption that the dictate of the state will be implemented without mediation. These processes are most in evidence at the local level, where practices have evolved most rapidly. There is an explicitly democratic version of this participatory governance. Theories of democratic deliberation have produced institutional innovations such as citizens' juries, local referenda, electronic democracy and civic fora (Font 2007; Roger 2007; Saurugger 2007). The theory of democratic deliberation, rooted in Habermas' notion of the public sphere, assumes that the act of deliberation can shift actor preferences and produce convergence and compromise (Habermas 1993). In this, democratic deliberation distinguishes itself from rational-choice bargaining, which considers preferences and choices to be exogenous to the process of deliberation itself. In other words, democratic fora contain within them the capacity to improve the quality of public debate. On the other hand, the linkage between governance and democracy is tenuous. Policy networks can operate as private forms of oligarchic government. Governance can escape from the public arena or, in Habermas' sense, from the public sphere (François and Neveu 1999).

An alternative reading of governance is as a means for enhancing the efficiency of the state. New policy instruments, management reforms or delegation to lower echelons of public administration are designed to enhance the productivity of the state and restore capacity to it. At the heart of governance is the desire of the state to decentre its own activity, to seek out more efficient means of providing collective goods. The state no longer directly administers, but provides for detailed regulation of service delivery. The regulatory state ensures compliance with its directives through standard-setting, performance indicators and the oversight of a growing number of independent agencies. The regulatory state itself is regulated in most of its fields of activity by the European Commission, the European Court of Justice, the European Central Bank and associated EU-level agencies. The regulatory mode of governance is the prevalent form in the field of competition policy, the environment, technical standards or banking in particular. In theory, regulation can replace orders by recommendations and is more accommodating of forms of soft law. In practice, the distinction between hard and soft law is not always easy to maintain.

Modern states no longer steer market capitalism, but they provide a market-supporting orientation. The state capacity argument centres on the proposition that there has been a 'shift in the purposes and modalities of contemporary state intervention' (Levy 2006: 2). Levy emphasises four new state missions: repairing the 'three varieties of capitalism'; making labour markets more employment friendly; recasting regulatory frameworks; and expanding market competition.[12] For the current argument, these might be reformulated in terms

---

[12] Levy describes the 'three varieties' of capitalism as (French) statism, (German) corporatism and (Anglo-American) neo-liberalism. He breaks with Hall and

of a spectrum ranging from the compensation state to the regulatory state. The compensation state corrects the dysfunctions of modern capitalism. Even in apparently harsh neo-liberal regimes, such as that of Thatcher in the UK, the state has intervened by providing support for the losers in economic modernisation, and shielding the weakest from market forces. It is no coincidence that the large trading countries have developed sophisticated welfare states. Somewhat further along the compensatory end of the spectrum, modern states have intervened to train displaced workers to take up new employment opportunities and impose new responsibilities as a condition of obtaining welfare benefits. States have attempted to direct labour markets and to make them more employment friendly. As Howell (2008) argues, the state cannot afford not to intervene in industrial relations systems. In the case of France, Howell (2008), Lalliement (2006) and others demonstrate how the state has intervened to expand labour market flexibility and expand decentralised collective bargaining.

Moving to the regulatory end of the spectrum, economic liberalisation not only constrains, but also provides opportunities for new state activities. Though from a political economy perspective globalisation is usually considered to weaken the state, it can also create new opportunities for state interventionism. Global markets require strong regulatory states, able to ensure that rules are respected, that commitments entered into are delivered, that the rules of market competition are fair. International investors possess limited local knowledge, and hence need to rely on high standards of corporate governance that are ensured by state activity. In developed countries there have been moves to prevent insider trading, standardise accounting procedures and enhance transparency and discipline. The regulatory hand of the state has been strengthened, and the state has introduced itself into the most private affairs of multi-national firms. The most neo-liberal economies have arguably strengthened the state at the expense of societal networks, the case in post-Thatcher Britain in particular. Strong states are needed to control public expenditure, rein in local authority spending and create targets for performance. Even in areas of deregulation – such as telecommunications – the

Soskice (2001), who speak only of coordinated market economies and liberal market economies, losing the 'statist' model somewhere along the way.

state has had to act in a regulatory sense to ensure that the rules are respected. The US and EU have had to develop new regulatory capacities to ensure equitable competition.

The European Union is the model for this mode of regulatory governance. With few budgetary or administrative means at its disposal, the EU mainly regulates, rather than administers or redistributes. It sets rules that must, in theory, be acted upon by national officials, controlled by national and European judges. Regulatory governance has an instrumental logic: its core justification is that of respecting 'Pareto-efficient' formulae for the operation of markets and devising performance indicators as neutral forms of arbitration (Leca 1996).[13] The European Union, conscious of criticisms of its own democratic deficit, is also the site where competing versions of participatory governance are tested. Building capacity through a permanent dialogue with core interests and associations from civil society is a proxy for the operation of the European Union as a genuine system of representative and responsible government.

Studying governance in France: a framework for analysis

Governance sits very uneasily with the mainstream French public law tradition, which emphasises the autonomy of the state, the superior legitimacy of state actors, the pyramid of laws and the necessary preservation of a distinct system of public law. The most conservative French public lawyers quite simply refuse to admit that anything has changed (Caillose 2007). The concept of governance challenges many underlying normative assumptions about France shared by public lawyers and orthodox political scientists alike. A political scientist such as Friedberg (1993), for instance, takes exception to the notion of governance, arguing that it denies the legal and institutional bases of public action that cannot be reified into abstract economic and social forces. For an orthodox writer such as Mabileau (1997) governance simply does not fit with French political traditions, based on an active central state, an embedded ethos of public service and an administered society. That governance is essentially neo-liberal and normative is a theme repeated by Gaudin (1999, 2002), Jouve and Léfèvre (1999) and

---

[13] 'Pareto-efficient', the optimal point for a community, signifies a situation where no one loses.

Rangeon (1996). The emphasis on 'good governance' in particular embeds a neo-liberal frame (Chevallier 2003a).

It is tempting to believe that because governance was so derided by public lawyers, it began to gain respectability among some political scientists. A number of writers, such as Chevallier (2003a), Gaudin (2002), Le Galès (1995, 1999) Padioleau (1999) or Pasquier and Weisbein (2007), apply different arguments for governance to the French case. Padioleau (1999) distinguishes between instrumentalised governance, whereby the state seeks to associate other actors in policy development in order to improve its own knowledge, and procedural governance, where the process of associating stakeholders is important for its own sake. Chevallier (2003a) associates governance in France not only with a widening of the range of actors associated with decision-making processes, but also with the emergence of more consensual, negotiated policies. In the realm of sub-national politics, Le Galès (1995) contrasts traditional local government with local governance. Local government refers to a rational, organised form of public administration, where the local authority is the only legitimate site of local power and policy. Local governance, on the other hand, signifies a much broader community of local stakeholders, composed not only of local authorities, but also of private firms, public and semi-public agencies, state field services, consultancies, research institutes and associations. In one of the most sustained accounts, Gaudin (2002) identifies three features of contemporary French governance: cooperation between public and private actors; ongoing interactions in defining and coordinating public policies; and the development of collectively negotiated and developed codes of behaviour and part-nership. Using governance in the French case is appropriate, in so far as it focuses attention on the importance of negotiation, rather than hierarchy.

Understanding governing as governance in France is no different in many respects from observing interactions in comparable European countries. Comparing French-style governance with that of similar countries involves conceptualising *degrees of (discursive) difference*, an exercise that is formalised in Chapter 8. There are dangers in attributing mechanical effects to movements such as Europeanisation, globalisa-tion or even decentralisation; these constructions are interpreted and mediated in different ways in specific contexts, whether that context be organisational, sectoral or the form of the state. Policy-making takes place within a realm of discourse, a system of ideas and representations that is comprehensible to the actors involved (Muller 2000, 2005). In subsequent chapters, the case will be made for the emergence of a contextualised French version of governance that contains numerous internal contradictions and that is mediated by institutional, interest-based and ideational pressures. Change does not occur on a *tabula rasa*. It is processed, in the main, by existing political institutions. It is interpreted by reference to sets of ingrained ideas and referential frames. It braves the reaction of established interests. Convergent pressures are mediated in ways consistent with prevailing ways of understanding the world.

A number of formal hypotheses facilitate our understanding of governing as governance in France. Each accepts two fundamental premises: that the state is embedded in a complex system of multiple legal orders and interdependent relationships; and that governance in France is mediated by institutions, ideas and interests. Our hypotheses are embedded in four axes. They comprise (1) new modes of partici-pation and regulation; (2) multi-level/multi-actor dynamics; (3) state capacity and the hollow state; and (4) sector specific and cross-sectoral dynamics. These axes provide an analytical grid to compare the various cases to be investigated empirically throughout the book, to place France in comparative context and to theorise about the internal consistencies and priorities of French-style governance.

Our first and second hypotheses posit that new modes of participa-tion and regulation are germane to the process of governing France. Along with all other member-states of the EU, France is caught between the conflicting participatory and regulatory modes of modern gover-nance, themes to be investigated in Chapters 2, 3, 4 and 6 especially.

Our third and fourth hypotheses posit the weakening centrality of the state in interactions affecting policy and process. Hypothesis 3 is that of *multi-level dynamics*. Governance is best understood as involving multi-level dynamics across a broad range of policy fields, a line of inquiry pursued in Chapters 2, 3, 4 and 6. Hypothesis 4 is that of *multi-actor coordination*. Governance is best understood in terms of the social and political coordination of the public, private and hybrid actors involved in modern policy-making, themes developed in Chapters 2–6.

Our fifth and sixth hypotheses relate to the state. Hypothesis 5 is that of the hollow state, inspired by the analytical tradition of *political economy*. Governance is the residue of the political sphere, the hollow state that has been emptied of its substance by the international political economy. Hypothesis 6 is that of *state capacity*. The metaphor of the hollow state underplays the efforts undertaken by central governors to build state capacity, to invent new forms of political steering and to discover new activities. State capacity-building involves developing new forms of interaction between the state and civil society, elaborating new instruments of coordination or simply engaging in new activities.

Our seventh and eighth hypotheses provide variations on forms of sector-specific dynamics. Our seventh hypothesis envisages governance as a form of functionalism, embedded within policy sectors that are highly resistant to political oversight. Powerful networks are able to resist governance as state capacity-building through developing sector-specific forms of private government. Our eighth hypothesis involves the pooling of expertise across strict professional boundaries, the democratisation of expertise and new cross-sectoral interactions between associations, professional bodies and political authorities.

These hypotheses are not mutually exclusive and each will find some support from the evidence presented in the book. Subsequent chapters will attempt to elaborate each of these dimensions and to suggest relationships between them. Governance as an overarching meta-frame has already been rejected. In the language of political science, governance is conceptualised as a dependent variable, something to be explained by a range of competing causal narratives. Governance is also syncretic, in that it integrates diverse influences and advances propositions that can appear logically inconsistent with each other. Understanding governing as governance in contemporary France requires the conceptualisation of a convincing mix, or, more realistically, mixes of the variables mentioned above. The challenge is to understand how and when sectors, actors, levels, institutions or interests matter and how best the relationships between them in the context of French politics should be conceptualised.

2 | Reforming the state

The 'reform of the state' is one of the most powerful contemporary narratives in French politics, but it is deeply ambivalent. It rests upon the assumption that the state needs reforming, a diagnosis contested by public sector workers, mid-ranking civil servants and much of public opinion, but central to official reports such as the Picq report of 1994. In the largely constructivist French political science tradition, writers such as Rouban (1997, 2003) emphasise that a convincing discourse is needed to legitimise state reform in France, a discourse that is consistent with pre-existing ideational frames and institutional orders. Yet there is no commonly accepted overarching *référentiel*, or framework of ideas, in the field of state reform. In Chapter 2, three distinctive but interconnected versions of the reform of the state programmes are presented, based on administrative modernisation, contractualisation and budgetary reform. These cases each illustrate an important dimension of governance in France: the attempt by governmental elites to redefine the core of state activity to give a strategic sense to the centre under threat. The chapter begins by setting out in some detail the state-centric model in France and its limits. It then considers in turn administrative modernisation and instrumentation, contractualisation and budgetary reform as attempts by powerful actors at the core of the state to reaffirm their centrality. It concludes by relating the evidence from the state reform case to the framework of analysis defined in Chapter 1.

The state-centric model and its limits

There is a rich debate among specialists over whether France has a strong state, a weak state or a disjointed state (see Elgie and Griggs 2000 for a good summary). Empirical evidence can support differential interpretations. In contrast with the Anglo-Saxon pluralist and rational choice or German corporatist traditions, much French public policy analysis was traditionally state-centric in its focus. Representations of the strong state focused upon the ambitions of an activist state in industrial policy (Cohen 1996), on the role of a French model of state elitism (Kessler 1986; Crozier and Tilliette 2000) or on the enduring centrality of the state in the French model of territorial administration (Mabileau 1991, 1997). In each of these areas the 'strength' of the state has been challenged over the past two or three decades, but the conceptual lens remains state-centric. The quest for overarching regulation and the reconceptualisation of a coherent centre describes well the reactions of leading French political and administrative actors to many of the challenges faced by contemporary France.

Though there is a state-centred tradition, developments since the early 1980s have revealed the complexity of French public-policy making. Economic globalisation, Europeanisation and political and administrative decentralisation have multiplied and shifted the centres of decision-making, and modified the control capacity of the central state (Gaudin 1999; Muller 2000; Irondelle 2005; Smith 2005; Culpepper, Hall and Palier 2006; Le Galès 2006). A more varied analysis of French public policy is emerging, one that is less state-centred, more open to the emergence of cross-sectoral public policies, horizontally organised networks and multiple levels of interaction. Even more traditional state-centric approaches have emphasised the disaggregated character of the French state, divided between rival *corps* and bureaucratic divisions and subject to routine political interference (Bézès 2006). French organisational sociologists have long challenged representations of the uniform Weberian state and emphasised the importance of individual actor strategies within complex bureaucratic systems (Crozier and Friedberg 1977; Friedberg 1993). Researchers into the French welfare state have adopted a different approach. Writers such as Smith (2004) have argued that the state does not perform a particularly important role in welfare and is hostage to the established interests that have captured the system of social protection. A rather similar argument is used by those focusing on the importance of direct action and regretting the incapacity of French governments to stand up to mobilised groups of protesters.

The state-centred intellectual tradition is rooted in French history, especially the Jacobin version of it that equates the existence of a powerful central state with the process of nation-building. The social demand for centralisation has been fairly constant, notwithstanding

changing ideological and intellectual fashions. In this tradition, centralisation has been interpreted as the true Revolutionary legacy of
1789, though the French Revolution had a Girondin as well as a
Jacobin phase (Nemery 2003). Other versions of the strong state are
much more recent. Though France in the nineteenth century practised
protectionism, the tradition of active state economic interventionism is
a post-war phenomenon. The *dirigiste* model identified by Cohen
(1996) and Schmidt (2002), whereby the role of the state was to lead
and to compensate for the lack of dynamism of domestic capitalism, in
reality only lasted for four decades and was always contested by
powerful forces within the French economic establishment (the *Trésor*
notably) (Dyson and Featherstone 1999; Howarth 2001). French
governments no longer have the political or economic capacity to
direct the French economy (Levy 2005; Culpepper 2006).

Another version of the strong state as centralisation model stresses
the importance of a tight politico-administrative elite. Heavily influenced by the traditions of Hegel, Durkheim and Weber, the state-
centric model focuses upon the role of elites at the heart of the state
(Jobert and Muller 1987; Muller 1992). Writers such as Crozier and
Tilliette (2000) and Suleiman (1974) emphasise the importance, in
comparative terms, of a relatively homogeneous political and administrative elite, rigorously selected through a system of elite schools and
competitive examinations. The role of the National Administration
School (ENA) is highlighted as comprising the core of this French
version of meritocratic elitism. ENA graduates occupy key positions in
politics, the administration and business and typify a French model of
elitism that allows for interaction and coherence within the politico-
administrative system. In one study, Muller (1990a) identified the
existence of three partly interconnected, in part rival elites at the heart
of the state, based on the professions, the administration and politics.

At the heart of the Jacobin reading of French history is an emphasis
on the undivided nature of political legitimacy and the weakness of
the *corps* intermediaries. This reading is influenced by Rousseauian
general will, rather than the checks and balances advocated by
Montesquieu, or the necessity for intermediary institutions between
citizen and state much admired by Tocqueville in his observation of
early nineteenth-century America (Levy 1999). In its purest form, this
republican model is deeply suspicious of intermediary institutions,
such as parties, groups and regions, as unwelcome barriers between

the state and the citizen. As a counterpart to the strong version of the republican state, there is a rather weak bargaining culture. In classic representations of French political culture, governments have an authoritarian decision-making style. French governments prepare decisions in a secretive manner, in the hope that they will not be contested (Hoffmann 1965; Crozier 1970; Jobert and Muller 1987). They do not like to negotiate solutions, but rather to decree a general norm and, if necessary, admit exceptions to the norm (Dupuy and Thœnig 1985). Throughout post-1789 French history, this authoritarian style has provoked sporadic revolts against secretive decision-making, the street acting as a counterweight to a bureaucratic model of decision-making. The accepted modes of collective action remain largely focused on the French state, however defined, far more than on local/regional authorities or even on Brussels.

The ideational context within which political battles in France are fought is heavily imbued with the belief that governments ought to act to solve ingrained social problems. Perceptions of a powerful state might matter more than any objective loss of state capacity. The perception of a strong centre is rooted in the political discourse of *voluntarisme* and the autonomy of the political sphere that is hegemonic among France's political parties. The crisis of state capacity is the counterpart to the lasting perception of a strong centre, able and apt to dispense territorial justice, ensure equal welfare provision, protect labour rights and provide employment. The metaphor of the 'social anesthesia state' used by Levy (2005) captures well the complex relationship between perceptions of state puissance and loss of capacity. They are two sides of the same coin – the difficult adjustment of the traditional French state-centric model to a changed and challenging domestic and international context. Thus, though the debate about strong state/weak state rather misses the point, the construction of the French polity has usually involved conceptualising a coherent centre over and above conflicting societal, professional and territorial interests (Muller and Surel 2002).

Reforming the state: from administrative modernisation to the regulatory state

In one of its narrowest uses, the reform of the state refers to a process of modernisation within the civil service, defined narrowly in terms of central departments, their field services and the processes of management reform therein. The modernisation of the civil service has been a preoccupation of all recent governments. No fewer than eight different reform programmes have been implemented since 1981, with varying degrees of success. It is possible to identify a spectrum of reforms, from 'soft' measures to improve user friendliness to much harder-edged attempts to introduce audit, or to change the terms and conditions of government workers. Reform programmes have usually included reference to 'modernity markers' such as evaluation, personnel management, contractualisation and benchmarking (Rouban 2003). In the soft register, each reform programme has emphasised the need for a more user-friendly administration. Thus, a charter for public services was created under Premier Rocard in 1992. Premier Juppé (1995) insisted upon the need to simplify administrative procedures, notably by creating one-stop shops (*maisons des services publics*) for citizens to deal with the administration. In a major symbolic reform, the Jospin government abolished the *État-civil* in 2002. The Raffarin government (2002–5) pledged to obtain a better use of human resources and improve user satisfaction. Civil servants are encouraged to see themselves not only as vested with public authority, but also as efficient service providers. These soft reforms were relatively uncontroversial, real resistance arising when staff terms and conditions were threatened.

Somewhat further along the spectrum, other state reform programmes attempt to influence the behaviour of agents through new forms of dialogue and interaction. The Rocard programme of 1988–9 was the best example of such a programme, relying on mobilising agents in pursuit of collectively defined service goals. The Rocard reform created two new instruments that were meant to empower mid-ranking agents: service plans (*projets de services*) and cost centres (*centres de responsabilité*). Service plans involved all staff in ministerial field services in defining key functions and performance indicators by which their action would be judged. By 1991, 470 service plans, which were intended to encourage dialogue within field units, had been signed (Jones 2003). The cost-centre scheme gave lower units more flexibility in staff management, as well as more control over local budgets. Both schemes were voluntary, however, and both met with internal resistance from the middle ranks of the bureaucracy, a defensive reaction considered in more detail in Chapter 7. These voluntary schemes, relying on horizontal cooperation rather than precise statutory obligations, had a limited impact.

There has also been an important territorial dimension to the reform of the state. Reforms within the state have centred upon the need to 'responsibilise' lower political and administrative echelons. Central governments have attempted to transfer more functions to lower administrative units (or to local authorities), closer to the populations they are supposed to serve. The political decentralisation reforms of the early 1980s were in part inspired by ideas of modern management, namely that proximity allows more efficient service delivery (Marcou 1992). While local and regional authorities were strengthened during the 1980s, the ministerial field services were initially disorientated. Decentralisation was experienced as a zero-sum game by members of the *grands corps*, by officials of the Interior ministry and within some of the more powerful field services.[1] Reforms in the state machinery during the early 1990s were intended both to strengthen and make more autonomous the local and regional field services of government departments and to reinforce the capacity of the state on the ground. In the key 1992 reform, the prefect was vested with the role of coordinator of governmental services at the departmental level (Bernard 1992). In theory, the ministerial field services were now required to submit to the coordinating role of the prefect, rather than operating as semi-autonomous outposts of central government departments. In practice the field services often retained an independent outlook. Field officials interviewed in 1995 resented the coordinating pretensions of the prefectures. For his part, one regional prefect interviewed in 1995 complained of being ignored by the lead field officials from the Infrastructure ministry on account of their belonging to a separate *corps* (Highways and Bridges, rather than the prefectoral *corps*).[2] In this case, membership of a corps dictated 'appropriate behaviour', rather than the written rule that prefects are supposed to have a responsibility to coordinate all government services on the ground.

The reform of the state refers also to management reforms within the administration. Traditional accounts (Stevens 2003) emphasise the

[1] Interviews, 1995, in the Regional Economic and Social Council and Regional Prefecture in Brittany in particular.
[2] Interview with a regional prefect, 1995.

importance of internal controls within French administration, ensured through a dual process of internal inspection and financial or administrative audit through bodies such as the Council of State or the Court of Accounts. Internal inspectorates in the fields of education (IGEN, IGAEN), social affairs (IGAS) or the police (IGPN) operate a long-established form of professional self-regulation that combines *corps* solidarity with independence.[3] In recent years, formal inspectorates have lost influence to harder-edged institutional audits, sometimes carried out by private sector contractors. The principle of audit was promoted robustly by Jean-François Copé, Minister for State Reform from 2005–7. During his tenure, some 127 audits were carried out across a wide range of state activities: from the cost of replacement teachers, through the adult handicap allowance, to the effectiveness of state publishing firms (Gueland 2007). Audits were openly discussed in terms of the productivity gains they could produce in the operation of the state. Even the Finance Ministry had to accept a full-scale institutional audit by Cap Gemini, a leading auditing firm.

Other indicators of the concern for state productivity are the increasing use of agencies to manage public services and the principle of the independent administrative authority. The principle of the independent administrative authority is not that new. Since the 1970s, there have been several examples of independent administrative authorities operating alongside the traditional inspectorates (Guettier 2006). For example, the ombudsman (*médiateur*) deals with cases involving breakdown of relations between individual citizens and the administration. The CNIL (*Commission Nationale de l'Informatique et Liberté*) oversees the rights of citizens to access their computerised data and the CADA (*Commission de l'Accès aux Documents Administratifs*) performs a similar role with respect to administrative documents. Created under the Socialists in 1982, the CSA (*Conseil Supérieur de l'Audiovisuel*) was created to ensure the political autonomy and neutrality of public service broadcasting. The CSA supervises audiovisual media, safeguards (in theory and usually in practice) against abusive intrusion from the state and generally ensures fair access for France's political parties. The COB (*Commission des Opérations de Bourse*) polices the operation of the stock

---

[3] Interviews with the evaluation division and within the educational inspectorates (IGEN and IGAEN), national Education ministry, October 1999.

market and aims to combat insider trading (Jones 2003; Stevens 2003).

A wave of more muscular, competition-minded agencies emerged in the 1990s, driven in part by the requirements of EU competition policy.[4] The ART (*Agence de la Régulation des Télécommunications*) provides one example that, contrary to many expectations, has presided over the almost complete liberalisation of the telecoms market. In the field of food safety, AFSSA (*Agence Française de Securité Sanitaire des Aliments*) has shown itself to be an organisation resolutely independent of political pressures. Under the 2002–7 government, there was a noticeable acceleration in the rhythm of creation of new agencies and, above all, a shift in the nature of the agencies created. There was, in particular, a rapid expansion in the number of agencies in the broad field of spatial and territorial policy, specifically in the areas of urban and rural regeneration (ANRU – *Agence Nationale pour la Rénovation Urbaine*), industrial innovation (AII – *Agence d'Innovation Industrielle*), transport (AFITF – *Agence de Financement des Infrastructures de Transport de France*), social cohesion (ANCS – *Agence Nationale pour la Cohésion sociale*) and research (ANR – *Agence Nationale pour la Recherche*) (Epstein 2005, 2006; Guettier 2006). Agencies are created by legislative or administrative acts. They are national in their scope and often guarantee a high degree of organisational autonomy. They use new techniques and policy instruments to achieve their objectives, notably tendering (*appels d'offres*), monitoring and performance indicators (Bureau and Mougeot 2007). On the other hand, there is no single agency model of governance; the hundred or so agencies that currently exist are regulated by different legal statutes, with more or less operational autonomy from government (Guettier 2006).[5]

---

[4] This trend has imitated that of the EU itself. In the first pillar, there are now twenty-one agencies, with specific legal tasks. There are three each under the second and third pillars.

[5] What's in a name? Most ministries have technical services that bear the name 'agency', but they do not have their own legal character (*régie directe*). Many agencies are semi-autonomous bodies, organised as *établissements publics*, with their own moral personality and financial autonomy, but dependent upon a specific ministry. A number have the legal status of partnerships (*Groupement d'Interet Public* – GIP). The GIP is a formula that allows the development of partnerships between public and private actors that manage services. The GIP is an alternative to the 1901 association format, regularly criticised by the Court of

The growing delegation of regulatory tasks to semi-independent agencies represents an important break with French administrative traditions of uniformity, hierarchy and clear bureaucratic chains of command. French public administration has moved closer to European norms, to the mode of agency governance preferred by the European Commission itself for many of its activities. This development brings France much closer to the new public management norm. There are echoes of UK-style new public management in the definition of national targets (rather than their coproduction by social partners), in the principles of agency monitoring and use of the nationally defined performance indicators that have replaced softer notions of pluralistic self-evaluation (Fontaine and Warin 2000). Embracing competition and introducing competitive bidding between cities and rural areas recall programmes such as City Challenge in the UK.

Performance evaluation has even begun to make timid inroads into a classic administered sector such as French education (Fixari and Kletz 1996). At the level of the school, there has been an increasing use of institutional audits. Since 1995, the Education ministry has published league tables of school performance, classifying schools both in relation to their absolute and 'value-added' performance. In the sphere of higher education, evaluation was first introduced in the Savary law of 1984, which set up a National Evaluation Committee (*Commission Nationale d'Evaluation* – CNE) for universities. Universities are evaluated both in relation to their environment (their local political, cultural and economic contexts) and with respect to particular disciplines, where university departments are beginning to be measured on a scale from 4 (excellent) to 1 (inadequate) (Deer 2002). By comparison with the UK, evaluation is soft, but these soft performance indicators are increasingly hardening. The creation of new bodies such as the Research Evaluation Authority (*Agence d'Evaluation de la recherche et de l'enseignement superieur*) is likely to continue this trend, constraining universities to bid for funds and tightening evaluation in the process.

Accounts. One of the lead agencies to be organised thus is the ARH, created by decree in 1996 to take over functions previously exercised by the health branch of the social security and the prefectures. According to Guettier (2006), there is only one independent administrative authority, the Research Evaluation Authority (*Agence d'Évaluation de la recherche et de l'enseignement superieur*).

The logic of technical choices: policy instruments and the regulatory state

The debate in France over policy instruments and the regulatory state follows naturally from the previous discussion. Lascoumes and Le Galès (2004) identify the revival of interest in policy instruments in part as a rediscovery of Max Weber and Michel Foucault. Weber emphasised the importance of legal-rational forms in modern bureaucracy and referred to the techniques of government as hidden forms of domination. Foucault, in his works on power, insisted on the importance of technical procedures in the broader process of the study of government. An emphasis on policy instruments fits in well with the direction of debates on new public management that have become omnipresent in public administration and management studies (Hood 2007). It is also a central component of new institutionalist thinking, especially that of Peter Hall (Hall 1993). In his classic formulation, Hall distinguished between policy goals, which remain relatively stable over time, and the techniques or policy instruments used to attain these goals, which are more amenable to change. Policy instruments are technical rules, norms, organisations or procedures. Particular instruments are created because it is assumed they will produce certain effects, for example, removing areas of inflationary expenditure from local or even national government. The focus on the technical qualities of instruments suggests processes of automatic government, of removing areas of public policy from political oversight and democratic accountability (Weaver 1988). Apparently technical choices can be highly political and can tie in future generations to initial choices (Pierson 2000).

In the French regulatory state, as elsewhere, the choice of specific instruments can provide a means of sidestepping established interests and introducing new organisational and management ideas that are unlikely to be embraced by established networks. Though the debate on instruments allows for a plurality of organisational forms, new instruments are usually associated either with France's European and international obligations (in the case of monetary policy, for example) or with domestic 'neo-liberal' policy choices. Sometimes new organisations are imposed on the French government by pressures from EU partners and institutions. Thus, the model of the independent monetary authority that has accompanied the introduction and management of the euro was not an initial French preference and has caused ongoing difficulties (Butzbach and Grossman 2004). The principle of the Open Method of Coordination (OMC) enshrined in the Lisbon summit in 2000 has similarly been experienced as a constraint (Dehousse 2004). The numerous semi-autonomous agencies that were created during the 2002–7 period, on the other hand, can be interpreted in terms of central state actors devising new forms of central steering. These new instruments are the organisational form of the regulatory state.

Contractualisation and governance

Though the creators of the Fifth Republic explicitly set about to restore the authority of the state, by the turn of the century it was 'generally accepted that the State had to negotiate just about everything' (Richter 2004: 21). Contracts and contractualisation have become a central feature of French governance. Richter (2004) identifies three broad phases of post-war contractualisation, spanning the contractual economy (1960–82), the phase of territorial contractualisation (1982–92) and the phase of contractual spillover (1992–2002), when contractual processes became disseminated into every aspect of administration. Since the late 1980s, the EU has provided an additional dimension to the contractual process, with negotiation of the six-yearly structural funds cycle closely tied into the French government's own state–region planning exercise. A fourth phase, since 2002, has witnessed a move away from notions of contractual cohesion in favour of more openly 'neo-liberal' tools of bidding, competition and choice.

There is such a wide use of the notion of the contract that some clarifications are immediately required. Contractualisation as an instrument of governance is distinct from the role of private law contracts between individuals. In governance terms, contractualisation involves either the delivery of public services, the development of inter-organisational relationships or, in a more narrow sense, is used to describe relations between a government department and its territorial field offices. Even these understandings can be broken down. Thus, Gaudin (1999, 2004) draws distinctions between public service, public–private and public–public contracts. Public service contracts are formalised agreements to provide public services; typically they involve a public authority (local authority or government department) and a public agency or a private firm that wins the contract to deliver services.

This arrangement, known as the *concession*, is one of the more remarkable features of French governance. The private actors that hold the *concession* – typically utility firms – are vested with a public service mission and thereby subject to the protections and constraints of French administrative law. Public–private contracts also involve public authorities and private sector actors but these are routine private law contracts that do not offer the guarantees of public law. These public–private contracts are particularly present in the area of the environment or social policy. Sometimes they are the means through which the state signs contracts with voluntary associations (for example between the state and sporting federations). Public–public contracts are of various sorts. At their weakest, they are akin to mission statements and vague declarations. At their strongest, in areas such as health or social services, they are service delivery contracts that can be enforced legally and there are strict rules governing their operation. Jurisprudence from the Council of State has gone further, accepting that partnerships can make binding rules on participants, even if these were not clear from the outset. Other public–public contracts include those signed between the state and public corporations such as the SNCF.

Contracts have become key instruments in a range of areas of public service delivery. Contracts are the preferred instrument in areas where central state players have to negotiate and bargain with service providers, an interdependency well illustrated in the field of social security and health.[6] The 1996 decree creating regional hospital agencies (ARH), for example, required contracts to be signed between the state, the new agencies and individual hospitals (Lamarque 2004). In the field of social security, since the 1995 Juppé plan became law, the state and the mutual insurance funds (*caisses*) that run the system have signed conventions that are operational for a minimum of three years. These conventions set out medium-term objectives, contain performance indicators and introduce methods of evaluation. The contract is the instrument that allows the central state to give a steer to an important area of public policy and expenditure that can easily escape tight state stewardship. However, the importance of the contract in health or in social security must not be overestimated. In the field of social security, for example, the local and regional funds (*caisses*) have the real power and the state cannot possibly agree conventions with all of

[6] Interviews, regional Court of Accounts, Higher Normandy, July 2004.

them. Even in those domains where contracts are signed contractualisation can appear as an epiphenomenon: it tells us little about the underlying balance of power between actors. In the case of hospitals, for example, the role performed by the semi-autonomous regional hospital agencies (which distribute funds to and sign agreements with hospitals) is arguably more indicative of new modes of regulatory governance than the act of contractualisation itself.[7]

Contracts have become an essential feature of French territorial governance, though, as detailed in Chapter 3, during the 2002–7 government there was a move away from contractualisation towards competitive bidding. Territorial contracts are usually, but not always, of the public–public variety. They bring together public authorities, typically in the state–region plans, the *contrats de pays*, the *contrats d'agglomeration* or the cultural charters (*chartes culturels*). The state–region plans have attracted much attention and are considered in the next chapter. Less well known are the sector-specific contractual agreements that bind public and private partners in a territorial network. In the area of adult training, for example, the contract of objectives (*contrats d'objectives*) has become the framework that organises collaboration between the regional councils, trade unions, employers associations and state field services. This procedure was introduced in the 1993 Training Act and strengthened in 2004. In the field of training, contracts are signed between the state, the regional council and a particular profession; each party agrees specific commitments, financial or otherwise. In these contracts, the 'social partners' are involved with the state and the regional council in defining future training needs over the duration of a five-year planning contract. In the first agreement of its kind in France, in 1995 a contract of objectives was signed by the president of the Brittany Building Federation, by the French state (represented by the prefect and the rector) and by the president of the regional council. By 2003, fourteen similar training contracts had been signed in Brittany between employers' federations, the state and the regional council. These contracts were subsequently integrated into the main planning

---

[7] The ARH has the responsibility for defining and implementing a regional policy for hospital care, coordinating the activities of public and private hospitals, controlling their operation and determining their resources.

documents, the regional training plan (PRDF) and the state–region plan. This process was not welcomed by all concerned. One official closely involved in the process claimed that the professional branches did not know what they wanted, making it very difficult to agree contracts.[8]

Contractualisation within ministries: Infrastructure and Education compared

Richter argues strongly that when the state signs an agreement with itself, then this is an agreement, not a contract (Richter 2004). Be that as it may, the term 'contract' is used increasingly to codify relationships between central ministries and their decentralised field services. Whether or not these are called contracts, agreements between ministries and their territorial field services have become a routine feature of French governance, hence a phenomenon worthy of analysis. Drawing from examples in the field, the ensuing section compares contractual processes in two French ministries: Infrastructure and Education.

The Infrastructure ministry was the first to experiment with new forms of contractual agreement. The context of contractualisation within the Infrastructure ministry was one of budgetary retrenchment and a loss of statutory functions. The Infrastructure ministry was the most obviously affected by the decentralisation reforms of 1982. Prior to 1982, the departmental field services of the ministry, the DDE (*Directions Départementales de l'Équipment*), had occupied centre stage in the provision of local services, especially for small rural communes. The DDE delivered housing permit certificates, built and maintained roads, regulated road transport, approved the local council's local and structure plans and generally provided a repository of expertise. The 1982 decentralisation legislation provided a shock: the communes took over control of local plans and housing permits, and the departmental councils assumed new maintenance responsibilities for departmental roads. In some *départements*, the departmental council simply absorbed the services of the DDE, as they were entitled under the legislation. In most cases, the DDE survived, but occupied a weaker position in the prefectoral field services. At first, the

---

[8] Interviews in the training division of the Brittany regional council, July 2002.

DDE agents were 'completely destabilised' by decentralisation.[9] The organisational survival of the field services was under some doubt. Contractualisation can be read as one form of response by the Equipment ministry to the threat to the organisational species created by decentralisation. The instrument of contractualisation encouraged the central Infrastructure ministry to provide the base units – the DDE – with much greater operational autonomy, while retaining overall strategic direction. The DDE were given a greater say over recruiting local agents, most of whom were skilled workers (category C). In return for a large measure of functional autonomy and control over decentralised budgets, the directors were invited to sign three-year contracts with the central ministry in Paris. Each contracting DDE agreed to implement an action plan, with a timetable and performance indicators to be achieved within a three-year period. These indicators were discussed with the staff unions. By 1989, two-thirds of departmental directors had signed up for the contracts. The departmental director of one large field service – in the Nord *département*, one of the largest in France, with 2,500,000 inhabitants – claimed to have a completely free hand when developing and implementing the contract.[10] In the case of the Infrastructure ministry, contractualisation was openly framed in terms of the need for budgetary cutbacks, productivity gains and the adoption of robust performance indicators. In the minds of DDE agents, however, contractualisation was above all linked with staff cutbacks.

In the Education ministry, the process of contractualisation followed a rather different path. The first contractual experiments were carried out in the higher education sector (Cole 2005). Contractualisation within the Education ministry itself (as opposed to 'contracts' signed between the central ministry and the universities (semi-autonomous public establishments)) can be dated from the late 1990s, and interpreted as an attempt by Education ministers (especially Jospin and Allègre) and a small group of top officials (within the *cabinet*, the Schools and Evaluation divisions) to modernise the

---

[9] Interviews with a former divisional head in the Infrastructure ministry headquarters, July 2004, and within the regional field service of the Infrastructure ministry, Nord/Pas-de-Calais, November 1995.

[10] 'I enjoy very close relations with the director of personnel in Paris, who allows me complete freedom in negotiating my plan. All operational credits are delegated to me.' This confirmed the view of the relationship from Paris.

Education ministry. This process encountered resistance from other civil servants in the central ministry and the field services. Reforming the administration was a particular concern of Education Minister Allègre (1997–2000). Allègre introduced two specific types of contract: those agreed between the ministry and the regional field services of the Education ministry, and those – initially limited to four pilot regions – concluded between the academies and individual schools. Contractualisation survived the change of government in 2002 and the first round of contracts was completed by 2004. From the perspective of central government, contracts have been accepted across the administration as a useful management tool, as a 'modern' technique of central steering. From the perspective of local and regional actors, however, contracts open up new opportunities for building territorial coalitions around specific policy objectives that go beyond the capacity of any individual institutional actor.

Detailed interviews and participant observation accompanied the negotiation of the Education contracts in the 1999–2000 round.[11] The thirty-one academies differed markedly in their approach to the contracts. In the minister's circular of January 1999, it was stressed that teams should focus on their aims and objectives, and how to achieve these, rather than formulating demands for new resources (National Education Ministry 1999). Early on, Education ministry officials complained that the academies viewed the contractual process from a traditional resource-based perspective. As contractualisation progressed, however, ministry officials recognised that contracts had made a difference, some complaining about the 'Balkanisation' of French education, with local conditions mattering much more for field services than respect for administrative hierarchy. For their part, certain participants from the academies dismissed contractualisation as a distraction of marginal importance, compared with the principal business of the field services, namely staff management, examinations and the burning issue of security in schools. In some instances, the contracts produced more resources. The Lille Academy lost fewer teaching posts than it would otherwise have done, on account of the

---

[11] The author was a participant observer in October and November 1999 at the contractualisation meetings between the ministry's schools division (DESCO) and teams from the Brittany and Nord/Pas-de-Calais educational field services. Interviews were carried out over the next few days with representatives of the central division and the field services.

priorities outlined in its project and its participation as one of four pilot academies. In most instances, however, contractualisation was resource neutral. But there were some perceived benefits from the perspective of the regional and departmental field services.

Negotiating contracts allowed the departmental and regional field services to announce publicly their policy choices. In the Rennes Academy, for example, the Finistère field office (Academic Inspectorate) justified its choice to provide infants as young as two with schooling, a choice rejected in many other *départements*.

All parties interviewed considered that, whatever their limitations, these contractual procedures represented organisational innovation. A series of follow-up interviews in 2004 with a number of the key actors allowed a more nuanced view.[12] In a frank interview, arguably the key architect of the 1999–2000 process defended contractualisation in terms of the capacity it generated for organisational learning and for accommodating territorial differences into the processes of what is often (wrongly) regarded as a highly centralised ministry. On the other hand, to succeed contractualisation needed to be championed either by the minister (as it was by Allègre from 1997 to 2000) or by a separate horizontal structure within the ministry. The only horizontal structure is the *cabinet*, but the *cabinet* is a political office, orientated towards short-term political advantage, rather than medium- or long-term reflection. In the case of agreements between ministry headquarters and field services, moreover, any objective evaluation of contracts was impossible. There was no external agency to validate progress towards targets. Finally, contractualisation was undermined by the change in political majority in 2002. After the 2002 elections, the process lost its political and administrative champions. Those rectors who had been the most enthusiastic about the process in 1999–2000 were replaced after 2002. As in the example above of the Infrastructure ministry, once the initial enthusiasm had died down, negotiating contracts became a bureaucratic ritual that caused some internal resentment.

These two examples demonstrate the importance of timescale, internal dynamics and the interface with the external environment.

---

[12] The following is based on several interviews carried out in July 2004 in the Education ministry and with the key architect of the contractualisation programme, who was in the Culture ministry at the time of the interview.

In the case of Infrastructure, contractualisation was a form of organisational survival faced with a new institutional configuration. As far as Education was concerned, the process was much more in the spirit of the Rocard reform of the state programme, given a new lease of life by the Jospin government. In both instances, the process was driven by some central divisions and identifiable individuals, but this was countered by resistance from others. In both cases, there was resistance from within the field services, the area where implementation needed to succeed. One of the main innovations of contractualisation was to introduce financial planning over longer periods, escaping the annual round of the budget cycle. But the major budgetary reform now to be considered restated very powerfully the importance of annual budgetary responsibility.

Budgetary reform and the LOLF: a case-study of new public management?

Budgetary concerns have always featured prominently in discussions of state reform. One account describes efforts to reform the state after 1983 as part of the general effort at budgetary restraint imposed upon France's Socialist rulers. Budgetary cutbacks introduced by the 1981–6 government encouraged 'a move away from the traditional quantitative approach of seeking growth in the public sector to a qualitative strategy that emphasised the most efficient use of existing resources' (Jones 2003: 54). If the budgetary constraint is always present in the background, it was given a new saliency in the early 1990s, as a result of a deteriorating external context and strategic opportunity-taking by a coalition of economists and liberals at the heart of the state. The backdrop was one of budgetary crisis. In the early 1990s, the budgetary deficit began to spiral out of control, doubling from 1991 to 1995 (Bézès 2006). Respecting the Maastricht convergence criteria was a political imperative for the French government, which came under external pressure to reduce spending in order to join in the single currency. The internationalisation of the French economy and free capital flows from 1990 made the French government much more dependent than ever before on international money markets.

The key players in the process of budgetary reform were the budget division of the Finance ministry, expert advisors in and around the prime minister's office under Premiers Balladur and Juppé and a cross-partisan alliance of parliamentarians operating through the National Assembly's Finance Committee (Bézès 2006; Siné 2006). The Picq report of 1994, prepared for Balladur, represented a landmark document, which provided the inspiration for Juppé's reforms and thinking. Under Juppé's service contracts scheme (1996), ministerial divisions were obliged to sign contracts with the budget division, setting out precise targets. These contracts combined greater financial autonomy for government bureaux with more rigorous target-setting and control. The LOLF, considered in some detail below, was the most complete version of this.

The budget division acted as a political entrepreneur. It explicitly sought to link budgetary reform with value for money, the general introduction of performance indicators and a more efficient use of public resources. It openly advocated neo-liberal managerial reforms and referred to new public management as a means of rethinking the role of the state to take into account economic, institutional and territorial transformations. The use of budgetary policy instruments enhanced its own claim to pilot the reform of the state. Its success in agenda-setting was only assured, however, because a cross-party group of deputies in the French National Assembly argued strongly that government should be more responsible to parliament for its expenditure. Hence, the concerns of public management and political accountability converged. The *Loi Organique relative aux Lois de Finances* (hereafter the LOLF) was passed by an overwhelming majority of both houses of the French Parliament in June 2001 and approved shortly afterwards by the Constitutional Council (Bouvier 2003; Vallement 2004; Finance ministry 2005). This show of quasi-unanimity, rare in the annals of French politics, survived the change of government in 2002 and testified to a broad-based, cross-partisan commitment to change.

The new budgetary law has been operational since 1 January 2006. The LOLF repealed the *ordonnance* of 1959, which had provided a set of strict – and from a parliamentary perspective draconian – rules throughout the Fifth Republic (Feller 2006). The main principle of the 1959 *ordonnance* was that parliamentarians could not propose any amendments that would increase public expenditure. Deputies were, in effect, invited to approve or oppose the budget *en bloc*. Under the old procedure, deputies were asked to approve the recurrent expenditure of all ministries (the *services votés*, 90–95 per cent of the total budget) in one vote.[13] There was little evaluation of either policy objectives or expenditure incurred. The image of *cloissonnement* within the French administration was derived, in no small part, from the existence of up to 850 separate budgetary lines, with limited possibility for transfer across budgets, a situation producing bureaucratic rigidities, turf wars, budget maximising reflexes by bureau chiefs and a total lack of parliamentary oversight.

A new regime has been in operation since 1 January 2006. Under the new regime, budgetary means are allocated to missions and programmes, rather than ministries. Where there used to be 850 budgetary lines, generally corresponding to divisions within ministries, there are now 40 missions and 132 programmes that can cut across departments. The missions are broad areas of public policy. Each mission is supposed to cover a distinct public policy – for example research and university higher degrees – rather than a whole government department such as Education. Missions usually cut across government departments: in the case of research and university higher degrees, Education manages six of the thirteen programmes. One department is recognised as the lead ministry, however, and takes charge of the programme budget.

Ministries have far fewer missions than they have administrative divisions: in Justice, Culture or Education there are henceforth only three main missions. Below the mission, the core unit of budgetary accounting is henceforth the programme, much broader than the budgetary chapters they replace. The programmes are headed by new officials, the programme directors (*responsables du programme*), far fewer in number than the existing divisional heads (*directeurs*). The divisional heads are, as a group, weakened under the LOLF, since only the programme directors are vested with hierarchical authority over a programme. The operator of a public policy does not necessarily respond to a pre-existing position within the civil service hierarchy.

Each programme also has its own operating budget (*Budget Operationnel du Programme – BOP*). The programme directors have much greater leeway to manage budgets in accordance with their declared strategic aims. Whereas the boundaries between budgetary chapters used to be watertight, there is now greater latitude to transfer

---

[13] The *services votés* concerned salaries, pensions and reimbursement of the public debt.

funds between categories of expenditure within programmes (for example operations, investment and intervention). The key principle is that of asymmetrical 'fongibility'. Credits earmarked for staff costs can be transferred into non-staff items, but the reverse is not true: transfers from non-staff items cannot inflate staff budgets. As personnel costs represent 44 per cent of the public sector budget, the implication is that staff cuts can produce margins for other purposes, a clear affirmation of the productivity imperative.

Even before Sarkozy's election as President and the commitment not to replace one retiring civil servant in two, there was broad acceptance that the size of the public sector deficit could only be reduced by trimming the number of public sector employees. Not only does the LOLF provide incentives for officials to reduce staff costs, but the new budgetary law threatens the role performed by the *corps* in civil service recruitment. The 1959 *ordonnance* delegated the responsibility for recruitment and career management almost entirely to the *corps*, the budget announcing annually how many new posts they were allowed to recruit. The LOLF, in theory, changes radically the rules of the game. The budgetary law establishes the dual principles of the salaried mass (*masse salariale*) and full-time equivalent jobs (FTEs), which cover all jobs, including part-time and contractual ones. The FTE mode of calculation can allow ministries to shift jobs between *corps* and grades without having to get the express approval of parliament, as under the old regime. The FTE calculation also gives more flexibility for part-time and contractual arrangements (Chevallier 2006). Enhancing state productivity can also explain the introduction by the LOLF of a new accountancy procedure designed to bring the management of the state's budget much closer to the norms operated in the private sector (Feller 2006).

A number of in-depth interviews in 2004 and 2005 allowed invaluable insights into the preparations for implementing the LOLF across a range of ministries. In these interviews, the author set out to investigate how a sample of different ministries – Interior, Finance, Defence, Education and Culture – were planning to cope with the introduction of the LOLF. A number of key findings emerged from these interviews, since the LOLF is potentially important at several levels. First, in terms of the functioning of France's political institutions, the LOLF held the promise of a return to a functioning parliamentary democracy and an increased parliamentary oversight of the budget. Second, in relation to the daily functioning of the governmental machine, the LOLF introduced principles of (new) public management that its supporters argued would revolutionise the functioning of public administration. Third, the implementation of the LOLF would have an impact upon the internal administrative organisation of most minis- tries. Fourth, there remained many unanswered questions, both in terms of potential unintended consequences and healthy scepticism about the degree of change the LOLF would bring about.

The first dimension identified was that of enhanced parliamentary oversight. Under the LOLF, government departments have to present much more detailed accounts to parliament. The National Assembly has to approve each of the 132 programmes, based on detailed appraisal of objectives and performance indicators. Increasing parlia- mentary oversight of the budgetary procedure was an explicit aim of the framers of the LOLF, including deputies and senators from left and right. Deputies would henceforth vote programmes clause by clause. Each programme would be accompanied by a document explaining precise objectives in areas such as road security, tax collection, terri- torial planning or primary education (to take four programmes at random). Whereas under the 1959 *ordonnance* the government could raise more money simply by issuing a decree or by annulling voted credits, henceforth the Assembly would have to approve any departure from the agreed expenditure. One senior civil servant identified a 'sea change' in patterns of French governance: 'The LOLF introduces face to face contact for the first time between the civil servant and the parlia- mentarian.'[14] While officials had been able to hide behind ministers, they could now be directly accountable to parliamentary committees. Moreover, their carefully prepared budgets could be modified by parliamentary intervention, something previously extremely unlikely. On the other hand, most officials interviewed thought it rather unlikely that deputies would become budgetary zealots.

The second dimension identified above was that of new public management. Its main supporters saw in the LOLF a means of intro- ducing 'real new public management' into the French administration.[15] The LOLF requires a clear statement of the aims and objectives of each programme and the publication and approval of a set of performance

---

[14] Interview, budget division, Finance ministry, July 2005.
[15] Interview, budgetary reform division, Finance ministry, July 2005.

indicators. One interlocutor emphasised how difficult ministries found the task of defining strategic priorities.[16] The type of performance indicator varied according to the programmes delivered by a specific ministry. In the case of the Justice ministry, for example, the indicators included the number of provisional incarcerations, the levels of suicide or the educational opportunities provided for inmates. In the case of Defence, the LOLF forced the ministry to define precise performance indicators for the first time, 'quantifiable objectives such as the number of training days for the army, flight times for the airforce or submarine manœuvres for the navy'. In the Education ministry, there were three broad missions (teaching, higher education and research, youth and sports), twenty programmes[17] and several 'actions' under each programme, each of which is accompanied by precise performance indicators. Though resources cannot be transferred between programmes (between teaching and higher education) they can within programmes (between primary and secondary education).

The third dimension identified above was the impact of the LOLF upon the internal organisation within ministries. The LOLF represented a major threat to existing organisational charts in every ministry. The first threat was to the position of divisional head (*directeur*), the cornerstone of French public administration. There would be a new hierarchical distinction between those divisional heads who headed a programme (hence with their own budget) and those who did not. While there are 132 programme directors, there are over 400 divisional heads, not to mention the bureau chiefs and other lesser functionaries. As well as affecting officials of different grades, the LOLF would also have an impact upon the survival of some existing bureaucratic units. In some departments, the logical effect of the LOLF would be to merge bureaucratic divisions, while in others it could have the opposite effect. In the Finance ministry, two examples illustrate the contrasting effects of the LOLF, were it to be applied logically. The Finance ministry identified tax collection as a single

---

[16] My interlocutor within the budgetary reform division expressed it thus: 'There have been very few texts to accompany the implementation of the LOLF. The other ministries have criticised us for this. But we always answer the same thing: you need to reflect about the goals of policy and imagine what strategies need to be put into place to achieve these, then the indicators will come naturally.'

[17] The teaching mission, for example, has five programmes: primary schools, secondary schools, agricultural schools, private schools and pupils.

mission. Traditionally, this function had mobilised two rival divisions: the General Taxation Division (*Direction Générale des Impôts –* DGI), responsible for determining levels of taxation, and the Public Accounts Division (*Direction Générale de la Comptabilité Publique –* DGCP) in charge of collecting taxes. Attempts to merge these two divisions into one in 2000 badly backfired, producing strikes, a ministerial U-turn and the resignation of Finance Minister Sautter. The introduction of the LOLF once again put these two rival divisions under pressure to agree to a merger. In another part of the Finance ministry, however, the LOLF ought logically to have the opposing effect, challenging the survival of the Customs Division, a single *corps* with a 250-year-old history. In the opinion of one interlocutor, 'the Customs Division (*direction des douanes*) employs 18,000 people with two distinct functions: collecting taxes on petrol and cigarettes; and ensuring the functions of security and police. The logic of the LOLF is that we separate out these two functions, but there is much resistance to this.'[18]

In other examples, a mission can cut across the formal boundaries between departments, as in the case of the police and the gendarmerie. The security mission covers the police (part of the Interior ministry) and the gendarmerie (under control of the Defence ministry). In this instance, the mission is cross-ministerial and brings together within the same structure two rival *corps* with a long history of rivalry. There were bound to be conflicts, with Interior likely to win out at the expense of Defence in the opinion of one interlocutor.[19] The example of the Defence ministry also shows how there could be winners and losers within the same ministry. The chief of staff (*chef d'état major*) would now head a mission and have hierarchical control over the heads of the army, navy and air force. Though the service chiefs would themselves be programme directors, in charge of vast budgets, the chief of staff would centralise most administrative, financial and operational resources at the expense of the heads of the army, navy and air force. For the first time there would be an 'explicit vertical hierarchy'.[20]

Finally, some of the more extravagant claims about the likely effects of the LOLF appear unfounded, or at least difficult to verify.

---

[18] Interview, Interior ministry, July 2005.
[19] Interview, Interior ministry, July 2005.
[20] Interview, Defence ministry, July 2005.

Predictions that the LOLF will lead to a rediscovery of parliamentary institutions are optimistic: the Fifth Republic remains an executive-dominated system and the executive retains a battery of instruments to force reluctant deputies into line. That parliament no longer automatically approves the *services votés* does not mean that 'annual expenses' will disappear. Most public expenditure will continue to be spent on salaries, pensions and the reimbursement of public debt. Predictions about the evolution of the Court of Accounts into a French-style Audit Commission also appear somewhat far-fetched. Under article 47 of the 1958 Constitution, the Court is ultimately subordinate to the government of the day, which routinely ignores its reports. Most of all, to make a success of the LOLF presupposes a perfect implementation model. There was a great deal of scepticism among interviewees that civil servants would move from a resource-based culture to one based on results overnight. The LOLF was very likely to meet ongoing resistance. Its success depended upon civil servants feeling themselves to be deeply involved in new projects. Taken literally, the LOLF threatened to break apart the system of *corps* that lies at the heart of French public administration, a situation not likely to be tolerated by these powerful networks within the state. Above all, there were no sanctions for non-compliance: in the words of one interlocutor: 'At the end of the day the LOLF is completely silent about positive or negative sanctions.'

The governance of state reform

The evidence presented in this chapter lends more support to certain of the hypotheses presented in our framework of analysis than others. The most pertinent are those of regulatory governance, state capacity-building and, to a lesser degree, multi-actor coordination and political economy. In some important respects, the direction of change strongly supports the evolution towards a regulatory mode of modern governance, propelled by overarching changes in the international political economy that require a more productive state. Agencies, performance indicators, monitoring and budgetary autonomy all have the ring of a new public management ethos about them, whereby the productivity of the state is the core concern of those in the centre. On the other hand, contracts and contractualisation offer a more classic register for multi-actor coordination between levels and organisations, or procedural governance, to borrow Padioleau's categorisation. Common to each of these constructions of state reform is an attempt to reassert central state identity, faced with exogenous challenges (Europeanisation and globalisation), inter-ministerial rivalries within the state, the rise of territorial politics and players and the importance of private and semi-public actors. These cases illustrate an important dimension of governance in France: the attempt by governmental elites to redefine the core of state activity to give a strategic sense to the centre under threat.

Whether intention is followed by effect is less clear. Management reforms can take varying forms, some apparently contradictory. Thus, contracts represented a move away from annual budgets and a co-definition of resources, objectives and performance indicators. But the LOLF and the new agency model imply a move towards annual budgets and a standardised definition of performance indicators and new forms of central monitoring. Both types of response address similar questions. The state must manage a complex set of new interdependencies, both those extending beyond the state (in terms of financial markets and European integration) and those emerging within the state (as far as local authorities, agencies or social security bodies are concerned). Faced with unprecedented challenges, the central state has attempt to strengthen its indirect capacities to govern at a distance, by inventing new instruments to facilitate central regulation (Lascoumes and Le Galès 2004). Even contractualisation appears as an attempt by central actors to strengthen their oversight role in a complex multi-actor policy field.

3 | Decentralisation and local governance

Of all the leading European nations, France is usually taken as the model of the unitary state. The movement of decentralisation in France has been gathering pace since the 1960s, however, with the landmark reforms of 1982–3 and 2003–4 representing staging posts in an ongoing process of incremental change. How best can we understand decentralisation in France? In this chapter, decentralisation in France is viewed through three alternative prisms – central steering, territorial capacity-building and identity construction. The first understanding of decentralisation in France is as part of a broader programme of state reform, part of a drive by central governors to divest themselves of unwanted or inflationary functions. It is an exercise in steering at a distance, a close approximation of our hypotheses 2 (regulatory mode of governance) and 7 (state capacity-building). The second understanding of decentralisation is in terms of new forms of local and regional governance practices, most closely matching our hypotheses 1 (participatory mode of governance), 3 (multi-actor coordination) and, to a lesser extent, 4 (multi-level dynamics). The third understanding of decentralisation in France refers to new forms of identity-based territorial mobilisation, in part captured by our first hypothesis (participatory mode of governance). Interlocutors repeatedly interpreted decentralisation in terms of one (or more) of these three main understandings, each of which is also embedded in different academic literatures. The main body of the chapter will address the arguments for interpreting decentralisation in terms of these three alternative approaches that will be integrated in the overarching framework in the concluding section. The chapter begins with an introduction to the context of French centralisation and decentralisation.

Centralisation and decentralisation in France

France is traditionally presented as the paradigm of the unitary state. The French Revolution of 1789 (and its Napoleonic aftermath) swept away provincial autonomy and created a sophisticated administrative infrastructure throughout France, embodied in the figure of the prefect (Machin 1976), the state's representative in provincial France. The deep penetration of the state into civil society was characteristic of the Napoleonic model of state and society (Page 1991; Sharpe 1993). The French model of territorial administration (Sadran 1992) rested upon the principle of administrative uniformity across the nation. It recognised the superiority of central state interests over those of parties, interest groups and localities. It formed part of a hierarchical mode of top-down organisation, whereby public policies originated within government departments or administrative *corps*, were implemented in localities by state field agencies and local authorities, and were coordinated by the prefect, the representative of the French state in the *département*.

French local authorities have traditionally operated within the context of this centralising state tradition. In the 'one and indivisible' French Republic, local government units were classically considered to be the antennae of central government. The 36,500 municipal councils in the communes and the 96 general councils in the *départements* were first and foremost instruments of central regulation. There was a major difference between the *départements* and the communes, however. While the *départements* replaced the pre-revolutionary provinces and represented the territorial interests of the central state, the communes were based on the parishes of the pre-revolutionary regime. The communes remained the foci of local identities and community interests that persisted in spite of the centralising ambition of the Republic (Nemery 2003). All institutional trace of the pre-revolutionary French provinces was banished, however. Not until the post-war period did French regions made their timid reappearance.

In practice, centre–periphery relations were much more flexible than the Napoleonic model implied, as uncovered in the empirical studies undertaken by researchers in the Centre for the Sociology of Organisations (CSO) in the 1960s and 1970s (Worms 1966; Crozier and Thœnig 1975; Grémion 1976). Particularly influential, the 'cross-regulation' approach developed by Crozier and Thœnig (1975) described relations between local political and administrative actors in this state-centric and bureaucratic system. Three pillars supported the system. First, national politicians and officials defined the rules governing centre–periphery relations. While local politicians and officials could negotiate concessions and exceptions, the rules had to remain intact. Second, there was an ongoing interaction between state officials (notably the prefect) and leading *notables*. In Crozier and Friedberg's classic *L'Acteur et le système* (1977) local politico-administrative negotiations took place in 'action systems', tight territorial networks of state officials and prominent local politicians that would usually come to arrangements to adapt national regulations to local circumstances. Third, local relationships were limited to a 'dual elite' of political and administrative actors; there was no place for 'third parties, whether they be economic interests or voluntary associations' (Dupuy and Thœnig 1996: 588). The principal local relationships in this pattern of cross-regulation were between prefects and political *notables* (parliamentarians, mayors, departmental councillors). There was an incentive for ambitious politicians to accumulate elective offices (*cumul des mandats*) as office gave access to higher levels of authority and consolidated local power bases. This model of politico-administrative power was well captured in the metaphor of the 'honeycomb state' (Crozier and Friedberg 1977; Duran and Thœnig 1985) with actors systematically appealing to higher levels of political or administrative authority to enhance their bargaining power.

The model of cross-regulation applied mainly to rural and small-town France. It depended in part on the weakness of political parties and upon the *notable*'s domination of his local political community. While this was an accurate description of politico-administrative relations throughout most of the country, certain types of municipal government never corresponded to this model. Those cities (especially in the Paris region, in northern and in southern France) controlled by the Communists, for instance, became citadels of opposition to government policy, with the municipality subject to tight control by a disciplined party organisation. Party politics was always far more important in large cities, where the left-wing parties had a weighty presence. Rapid post-war urbanisation and industrialisation created more complex cities, and produced more specific politics in the large cities. If large cities fell outside the cross-regulation model, from the 1960s onwards the model of cross-regulation became less influential in rural areas and small towns as well. During the 1970s, the localist case began to be won at the level of ideas (Ohnet 1996; Bœuf 2004a). The watershed in the governance of French municipalities occurred in 1977, when the left captured control of almost three-quarters of large towns. During the 1970s, the French Socialist Party re-established itself within the municipalities (in 1971 and 1977) before achieving national victory in 1981. Old-style municipal socialists were gradually replaced by innovators determined to use local government as a policy laboratory. With the left in charge of most French cities and departmental councils by 1977, prefectoral authority was increasingly resented and effectively bypassed. Left-run municipalities were not content to engage in traditional lobbying practices. Many of the new municipal teams were strongly influenced by the ideas of the May '68 movement, notably those of self-management and social experimentation (Rosanvallon 1976). A belief in proximity, democratic empowerment, citizenship and local self-reliance were thus important facets of a changing ideological and policy climate that preceded the institutional reforms of the early 1980s.

Decentralisation Act 1, 1982–1983

The French Socialist government's reforms of 1982–3 were ambitious (Duran and Thœnig 1996; Mabileau 1997; Levy 2001; Gaudemet and Gohin 2004). The reforms both created new institutions (the twenty-two elected regional councils), and greatly enhanced the decision-making powers of existing players (the ninety-six departmental councils and the larger communes). The decentralisation reforms recognised local authorities as fully operational legal entities freed from a priori prefectoral control. The decision-making responsibilities of local and regional actors were increased, with the extension of sub-national influence into new policy areas such as social affairs, economic development and education. In most respects, the 'departmentalists' defeated the 'regionalists' in 1982–3, as they would again in 2003–4. The *départements* were given larger budgets, more staff and more service-delivery responsibilities than the regions. Central government preferred to deal with the relatively subservient *départements*, rather than strong regions which might contest its authority.

The 1982 reforms were guided by two rather contradictory principles: that types of decision should be attributed to specific 'levels' of public administration (communal, departmental, regional); but that all authorities should be free to develop policies in areas they deemed to be important for their constituents (Fonrojet 2004). The first of these principles enshrined the so-called blocks of competencies (*blocs de compétences*) signifying particular responsibilities carried out by the different levels. As a general rule, matters of immediate proximity (low-level social assistance, administrative port of first call, planning permission, waste) are the preserve of the communes and the various inter-communal bodies – SIVU,[1] SIVOM,[2] EPCI[3] – to which they delegate authority. Matters of intermediate proximity are the policy province of the ninety-six departmental councils, which manage large budgets and are major service delivery agencies (in social assistance, some intermediate education, social services, roads and the minimal income (RMA)). Matters deemed to be strategic are, in theory, the preserve of the regional councils: economic development, vocational training, infrastructure, some secondary education, some transport (notably regional rail services since 2002), with additional responsibilities in culture, the environment and health. The second principle – that of the 'free administration of local authorities' – cuts across the apparent clarity of the first. In practice, the various sub-national authorities have overlapping territorial jurisdictions and loosely defined spheres of competence. Moreover, there is no formal hierarchy between them. No single authority can impose its will on any other, or prevent a rival authority from adopting policies in competition with its own. Unlike in federal systems, the French regions do not exercise leadership over other local authorities; if anything, the French regions are dependent upon the cooperation of lower-level authorities – the *départements* in particular – for the successful implementation of their own policies. The various levels of sub-national government are presented in Table 3.1.

French sub-national governance rests upon a complex actor system, whereby policy is managed by actors and organisations with overlapping responsibilities. After the reforms of the 1980s, there remained much confusion about the division of policy-making and administrative tasks between central and sub-national units and among the

[1] *Syndicat Intercommunal à Vocation Unique.*
[2] *Syndicat Intercommunal à Vocation Multiple.*
[3] *Établissement Public de Coopération Intercommunale.*

Table 3.1. *Sub-national authorities in mainland France*

Type	Number	Functions
Communes	36,500	Varying services, including local plans, building permits, building and maintenance of primary schools, waste disposal, some welfare services
Voluntary inter-communal syndicates*	not available	Groups of communes with a single function (SIVU), or delivering multiple services (SIVOM)
Tax-raising inter-communal public corporations (EPCI)* Includes: urban communities, city-wide communities and communities of communes	c. 2,700	Permanent organisations in charge of inter-communal services such as fire-fighting, waste disposal, transport, economic development, housing
Departmental councils	96	Social affairs, some secondary education (*collèges*), road building and maintenance, RMA
Regional councils	22	Economic development, some transport, infrastructure, state–region plans, some secondary education (*lycées*), training, some health

* These organisations are legally considered local public establishments, rather than fully fledged local authorities

Source: Adapted from INSEE 2006–7, *Tableaux de l' Économie Française* (Paris: INSEE, 2007).

local authorities themselves. While decentralising major areas of responsibility, the 1982 laws did not specify clearly which body was responsible for what activity. Education, for instance, is divided between three levels of sub-national administration. The communes manage the primary schools, the departmental councils the *collèges* (11–15-year-olds) and the regional councils the *lycées*. Matters of curriculum and teaching staff management largely remain the policy preserve of the Education ministry, either in the regions (the rectorates and Academic Inspectorates) or in Paris (the central divisions of the Education ministry). There is an ongoing dispute about the extent of the regional councils' authority in matters of substantive educational content, and certain ambitious regions have laid a claim to influence classroom content (van Zanten 2006). The situation in the sphere of training is even more complicated. The regional councils are in charge of post-16 training and adult education, but they must contend with the powerful influence of firms, of the social partners (employers and trade unions), of the French state in its regional and central manifestations and of the employment service. These examples could be repeated across most other policy sectors.

Though there is broad consensus that there are too many layers of sub-national government in France, it has proved extremely difficult to reform the complex and confusing structure alluded to above. Each reform adds a new layer, but is incapable of dispensing with the old. Recent reforms – the Voynet and Chevènement laws of 1999 and the Raffarin reforms of 2003–4 that are considered below – have run true to form. They have introduced new structures (communities of communes, city communities) without fundamentally overhauling the pattern of territorial administration. Central governments are loath to challenge the role of the *départements*, because the organisation of the state's own field services – especially the prefectures – remain predicated upon those of the *départements*. The state can rely on the departments to be relatively compliant with its own interests – unlike some regions and the communes in larger cities.

Decentralisation Act 2, 2003–2004

What became known as Decentralisation Act 2 consisted of one constitutional reform (17/03/2003), one organic law to allow for local referendums (02/03/2003), one organic law on local government finances (29/07/2004) and one law on the transfers of competencies from central government to local authorities (13/08/2004). The constitutional reform of 2003 embedded the regions in the constitution and referred to the decentralised organisation of the Republic. The original version, proposed by Premier Raffarin, had proclaimed that 'France is an undivided, lay, democratic, social and decentralised Republic'. On the insistence of President Chirac, the new Article 1 of the Constitution now reads: 'France is an undivided, lay, democratic and social Republic. Its organisation is decentralised.' This weaker formulation does not challenge the hierarchical control of the state over its constituent regions and France remains very much a unitary state. The French constitution now recognises four levels of local authority: the commune, the *département*, the region (new) and those with a 'special statute'. The 'special statute' clause covers the various inter-communal bodies (EPCI) and also refers to the eventual merging of existing sub-national authorities into larger units, potentially a radical break with the past. The constitutional reform bill initially proposed two separate mechanisms for institutional adjustment: agreement between the elected representatives of two or more local authorities, or through a majority in a local referendum. Various ideas were launched in 2002–3, including the merging of separate councils into larger authorities in Brittany, Normandy, Savoy and Corsica. In July 2003, however, voters in Corsica narrowly rejected in a referendum the proposition that a single regional authority should replace the existing Haute-Corse and Corse-Sud *départements*, considerably dampening reformist enthusiasm elsewhere.

Once the dust had settled, the main innovations introduced in 2003–4 concerned the provisions for experimentation, the transfer of new functions to local and regional authorities and new constitutional rules governing local government finance. The first and most innovative, the constitutional reform and the law of 13 August 2004 introduced the possibility for the experimental transfer of functions. Experimentation empowers local and regional authorities through transferring powers in specific domains, admitting exceptions to general provisions or vesting a local or regional authority with the authority of the state (Nemery, Bricault and Thuriot 2005). Under article 72, any sub-national authority – a region, but also a *département*, an inter-communal structure or a commune – can bid to exercise a range of responsibilities that were previously in the policy domain of the central state or other public authorities such as the chambers of commerce. Since 2005, for example, the Brittany region has had responsibility for ports and canals, the Alsace region for managing European structural funds. Not only can local and regional authorities bid to run new functions, they can also derogate themselves from providing services on a case by case basis. Article 72 stipulates that experimental functions/derogations can remain in force for up to eight years, before any definitive decisions are made.[4] The proposals for experimentation were watered down in the course of the bill's passage through parliament, particularly after the serious doubts expressed by the Council of State. Even a conservative interpretation sees experimentation as a move away from the uniform application of rules associated with the republican territorial model.

Second, new competencies were transferred to local and regional authorities. Though the 2003–4 reforms promised clarification, they ultimately produced obfuscation (Le Galès 2006). As in 1982–3, the competition between regionalists and departmentalists prevented a clarification of roles. Former president of the Poitou-Charentes region, Premier Raffarin (2002–5) came to office committed to strengthening the regional councils and vesting them with a clear leadership role. As a long-standing senator, however, Raffarin was attentive to a strong rearguard action in the Senate, where most senators favoured *départements* over regions. In 2003, the idea of the region as lead authority (*chef de file*) was abandoned after objections from the Council of State. After the left's clean-sweep in the March 2004 regional election, the role of the regions was further downsized, with their proposed lead responsibility for economic development being changed to a coordinating role among all local authorities. In the law of 13 August 2004, the regions were strengthened in matters deemed to be strategic: economic development, education, training and transport. They were given responsibilities in some new areas, such as health, from which they had previously been excluded. The regions took over direct responsibility for managing school ancillary and catering workers, making them for the first time major employers in their own right. But the most significant transfers, involving large-scale service delivery responsibilities, were to the *départements*, which took over most roads and increased their responsibilities in social welfare, income support and intermediate education. The *départements* obtained 70 per cent of

---

[4] Though any sub-national authority can bid to run services on an experimental basis, this decision needs to be approved by parliament. Moreover, after a five-year period, the French parliament will then have to decide whether the transfer of functions should be made permanent. If so, the new policy responsibility will be transferred to all cognate sub-national authorities throughout France, thereby ensuring equal treatment.

transferred funds, as against 20 per cent for the regions and 10 per cent for the communes/EPCI. This 'victory' of the *départements* could be explained only in part by political choices. The basic institutional architecture of French sub-national governance, whereby the *départements* have a much more sophisticated administrative infrastructure than either the regions or communes, accounted in practice for the decision to transfer new responsibilities to the departmental councils. The regional councils are not major service deliverers or personnel managers, and the presidents of the regional councils were deeply ambivalent about assuming these new responsibilities.[5] Taking over the management of school technical and maintenance workers was a headache, with the regions having to create new personnel departments from scratch.

The third dimension of the second wave of decentralisation concerned local government finances (Hertzog 2004). The constitutional reform and the May 2004 law embed the principle of the financial autonomy of local authorities. The constitution now affirms that the principle of 'free administration' requires local and regional authorities to be responsible for raising the 'preponderant part' of their 'local resources' in local taxation. But there was no definition of what 'local resources' comprised and this ambiguity has given rise to ongoing disputes.[6] This provision, in theory designed to safeguard local fiscal autonomy, raised much opposition from local and regional politicians. The latter[7] feared that, as the state could not increase its percentage input into local resources, local taxes would have to rise to provide new services. The first two years of implementation of the new financial provisions witnessed rises of 30 per cent in the regional element of local taxation in 2004 and 2005, in addition to the regional councils levying the maximum legal fuel duty (1.75 centimes a litre).[8] The presidents of the twenty regional councils run by the left claimed they had no option, given the state's failure to fully compensate sub-national authorities for the transfer of their new competencies. For its part, the Villepin government commissioned the Richard report on local government finances. Richard criticised the increases in local

---

[5] Interview, president of the Brittany regional council, July 2002.
[6] Interview, Court of Accounts, Paris, July 2004.
[7] Interviews in Brittany region, 2002, 2003.
[8] Reported in the *Journal du Dimanche*, 18 December 2006.

taxes since the 2004 law and recommended that, in the interests of controlling overall public expenditure, local authorities could not be allowed to continue to increase taxes (Andréani 2007).

The 2003–4 decentralisation reforms did not alter the basic, highly fragmented structure of French local government. In contrast to the pattern of ongoing change in the United Kingdom, there has been no root-and-branch structural reform of local government in France. Rather, a process of incremental accretion has taken place. New structures have been added to existing ones, without a fundamental overhaul of the territorial system as a whole. This observation was as true in 2007 as twenty-five years earlier. 'Who does what?' is arguably not the most interesting question. French sub-national governance rests upon a complex actor system, whereby policy is managed by plural actors with overlapping responsibilities at several levels. Complex actor systems produce interdependent relationships, rather than clear-cut transfers of responsibilities. This interdependency can legitimately give rise to contrasting interpretations of decentralisation, three of which we now consider.

Decentralisation as steering at a distance?

If the cross-regulation model applied principally to the pre-Second World War period, the first thirty years of the post-war period were those of technocratic modernisation. The 'orthodox' account of French public policy, developed principally by Jobert and Muller in *L'Etat en action* (1987), describes determined central state action, uncovers the existence of tight policy communities located within the state and diagnoses a specific form of French state corporatism. This state-centric model had important ramifications for territorial public policy-making. Modernising state planners piloted most significant public policies in the 1950s and 1960s (Lorrain 1991). The French state combined various forms of direct and indirect control over territorial planning (*aménagement du territoire*). In a direct sense, central actors determined territorial planning priorities and ensured a steady flow of financial resources to fund centrally defined projects. Territorial planning activities were above all the policy province of the Bridges and Highways (*Ponts et Chaussées*) *corps* that controlled the engineers working in the Infrastructure ministry (Thœnig 1973). Indirect methods of control of central government were even more effective. Adopting a standard-setting role, central actors dictated technical norms in housing, road building and infrastructure. The state could rely on a network of state field services and agencies to implement its will in French localities. The most significant of these were the *Caisse des dépôts et de consignations*, the state lending bank that controlled most finance, the *Direction Départementale de l'Équipment* (DDE), the departmentally based field services of the Equipment ministry, and the DATAR. The DATAR was created in 1963 as a central state agency 'to accompany the development of the French desert around Paris'[9] through making strategic investments in economic development. Renamed DIACT in 2005, it remains a key player in the process of central steering, as demonstrated by its lead role in the competitive clusters (*pôles de compétitivité*) programme of the Villepin government. The state had a coherent discourse on urban planning: it implemented ambitious urban development policies with minimal local consultation. The mainstays of central policy included the creation of urban communities in 1968, the ambitious structure plans of the late 1960s, the creation of new towns (such as Villeneuve d'Ascq in Lille) and the establishment of the first generation of urban development agencies.

The top-down model was (initially) distrustful of local, regional or even administrative decentralisation. The gradual empowerment of a meso-level of public administration in the late 1950s and early 1960s reflected the inability of the central state to achieve its objectives alone. Regional structures were created as technocratic outposts of the French state, to assist in strategic functions of economic development, transport and territorial planning. The regional administrative constituencies (*Conférences Administratives Régionales* – CAR) set up in 1955 were the precursors of the first regional councils (*Établissements Publics Régionaux* – EPR) created in 1972 (Ohnet 1996; Dumont 2005). In time, these nominated bodies became directly elected levels of sub-national government from 1986 onwards. Administrative decentralisation (*déconcentration*) preceded political decentralisation by two decades, however. The creation of the regional prefectures in 1964 marked the first significant regionalisation of state structures. Rather like the regional councils later, the regional prefectures were

---

[9] Interview in the DATAR, July 2005.

light, strategic bodies that could coordinate the activities of the much weightier departmental prefectures.

This phase of ambitious top-down urban expansion was interrupted by the economic crisis of the 1970s. From the 1970s onwards, the state no longer had the means to realise its ambitions; in this sense Crozier's (1992) description of decentralisation as a 'reform of the state' was accurate. The growing complexity of decision-making called into question the central state's capacity to deliver services alone. The belief was widespread that excessive centralisation in service delivery produced inefficient services, interminable delays and a lack of flexibility to deal with local circumstances. This was manifest in a domain such as secondary education, where exclusive central state control left school buildings in desperate need of repair (Marcou 1992). Proximity itself was a means of improving the quality of public services; this belief came to be shared not just by local policy actors but by powerful interests within the state.

Once decentralisation had been implemented in the early 1980s, central government began to change the mode of its intervention in French localities and regions. In the early years after 1982, decentralisation was experienced as a loss of prestige by certain state *corps* (Highways and Bridges, notably). Bringing the state back in the governance of French localities and regions was achieved by the state–region plans, introduced in the 1982 decentralisation law (Pontier 1998; Gaudin 1999; Pasquier 2004). Under the terms of the 1982 law, the regional council first draws up a regional plan and then negotiates with the state-in-region, represented by the regional prefecture. One interpretation of state–region planning is as a new form of central steering, with the infrastructure of the regional prefectures used to direct regional policy choices. Through the state–region plans, the central state has been able to impose some of its own priorities on the regions, notably in the fields of higher education[10] and transport.[11]

---

[10] The University 2000 programme during the 1990s was a particular case in point. Across France, local and regional authorities built new universities in partnership with the central state. Ambitious regions, such as those in Nord/Pas-de-Calais and Brittany, enthusiastically participated, viewing the process in terms of instituional legitimisation.

[11] In Nord/Pas-de-Calais, a number of interviewees complained that the 1994–9 state–region plan was used to force the regional council to invest in road-building programmes, though they have no legal responsibility for roads. In

For a number of interlocutors in the French regions, the state–region plans are a means for central government to mobilise the financial resources of local and regional government in the pursuit of its own objectives. Regional council ownership of the plans is limited by the fact that all plans have to be agreed by the Inter-ministerial Territorial Planning Committee (CIACT since 2005), a structure attached to the prime minister's office from which the regional presidents are excluded. State–region plans cannot, however, be reduced to crude central steering. Through its use of contracts, the French state has operated in a more flexible manner in an attempt to mobilise resources beyond its control. Since 2003, there has been a movement away from contractualisation. The state–region plans have been relabelled state–region projects, with much stricter national criteria governing their operation and less room for adaptation to local and regional circumstances.[12]

The belief gained ground during the 2002–7 government that competition improves efficiency and that targeted investment in either high performing or underprivileged territories would contribute to national efficiency. Epstein (2005, 2006) interprets this in terms of a neo-liberal paradigm of competitiveness replacing the Keynesian belief in social and territorial cohesion. Thus, in 2005 the DATAR was renamed DIACT (Interministerial Delegation for the Planning and Competitiveness of Territories), replacing the old reference to regional action in its title with that of competitiveness (Nemery, Bricault and Thuriot 2005). The Villepin government's competitive cluster (*pôle de compétitivité*) programme invited local partnerships (typically local authorities, universities and firms) to bid for central funds on the basis of indicators defined by the centre. Though the process was intended to be highly competitive and to get territories bidding against each other, in practice the state co-financed sixty-six economic projects throughout France, too many for a genuine programme of competitive clusters.

Perhaps most important of all was the creation in 2004 of a new agency, the National Agency for Urban Regeneration (*Agence Nationale pour la Rénovation Urbaine* – ANRU) as a one-stop-shop that

Brittany, on the other hand, the regional council itself insisted that the road-building programme should be the main priority of the plan.
[12] Interview, DIACT, May 2007.

brings together a number of government programmes for poor inner-city suburbs that were previously dispersed across separate ministries (ANRU, 2004). The ANRU has rightly been identified as a core case-study for the new phase of urban regeneration policy in France (Epstein 2006). It combines the agency principle with a high degree of political intervention and ministerial steering. The ANRU, created by the Social Cohesion law of 1 August 2003, manages all state funds destined for deprived urban areas (*zones urbaines sensibles*). Though it carries the title agency, it has the legal status of a public body (EPIC) and its director is named in the Council of Ministers. The agency responds directly to orders from the Social cohesion ministry in the form of ministerial letters. The agency determined its 188 'highest priority' areas for its first years on the basis of a formal letter written by Borloo, then Social Cohesion minister (ANRU, 2004). Though referring to the partnership principle, the agency reverts in important respects to a traditional form of territorial management. The inter-locutors in the localities are the departmental prefects (who double as territorial delegates of the ANRU) and the departmental field services of the Infrastructure ministry (the DDE). As territorial delegate, the departmental prefect determines whether or not projects submitted by local authorities should be referred up to the full national level for a decision. The prefect then transmits eligible projects to the national committee of the agency. The key partners at a national level are the traditional allies of the central state: the *Caisse des dépôts*, the housing trusts and social housing professionals. It is noteworthy that the professional associations of local and regional authorities are not represented on the governing council of the agency. The input of local and regional authorities was limited to that of preparing bids for co-funding in the area of the agency's remit, mainly social housing.

As in the UK, the agency principle is now firmly established as a tool of territorial management. The central state has thus attempted to strengthen its indirect capacities to govern at a distance, by inventing new instruments that can accelerate decision-making in line with central government priorities and that lessen the need to maintain a dense network of relationships at the local and meso-levels. The losers in this new arrangement are the local and regional state field services, including the regional (but not the departmental) prefectures. Though it is too early to detect any lasting impact, these moves represent a significant shift in emphasis.

Steering at a distance is best understood as the top-down impulse of delegating difficult decisions to lower echelons of public administration. Nowhere was this rationale more apparent than in the 2004 Decentralisation Act. An internal circular within the prime minister's office that accompanied the publication of the *proposition de loi* in December 2002 referred to those areas to be transferred as those which were 'technically and socially the most difficult'.[13] Deep suspicions of central government motives were raised in interviews in the summer of 2002 concerning the future reform. As the decentralisation debates unfolded in 2003/4, opposition hardened to the transfer of functions and personnel, particularly in the sensitive areas of educational and health staff. The core of the 'steering at a distance' claim lies in the financial disengagement of the state (Ba 2004; Connétable 2004). The sentiment was repeatedly expressed in interviews in 2002 that functions must not be decentralised without complete financial compensation. Since the implementation of the law of 29 July 2004, the twenty PS regional presidents have complained bitterly that financial transfers from central government have been inadequate to cover the cost of their new responsibilities (Le Lidec 2007). Thus, the regional councils' professional association, the ARF, complained that regions have had to spend 50 per cent more to run the regional rail services than the sum transferred (Andréani 2007). A parliamentary report by a UMP senator calculated that the transfers from the state in 2005 covered only 85 per cent of the real charge.[14] Worse, in 2006 the Council of State ruled that the local authorities' pension fund would have to pay the pensions of the transferred technical and school ancillary workers without having received any of the contributions previously paid into the state's own fund (Conseil d' État, 29 August 2006).

Decentralisation as 'steering at a distance' has a powerful resonance. The delegation of new service delivery responsibilities forms part of a broader process of state reform, the perennial preoccupation of policy-makers in France. In the debate on local finances, there were echoes of British-style new public management, in so far as government ministers welcomed the prospect that local financial accountability would be enhanced. Steering at a distance was not in the least a

[13] Reported in *Le Monde*, 13 December 2002.
[14] Reported in *Le Monde*, 10 November 2006.

federal conception. Services would be delivered at a regional, departmental or local level in ways that were closely regulated and defined by the central state.

Decentralisation as territorial capacity building?

At the heart of the governance approach presented in Chapter 1, it was argued that the state is embedded in a complex system of multiple legal orders and interdependent relationships. Rather like the central state, local authorities have to react to their external environment in order to build their own governing capacity. Innovation in France's regions and localities has been driven by the emergence of more cohesive local government structures, the development of local technical expertise, the strengthening of local political leadership and the invention of more entrepreneurial forms of policy-making. In terms of our framework of analysis, localities and regions have become *multi-actor* arenas engaged in *multi-level* and *cross-sectoral* dynamics, and involved in new forms of *asymmetrical* policy delivery. Local governments have also sometimes (though not always) been the institutional arenas for more *participatory* and *deliberative* politics.

The emergence of more cohesive local government structures is the first key dimension of this process of governance capacity-building. French sub-national governance has traditionally been characterised by resource-based competition between overlapping layers of public administration, the 36,500 communes, 2,500 or so inter-communal bodies, 96 *départements* and 22 regions in mainland France. This institutional diversity is made even more complex by the penetration of the central state's ministerial field services into the smallest French towns. This pattern of public administration has had many zero-sum qualities, as embodied in damaging tax competition between communes, overlapping and competitive modes of service delivery between layers of local government and institutional turf wars between local authorities and state field services. More cohesive local government structures have developed in recent years. They are rooted in urban governance and processes of metropolitanisation (Ascher 1998; Le Galès 2002). In France's urban areas, successive laws and regulations since the 1960s have attempted to adapt local government structures to take account of sociological and demographic change. While large cities typically contain between thirty and eighty communes, public policy problems do not respect such small communal boundaries. There has been a growing impetus behind the development of city-wide local government structures as a tool for tackling problems of urban governance. The most complex of these city-wide inter-communal structures are the urban communities, created in 1968, that administer many of the traditional communal functions in France's largest cities, such as Lyons, Marseilles and Lille. Reforms in the 1990s strengthened further city governments, particularly through developing the inter-communal public corporations (*Établissements Publics de Coopération Intercommunale* – EPCI) (Bœuf 2004b; Marcou 2004). Most medium-sized and large cities are now administered by these (indirectly elected) public corporations which are vested with tax-varying and service delivery powers.

One core dimension of local governance is the development of the technical expertise upon which France's cities can now rely. The rise, almost everywhere, of urban development agencies (staffed by planning experts, economists and urban geographers) bears testimony to this.[15] Such agencies have reduced the reliance on state field services, especially those of the Infrastructure ministry. Large communes have also developed sophisticated place-marketing agencies, often in association with business interests, and on occasion in competition with the state's own agencies.[16] There has been a flourishing of think tanks, advisory committees, public fora and local panels. In the major French cities, networks of experts and professionals have emerged whose role is to offer advice to municipal teams, identify problems and propose solutions. Studies carried out across France (in Poitiers, Bordeaux, Nantes, Rennes, Lille and elsewhere) have identified new policy communities of consultants, urban planners, property developers, architects, lawyers, economists, university experts and expert elected councillors (Cole and John 2001; Le Galès 2002; Cadiou 2007). In cities across France, there is now a systematic recourse to an evidence-base to justify municipal decision-making.

Interconnectivity provides a variation on the theme of local and regional capacity. Local and regional authorities need to develop

[15] There has been a profusion of urban development agencies everywhere: Taiclet (2007) reports the existence of nine in the department of the Saone and Loire alone.

[16] The case for the Lille metropolitan area, notably. Interviews December 1994, January 1995.

efficient horizontal and vertical relationships – or at least to avoid damaging zero-sum disputes – if they are to carry out their minimal duties. Good relationships are required to make the institutions of French sub-national governance function effectively. Relationships between levels of meso-level governance (local, departmental, regional) are not necessarily played out as a zero-sum game. The ability of a regional council, for example, to articulate an overarching territorial vision might be enhanced by strengthening inter-communal collaboration. Inter-communal structures, usually based on employment or training zones that are substantially larger than traditional communal boundaries, are generally consistent with the region's own planning on a sub-regional level. More cohesive local government structures thus allow for meaningful negotiations to take place between the regional council and the varied territorial interests in their midst. The state of inter-institutional linkages varies in accordance with local and regional circumstances. Empirical investigation carried out in two French regions revealed very contrasting patterns (Cole and John 2001; Cole 2006). The Brittany region stands out for its high level of cross-communal cooperation, not only in urban centres such as Rennes, but in the rural hinterland as well. In Nord/Pas-de-Calais, on the other hand, a long tradition of urban rivalry, fractious state–region relationships and poor relationships between local politicians and business actors traditionally produced sub-optimal local outcomes.

More cohesive local government structures have encouraged stronger local political leadership, another key dimension of capacity-building. The local government route can produce political leaders with international reputations, such as Bertrand Delanoë in Paris. The mayoral office, rather than the presidency of a departmental or a regional council, continues to be the most coveted by politicians with a base in local government. Decentralisation enhanced the power of urban mayors by loosening tight state controls on their financial capacity and by increasing their legal and political scope for innovation. Across France, mayors have placed themselves at the head of new-style development coalitions, mobilising large-scale public and private resources for ambitious development projects. Mayors of big cities in the public limelight have also had to face unprecedented new challenges and to weigh the imperative of social cohesion against the promise of economic growth and prosperity. The urban riots of 2005 demonstrated that in poor suburbs social cohesion was a greater immediate concern than the remote chance of inward investment or endogenous forms of economic development.

On the other hand, the more composite environment produced by decentralisation has made the mayoral function far more complex. It has become unrealistic to conceive of mayors as exercising a tight personal control over all aspects of local policy-making. Specialisation has diversified the structures of local power. In the model of cross-regulation, local interactions were mainly limited to those between mayors and prefects (Crozier and Friedberg 1975, 1977). Since decentralisation, local networks have become much broader, to encompass mayors and their *adjoints*, representative of local economic power (chambers, employers' associations, individual businesses), associations and public–private partnerships, either mixed economy societies or formal public–private partnerships (Cole and John 1995; Le Galès 1995; Gaudin 1999; Groud 2006). Local power has become more complex, and successful mayors are those powerful enough to pull the shifting framework together.

Local and regional authorities have become more entrepreneurial, a fourth key dimension of capacity-building. Joint venture companies (known as 'mixed economy societies') have allowed local (and in some cases regional) authorities to launch ambitious development projects part-financed by private capital. Such joint ventures are not new, tracing their history back to 1926, but decentralisation loosened considerably the administrative constraints conditioning their operation. As mixed economy societies are subject to civil rather than to administrative law, they are much more flexible than local authorities themselves. Joint ventures have been used for purposes of transport, museums, theatres, sporting facilities, tourism, conference centres, even hotel chains (Lorrain 1991, 1993; Heinz 1994; Ascher 1998). At their most ambitious, mixed economy societies have acted as a conduit for large-scale foreign direct investment into French localities. Mixed economy societies have facilitated the introduction of private sector management techniques (such as the freedom to recruit part-time and temporary workers and more flexible accounting practices), while retaining overall public sector control of joint ventures.[17]

[17] The mixed economy societies are joint venture companies between public and private partners, within which local authorities hold a majority of the capital.

Theses of local, and specifically urban, governance emphasise above all the priority given to economic development and the emergence of new forms of interaction between local authorities and private interests.[18] Evidence from fieldwork undertaken in 1994–6 in two French cities, Lille and Rennes, provided some precise examples of the variety of forms that such public–private interactions could take: from broad-based territorial advocacy, through public–private infrastructure development to a near total breakdown of confidence between political and business leaders (Cole and John 2001). Territorial advocacy involves, at the very minimum, public declarations of common purpose by a city's leading political and business leaders. In Lille, a history of mutual suspicion between local politicians and business leaders gave way in the mid-1980s to an atmosphere of closer cooperation. The city's key political and economic decision-makers lobbied hard in favour of the Channel tunnel and then combined forces to argue in favour of bringing the high-speed train (TGV) to Lille, rather than rival Amiens (Holliday, Marcou and Vickerman 1991). Though divided subsequently over the Euralille development (see below), the experience of broad-based territorial advocacy survived. In 1994, the Greater Lille Committee was created on the initiative of local industrialist Bruno Bonduelle as a forum involving public and private sector actors, to promote the interests of the Lille metropolitan area and, specifically, to heighten city visibility in international business circles.[19] The Greater Lille Committee was the driving force behind Lille's ultimately unsuccessful bid to host the 2004 Olympic games.

Major development projects can also divide local business interests, as the case of the Euralille development illustrated. Once the Channel rail link had been secured, the mayor of Lille, former Premier Pierre Mauroy, next proposed a massive new commercial and property development known as Euralille. This proposed office and commercial complex adjacent to the new high-speed train station divided the local

[18] Moreover, cities have competed to attract the 'right' middle-class inhabitants, which involves providing leisure and cultural facilities. There is a strong linkage between social exclusion and economic problems; the salaried middle classes desert areas with social problems. The central challenge facing urban governments is to balance the requirements of economic competition with those of social cohesion.

[19] Interviews. In November 1995, this committee was composed of 272 local decision-makers, drawn from the spheres of politics, culture, industry and higher education.

business community, though it mobilised national and international firms and banks.[20] The technical details of the Euralille project were indicative of new patterns of French local governance, notably the role of the mixed economy societies as public–private developers. The mixed economy society SEM Euralille was a 'high risk' joint venture, whereby the society had to agree to underwrite the commercial development and accept there would be no local authority guarantees in the event of financial collapse. Euralille can be offered as a good example of an innovative new form of economic development facilitated by decentralisation, though it is more doubtful whether it can be used to support urban regime theory (Stone 1989).[21]

The final example from fieldwork is one of (temporary) breakdown. In contrast to Lille, in the city of Rennes there was a tradition of close cooperation between politicians, businesses and voluntary associations to promote the city's economic development and to achieve social progress. During fieldwork in 1995, however, the local business community was almost unanimously opposed to a proposed new underground transport system, business opposition being coordinated by the managing director of the Citroën car plant, the major Rennes employer. Business anger was rooted in opposition to the increase in the transport levy that the development would incur. The project was pushed through anyway by a determined mayor, Edmond Hervé. These examples demonstrate the limits of territorial path dependency arguments. A long history of distrust in Lille did not foreclose closer cooperation in response to strategic economic development opportunities from the mid-1980s to the mid-1990s, while a history of close relations was unable to prevent a (temporary) breakdown in relations in Rennes.

Multi-level dynamics are germane to arguments about new forms of territorial governance. The European dimension provides some limited evidence of capacity-building. France has traditionally had one of the tightest, most state-centric forms of interaction with Brussels. At an

---

[20] Local shopkeepers and small businesses in old Lille were opposed to the Euralille complex, which they considered threatened their trade. Most partners in the SEM Euralille were national or international rather than Lille-based.

[21] Urban regime theory, as conceptualised by Clarence Stone in *Regime Politics* (1989), relies on a long-term alliance between local businesses and local government, with business interests exercising the core role of leadership over the medium and long term.

official inter-governmental level, all interactions are supposed to be cleared by the SGAE. Another central state agency dependent upon the prime minister, the DIACT, coordinates local and regional bids for EU funding, in close liaison with the regional prefectures, the SGAR. In practice, bound by EU rules, the regional prefectures have associated the regional councils (especially) with the definition and the implementation of structural funds.[22] Since the passage of the 2004 decentralisation law, indeed, French regions have been allowed to bid to exercise complete control over the management of structural funds on an experimental basis (the first being Alsace). The direction of change is clear, even though French administrative and political elites continue to resist this development.[23]

There has been some development of local and regional capacity in the European sphere. The 1982 Act allowed French local and regional authorities to set up offices in Brussels. Where they exist (as in the case of Brittany) these offices perform a restricted role, limited to information gathering, anticipation of future developments and organising meetings for local and regional politicians with the relevant officials from the Commission.[24] Unlike their counterparts in some countries, French sub-national offices have no access to diplomatic papers or officials. Local or regional politicians are not present in the Council working groups, nor do they represent France in inter-governmental committee structures (as the devolved authorities can do in the UK). The representation of France in Brussels remains, in comparative terms, a state-centric affair. If the institutional avenues for formal expression are modest, however, interviews uncovered a rich stream of more covert forms of influence.[25]

If governance requires evidence of new forms of deliberation and participation, these are most likely to be forthcoming in the local arena. Decentralisation has often been justified in terms of bringing decisions closer to the people, with the (unproven) causal belief that

---

[22] Interviews in the regional prefectures in Brittany (2001, 1995) and Nord/Pas-de-Calais (1994).

[23] Interviews in the General Secretariat for European Affairs, October 2006.

[24] Interviews in the Bretagne/Pays de la Loire European Office, Brussels, March 2004.

[25] One interlocutor referred at length to the informal linkages between Breton local authorities and well-placed Bretons within the Commission, praising the helpful role of Commission officials in preparing urban dossiers.

proximity equates with democracy. The Jospin government (1997–2002) introduced a number of measures designed to strengthen local community expression and build direct and participative forms of democracy (Milner 2006). A 2001 law encouraged local democracy by making neighbourhood councils (*conseils de quartiers*) obligatory in communes with over 20,000 citizens. Whether this represents a real empowerment of local communities remains unclear, however, as local councils nominate at least half of the members of neighbourhood councils. Capacity-building must not be confused with democracy. The strengthening of the inter-communal public corporations (EPCI) since 1999 has not been accompanied by their direct democratic election. Councillors serving on the EPCI are indirectly elected through their communes, which are proportionately represented according to size. This vital layer of sub-national government is unelected and unaccountable. Though direct election was advocated in the Mauroy report of 2000 (Mauroy 2000) and formed part of the 2002 bill, the provision was rejected by the Senate (Milner 2006).

Linked to participation, public debate (*délibération*) is a key feature of arguments about governance. The process of *délibération* is central to local government, in large cities especially. Nearly all French cities have their own urban 'projects', which typically set out a city vision for the next decade and rely upon the consultation and involvement of key local stakeholders. A number of the new contractual processes require public fora to be organised to gather evidence; this is especially the case for the city contracts introduced in the Voynet law of 1999. Interaction occurs through formal committees, as well as seminars, working groups or public fora. Public enquiries around major development projects can also offer the occasion for opposition on the part of social movements (Rui 2004). There are two rather different readings of these processes. Some case-studies interpret the deliberative aspects of local consultation as a new form of pluralism. The process of deliberation is primarily important because it mobilises the main stakeholders behind collectively defined city visions. In some respects, these new modes respond to a normative deliberative logic: local projects *ought* to be debated and legitimised in the public sphere. This deliberative exercise is more important as a process than the specific outcomes produced by debate. Other interpretations point to the instrumental use of public debate by municipal majorities. Fine-grained studies identify a core elite of technical advisors around the mayor as performing the major role of agenda-setting and problem-definition (Cadiou 2007). As networks of experts depend upon the municipal majority, local politicians retain a key role in determining which expertise to use and which interests to consult. Even if this interpretation is accepted, and even if local leaders consume expertise mainly for instrumental reasons, they are forced to justify decisions by reference to experts and make evidence-based arguments.

Taken together, these various dimensions of sub-national capacity-building present a powerful counterweight to technocratic central steering as an explanation of decentralisation.

Decentralisation and identity construction

Has decentralisation in France been shaped by new forms of identity-based territorial mobilisation? The hypothesis is not implausible. Minority nationalist writers argue that almost everywhere there has been a revival of ethno-territorial identities and a challenge to the centralist model of the unitary state (de Winter and Türsan 1998; Keating 1998; Loughlin 2001; McEwen and Moreno 2005). Ethno-territorial identities are reflected in different party systems, language rights movements, cultural traditions or specific forms of elite accommodation (Cole and Evans forthcoming). These arguments were developed to understand the union states of the United Kingdom and Spain, and later adapted to Belgium, Germany and Italy. Research into compound identities is much rarer in France. In the mainstream French republican tradition, territorial (especially regional) or ethnic identities are considered a threat to a neutral public sphere that can alone guarantee political and civil rights (Raymond 2006). Researchers working in this area face numerous obstacles, as France does not allow the collection of statistical data on the basis of 'ethnic' or linguistic criteria, only those of nationality (Reverchon 2005). In the one and indivisible Republic, there can only be one identity and one language.[26]

The intuitive response is to reject the identity construction hypothesis. The examples of territorial asymmetry explored above were linked to efficient service delivery, or to political entrepreneurship, not

---

[26] The census does not collect information on how many people speak languages other than French, which, in article 2 of the French constitution, is the only language of the Republic. Moreover, it does not ask any 'ethnic' questions.

to identity politics. More robust attempts at introducing new forms of asymmetrical devolution in France have run against serious obstacles. The Matignon process undertaken by the Jospin government in 2001 was a bold attempt to introduce the principle of legislative asymmetry. This aborted process had envisaged transferring regulatory, then legislative powers to the Corsican Assembly, until the Council of State objected and the Constitutional Council ruled the process unconstitutional. Given its reaction to the Corsican example, it is highly likely that any attempt to derogate too seriously from the norm of uniformity will be resisted by the Council of State, the guardian of France's conservative public law tradition.

The French republican model emphasises formal equality and individual rights, rather than territorial equity and group identities (Levy, Cole and Le Galès 2005). The history of regionalisation in France bears the imprint of the centralising French republican tradition. French regions were imagined as institutions without a link to territory (Nay 1997; Balme 1999; Pasquier 2004; Zeller and Stussi 2002). They were created in a standardised form throughout France, including areas where no regional tradition existed. With the partial exception of Brittany, Alsace, Normandy and Corsica, France's historical regions and communities do not enjoy institutional expression. The Basque movement has so far failed in its minimal demand for a Basque *départements*. There is a small electoral clientele for regionalism in Alsace, Savoy, Brittany, Normandy, the Basque country and French Catalonia. Regionalist or autonomist parties have occasionally elected representatives to local and regional councils, but they have found it difficult to operate independently of the main French parties (Ruane, Todd and Mandeville 2003; Charette 2005).

On the other hand, strong cultural, language and territorial defence movements have emerged since the 1970s (Cole and Williams 2004). New forms of collective mobilisation have raised the status of the Breton, Occitan and Basque languages. Cultural regionalism has emerged as a powerful force in Brittany, the Basque country and Alsace, and to a lesser extent in Savoy, Normandy, Occitania, Flanders and French Catalonia (Chartier and Larvor 2004). There has been a revival of regional cultural traditions, languages and historical identities.

The official resistance to recognising compound identities makes the French case an interesting one. For Moreno (forthcoming), France provides the counter-example, the one case where the unitary state tradition has repressed particularistic identities and where there is a lack of correspondence between territorial units and 'natural' identity communities. If compound identities feed into institution-building anywhere on the French mainland, they are likely to do so in Brittany, which is identified from the existing literature as the region in mainland France with the most distinctive sense of its own identity (Le Coadic 1998; Pasquier 2004). In theory, Brittany possesses key features identified by Moreno (forthcoming) to develop an 'ethno-territorial' identity: a pre-state political existence,[27] an autonomist Breton political movement, a language rights movement, strong cultural traditions and specific forms of elite accommodation. Brittany is also one of the few regions where political institutions refer to a distinctive political region.[28] There is a complex pattern of multiple Breton identities and a willingness to envisage more advanced forms of political decentralisation than elsewhere in France (Le Coadic 1998). Brittany therefore provides a robust case for testing the importance and limitations of the relationship between territorial identities and political institutions, and for pinning down the sources of support for regional political institutions.

To investigate further, a polling organisation was commissioned to carry out a survey in June 2001.[29] Findings are now presented relating

[27] First an independent monarchy (845–938), then a duchy (from 938 to 1532), then a French province with special prerogatives (1532–1789), reduced for long to being a collection of disparate *départements* before becoming an administrative (1972) then political region (1982), modern Brittany is a French region with a difference.

[28] The term 'region', as applied to Brittany, is ambiguous, as it can refer to both the institution embodied in the current regional council with its four departments (Côtes-d'Armor, Finistère, Ille-et-Vilaine and Morbihan) and to the geographically wider historical 'region', including the Loire Atlantique *département*, corresponding more or less to the ancient duchy of Brittany. The survey to which this article refers was carried out in the area covered by the existing region, known sometimes as B4.

[29] Efficience 3 interviewed a representative sample of 1,007 individuals, selected by quotas of age, gender, socio-economic group and locality. Interviews were by telephone, using the CATI method. The dataset produced by the survey consists of 1,007 cases and 60 variables (Cole 2004). The dataset is divided into socio-demographic and attitudinal variables. The socio-demographic variables are those of region, locality, gender, occupation of the chief income earner, level of education, country of birth, intended vote in a general (parliamentary) election, intended vote in a regional council election, working status, time spent in Brittany, age, marital status, children in full-time education and level of interest in politics. Most of the survey material is in

Table 3.2. *The 'Moreno' identity scale in Brittany (n. 1,007)*

	%
Breton, not French	2
More Breton than French	15
Equally Breton and French	57
More French than Breton	17
French, not Breton	7
Don't know	2

Figures rounded up or down to the nearest percentage point for ease of comprehension.

to compound identities and institutional preferences, and a number of deductions made about regional/ethno-territorial politics and the political opportunity structure. We measured identity by using the Moreno scale, which asked respondents to situate themselves along a five-point continuum ('Breton, not French', 'More Breton than French', 'Equally Breton and French', 'More French than Breton', 'French, not Breton'), providing insights into their preferential mix of regional and national identities. The results of the Moreno questionnaire in Brittany are presented in Table 3.2.

Brittany has the optimum identity spread: a powerful sense of territorial identity, which is easily accommodated within the framework of the existing French state. There is little perceived conflict

the form of detailed analysis of attitudinal and opinion variables on matters relating to decentralisation, Breton identity and attitudes (preferences) towards issues of the Breton language, education and training. The principal attitudinal questions investigate views on decentralisation in Brittany; the 'Moreno' identity scale; the Loire-Atlantique and the administrative region of Brittany; views on the performance of the Brittany regional council; future expenditure priorities; preferences for regional political institutions; relations between the Brittany regional council and similar bodies elsewhere in Europe; understanding of the Breton language; views on the Breton language; public policy and the Breton language; decision-making arenas and the Breton language; Breton language in schools; attendance at a training course in the past 24 months; priorities for spending money on training in Brittany; decision-making arenas and training in Brittany; priorities for improving the training of young people; and attitudes towards the importance of qualifications as against employment aged 16 and above.

Table 3.3. *Institutional preferences in Brittany*

Q. There is a debate today in France on the future of decentralisation. Which one of the following options do you prefer?	Brittany (n. 1,007) %
'Abolish the regional council'	2
'Retain a regional council with limited powers'	44
'Create an elected parliament with tax-varying and legislative powers'	34
'An autonomous Brittany'	12
Don't know	8

Figures rounded up or down to the nearest percentage point for ease of comprehension.

between being Breton and being French, the median position ('Equally Breton and French') being the overwhelming favourite. On the other hand, our findings explode the myth that there is only one French identity: three-quarters of the survey declared themselves to feel at least as Breton as French. These findings back up the common perception that Brittany is a 'strong identity' region. Though the sense of regional identity is strong, however, this is not considered as being in opposition to an overarching French nationhood.

Brittany is also the birthplace of the idea of regional political institutions in France (Pasquier 2004). The survey captured institutional preferences for the future in Brittany that are presented in Table 3.3. It reveals a strong demand in Brittany for consolidating or strengthening existing regional institutions, with a firm foundation of support for more enhanced forms of regional governance. Cross-tabulations demonstrate a convergence towards the median identity position – 'Equally Breton and French' – and support for either retaining the existing regional institutions, or moving towards a more powerful regional body with legislative and tax varying powers.[30]

[30] The 'Equally Breton and French' group, which represented 57 per cent of respondents, divided its preferences as follows: 'retain the existing regional council' (42.2 per cent); 'give the regional council law-making and tax varying powers' (36.4 per cent); an automous Brittany (10.1 per cent); don't know (9 per cent); and abolish the regional council (2.3 per cent).

What variables came into play when supporting these varying degrees of political autonomy? To obtain answers, we undertook logistic regression, with a view to elucidating differing attitudes to the hypothetical situations of political independence, full legislative devolution, limited decentralisation and opposition to any form of regional political institution.[31] A number of independent variables were identified, such as age, gender, education and place of birth. The attitudinal and opinion variables of identity, aptitude in the Breton languages, preferred level of decision for policies and intended voting behaviour in a regional and general election were also included. Table 3.4 provides the logistic regression estimates for Brittany.

A number of conclusions emerge. There is a significant relationship between the intensity of feelings of identity and support for autonomy (the small proportion of the 'Breton, not French' group being much more favourable to autonomy than any other). But the small number of respondents falling into this category urges caution. Other identity markers are less obviously correlated with support for political autonomy or enhanced decentralisation. Counter-intuitively, there is a negative relationship between Breton language competency and support for autonomy or for enhanced forms of devolution. This finding backs up the traditional literature in the field, emphasising a lingering

---

[31] The data are based on 1,007 individuals in Brittany aged 16 and above. Interviews were carried out in June 2001. The survey was divided roughly into four parts, corresponding to our research questions: namely, attitudes to political institutions, to language, to education and training issues, as well as socio-demographic characteristics. For the purposes of establishing relationships, we recoded our data to develop multivariate models of institutional preference. We ran logistic regression to explain individual support for each of the possible institutional situations. In Brittany, we extrapolated four different dependent variables from our institutional scale. We coded these as: 1 'independent Brittany', 0 'others' (autonomy column in Table); 1 'regional council with law-making and taxation powers', 0 'others' ('regional council with extended competencies' column); 1 'regional council with limited law-making and taxation powers', 0 'others' ('regional council with limited competencies' column); 1 'no regional council', 0 'others' ('no regional council' column). We selected the independent variables of age (3 '16–24 years', 2 '25–44 years', 1 '45 years and more'); gender (0 'male', 1 'female'); education (1 'lowest or no degree' to 6 'upper degree'); place of birth (0 'other', 1 'Brittany'); identity (1 'Breton not French', 2 'more Breton than French', 3 'equally Breton and French', 4 'more French than Breton'; 5 'French not Breton'); language (0 'not Breton speaker', 1 'Breton speaker'); level of decision for language and training (0 'other', 1 'Brittany'); and voting behaviour (1 'UDF', 2 'Socialist party', 3 'RPR', 4 'Regionalist party').

Table 3.4. *Logistic regression estimates for Brittany*

Variables	Autonomy	Regional council with extended competences	Regional council with limited competences	No regional council
Age	*** 0.668 (0.182)	** −0.421 (0.124)	0.168 (0.115)	−0.138 (0.391)
Gender	0.375 (0.264)	** −0.368 (0.169)	* 0.329 (0.163)	* −1.095 (0.605)
Education	*** 0.712 (0.130)	*** −0.247 (0.057)	0.025 (0.056)	0.128 (0.207)
Place of birth	* 0.511 (0.310)	− 0.016 (0.200)	−0.267 (0.194)	0.353 (0.622)
Identity	*** 0.863 (0.179)	** 0.255 (0.113)	*** −0.587 (0.113)	0.107 (0.321)
Language	−0.135 (0.447)	0.434 (0.267)	−0.314 (0.272)	−0.689 (0.990)
Attitude to devolution process	−0.481 (0.350)	0.391 (0.278)	0.243 (0.263)	** −1.700 (0.566)
Level of decision (language)	−0.293 (0.266)	0.141 (0.174)	0.040 (0.168)	−0.507 (0.595)
Level of decision (training)	−0.186 (0.278)	−0.018 (0.175)	0.151 (0.169)	* −1.282 (0.715)
Voting	−0.200 (0.165)	0.015 (0.094)	0.049 (0.091)	0.135 (0.294)
Constant	*** −9.225 (1.301)	** 0.227 (0.703)	1.084 (0.677)	−2.592 (2.090)
Log-likelihood	409.327	841.489	886.650	121.605
Predicted (%)	88.20	65.00	61.10	97.80
R2 Cox & Snell	0.118	0.072	0.063	0.030

* $p < 0.10$, ** $p < 0.05$, *** $p < 0.001$.

sense of shame and inferiority among native Breton speakers (almost by definition in the oldest age categories) and an over-compensation of loyalty to France and the French state (Hoare 2000).

Moreno identifies the other identity markers for stateless nations as political movements, cultural movements and elite accommodation. Support for decentralisation in Brittany is not a function of a powerful nationalist party. Though Brittany has a rich variety of small nationalist political organisations, political nationalism in Brittany has been a marginal political (as opposed to cultural) force and has exercised little agenda-setting influence. The main Breton 'ethnic-territorial' party, the Breton Democratic Union (*Union Démocratique Bretonne* – UDB), has a real but limited presence. The Breton cultural movement has been very powerful, on the other hand, performing an agenda-setting role in matters of bilingual education, cultural investment, the environment and the regional media. Our survey uncovered broad public support for measures to assist the Breton cultural movement, with strong majorities agreeing that Breton-medium cultural associations and media should be part-financed from public funds. There is clearly a latent Breton consciousness, kept alive by a dense network of cultural associations that might, in other circumstances, provide the basis for a distinctive ethno-territorial party.

This latent Breton consciousness is not a political resource that can be mobilised by any of the existing regionalist or nationalist parties such as the UDB (Cole 2006). The political and discursive opportunity structures in contemporary France are forbidding for explicit ethno-territorial politics or parties. Breton influence manifests itself most effectively at the level of elite accommodation. Brittany is a region with a strong identity, whose elites have become accustomed to operating in the broader French state (and European Union) context. In the real world of French politics, Breton politicians concentrate their primary efforts on Paris. An element of ambiguity is calculated to serve Brittany's interests. Playing up Breton identity encourages the central state to channel scarce resources to its peripheral region. Brittany's political elite has thus adapted to the French logic of territorial decentralisation, while framing political interactions at least in part in regional terms. Breton political capacity is real, but it is only partially articulated through the regional political institution created by the 1982 Decentralisation Act. The institutional and political structures of opportunities have emphasised the conquest of national

(French) power, and this has only partially been called into question with decentralisation.

The governance of decentralisation

This chapter set out to evaluate the relative importance of state reform, local and regional governance capacity and territorial identities as explanatory variables for understanding decentralisation in France. The first conclusion is that decentralisation in France needs to be read at different levels: in terms of actor motivations, institutional and policy outputs and political and partisan processes. The metaphor of steering at a distance captures well the motivations of key central state actors and the perceptions of these motivations from those operating at the micro- and meso-level. The capacity-building argument has little to say about motivations, but rather more about institutional and policy outcomes, and captures the iterative processes at work in local and regional capacity-building. The identity construction approach elucidates how ethno-territorial political processes can, in certain circumstances, impact upon the functioning of devolved political institutions.

Each argument can draw some support from the evidence presented. The third approach – that decentralisation in France is shaped by new forms of identity-based territorial mobilisation – is the weakest. Political movements based on territorial identity do exist in France, but they have been unsuccessful in shaping institutional responses, except arguably in Corsica. Even in a 'strong identity' region such as Brittany, regional advocacy has been promoted through the existing French political parties, rather than by nationalist or regionalist alternatives (Cole and Loughlin 2003). Though a distinctive form of sub-national governance has evolved in France, its precise form has been shaped by the opportunities provided and constraints imposed by the unitary state form. Unitary states can accommodate pragmatic policy differentiation, hence the move to a French-style local and regional governance since the early 1980s. But they allow much less scope for the construction of autonomous territorial-institutional futures than in union states, such as the United Kingdom and Spain, or in federations, such as Belgium.

Our first approach – that of steering at a distance – is very seductive. From the perspective of the central state, political and administrative decentralisation can produce beneficial fiscal and functional effects, improve public policies and shift blame. Shedding inflationary social assistance policies, for example, can allow more strategic thinking at the centre and offload tax increases onto local authorities. It is quite possible to interpret the decentralisation reforms of 1982–3 and 2003–4 as little more than a by-product of the perennial effort to reform the state. Reforms adopted in the field of territorial management since 2005 have been even more explicit in their intention of improving governability by setting precise targets for local and regional authorities. Taken together, this evidence provides support for the regulatory mode of governance and state capacity-building hypotheses that were outlined in Chapter 1.

In relation to our second approach, the evidence presented does not provide unqualified support to the strongest arguments that present governance as a new form of coordination that replaces hierarchies and markets (Taiclet 2007). French localities remain subject to both hierarchies and markets, and the metaphor of the US-style urban regime is rather implausible in nearly all French cities. In short, decentralisation in France falls somewhere between *régulation territorialisée*, the adapting of state policies to local circumstances, and the embrace of new forms of territorial governance. In terms of our framework of analysis, localities and regions have to some extent become *multi-actor* arenas engaged in *multi-level* and *cross-sectoral* dynamics, and involved in new forms of *asymmetrical* policy delivery. Local governments have also sometimes (though not always) been the institutional arenas for more *participatory* and *deliberative* politics. These processes ought to be understood in terms of meso-level analysis, rather than in terms of overarching narratives such as state capacity, territorial coordination or identity. They are incremental (the result of years of small changes) yet iterative (they have had a cumulative impact). The governance literature, with its disparate focus upon public–private synergies, multi-level interactions, territoriality, experimentation and organisational decentralisation, best captures the complexity uncovered throughout the chapter. In defence of the second approach, decentralisation must be read as a process, not a single event. Local and regional authorities have become entrepreneurial as they have gained experience and confidence. They have also learned from their own past errors, as well as from comparing their own experiences in policy fields such as education, welfare and transport. The preferred second approach does not facilitate drawing neat conclusions that are equally valid across country, sector or locality. The weight of local and regional variables depends upon precise configurations that vary across France. Political arrangements must be understood within the context of local (and sometimes regional) political traditions, social dynamics and economic change.

4 | *Europeanisation*

More than anything else, the success of the concept of Europeanisation in recent years is due to the realisation that EU policy has become domestic policy, with 80 per cent of all policy sectors influenced in one way or another by the Union. Such processes might better be described as 'EUisation', in so far as they refer to the impact of the institutions, actors and policies of the European Union on its member states. But most scholars prefer to reason in terms of Europeanisation and to avoid the unattractive phraseology of the alternative term (Börzel 2002; Featherstone and Radaelli 2004; Bulmer and Lequesne 2005). Among the various definitions of Europeanisation, a distinction is usually drawn between top-down and bottom-up processes. For Saurugger (2007) top-down Europeanisation can best be understood as a continuum at three levels: adaptation, inertia and resistance. *Adaptation* of preferences to the perceived requirements of integration is the strongest form of Europeanisation. There has been a proliferation of work looking at the domestic effects of European integration on political (typically executive) structures and on public policies. *Inertia* signifies the absence of any causal relationship between European-level and domestic change (Börzel 2002). Paradigmatic policy change, or changing relations between the state and non-state actors, for example, might have nothing to do with EU-level processes. *Rejection* is much stronger. Social movement and party actors use an anti-EU discourse to shape their own strategies, while policy-makers resist unwelcome developments in European integration by all means at their disposal. This approach to top-down Europeanisation will be employed as a basic model to structure findings in the latter part of this chapter. The top-down approach is not the only pertinent one, however. Europeanisation can also signify the *uploading* of state preferences or prevailing intellectual frames to the EU level, itself a measure of the competition between national models in the hybrid quasi-polity that the European Union has become.

Europeanisation can cut across most chapters in this book. As a quasi-polity, the EU mobilises political leadership, involves intense interaction through administrative circuits, promotes new forms of collective action and embeds a number of new principles (such as the EU as a legal order) that put domestic actors under intense pressure to act. In an earlier work, I identified a spectrum involving four main uses of Europeanisation: as an independent driver of policy and institutional change; as a form of emulative policy transfer and lesson drawing; as a convenient external constraint to justify domestic reform; and as a form of blame avoidance through scapegoating Brussels for the failure of French politicians to act (Cole and Drake 2000; Cole 2001b). More recent definitions have embellished further the concept, including ideas of top-down and bottom-up Europeanisation, uploading and down-loading preferences, cognitive convergence and 'tying hands'.[1] The chapter will draw both on my earlier work and on the conceptual innovations produced by other scholars. It starts by outlining France and Europe in national and institutional context. The chapter then considers Europeanisation from the perspective of uploading, adaptation, inertia and resistance. The chapter concludes by considering whether there is a misfit between Europeanisation as applied to the French case and the broader direction of European governance.

France and Europe: national and institutional context

France's relationship with Europe has often seemed a paradoxical one. The European Union appears simultaneously as a powerful constraint on domestic public policy and a source of unrivalled opportunity for contemporary French governments to exercise influence on a wider world stage. French discourses on European integration must be interpreted with caution: attitudes to Europe are continually evolving as domestic and external circumstances change and as the EU develops as a polity-like regime. French governmental perspectives on European integration are also closely related to perceptions of the country's leadership role within the Union. The EU was traditionally framed in national (and European) terms as a means whereby France could escape dependency, recover sovereignty and export its institutional and policy models to the supranational arena (Harmsen 1999; Balme

---

[1] Bulmer and Lequesne (2005) provide a useful summary of the main definitions.

and Woll 2005; Dulhpy and Manigand 2006). But as the EU has enlarged, and as the policy direction it has taken has shifted, European integration is now less likely to be framed in such positive terms. There has been a gradual shift in elite attitudes to European integration that has been amplified in public opinion. Traditionally favourable to integration, recent Eurobarometer and other surveys have revealed deep-seated unease about the direction of the European project (Sauger and Laurent 2005; Sauger, Brouard and Grossmann 2007). There remains deep unease with 'foreign' concepts such as federalism, subsidiarity or a Europe of the Regions that run counter to the grain of French republican traditions.

By the end of the twentieth century, traditional French understandings of what Europe was for had been challenged in several important respects. The experience of the left in power from 1981 to 1986 drove home the extent of France's economic and institutional interdependence. The economic U-turn of 1982–3 destroyed the French Socialists' illusions of economic independence and shook their faith in nationally distinctive paths to socialism (Cole 1994; Clift 2003). The linkage operated by President Mitterrand between domestic economic retrenchment and the relaunch of European integration was one important variable in explaining the closer policy convergence between leading EC states that produced the Single European Act (Moravscik 1998). The Single European Act was littered with unintended consequences, and the changes it inspired presented new challenges to domestic French political traditions and policy-making practices, particularly to those of the French left. German unification and its aftermath altered the internal equilibrium within the Franco-German alliance and shifted power away from Paris (Webber 1999; Hendriks and Morgan 2001). The Maastricht treaty of 1992, with its core single currency decision, also posed new challenges to the traditional French economic policy paradigms valued by many Socialists, such as the political direction of economic policy and governmental control over monetary policy instruments (Clift 2003).

With successive enlargements, the influence of the cherished Franco-German relationship has diminished (Hayward 2008). The widening of the EU in 1995, 2004 and 2007 gathered pace at the expense of its deepening, with French leaders fearful that widening would dilute French authority within the institutions of the European Union and its influence within and beyond Europe. Attempts to map French policy preferences and EU legislative outcomes in areas of qualified majority voting suggest that it does just that (Selck and Kaeding 2004). European policies such as the Common Agricultural Policy (CAP) that favoured France were challenged by new coalitions of states within the EU and the rise of new global forms of regulation without (Fouilleux 2003). Above all, the orthodox state-centric model of public policy was threatened by the activism of individual policy entrepreneurs in areas of sensitive domestic concern (such as competition policy and public services) and an emerging referential paradigm which challenged many French conceptions about the role and nature of the European Union.

While France was once looked upon by partners to produce new initiatives, French ideas and preferences have lost currency in important respects, most especially since the defeat of the referendum on the draft constitutional treaty in May 2005. The traditional French construction of Europe was as a tight, politically coherent group of western European states with similar levels of economic development. After the enlargements of 1973, 1981, 1986 and 1995, the arrival of twelve new states in 2004 and 2007 moved the EU even further away from this vision. The election of Nicolas Sarkozy as president in May 2007 ended a period of French isolation brought on by the defeat in the May 2005 referendum. Early evidence from the Sarkozy presidency could lend some support to the hypothesis of a return to French influence at the EU level: the new president was instrumental in obtaining agreement over the 'mini-treaty' at the Brussels summit of June 2007. But other episodes also demonstrated an ongoing inability to upload French monetary policy preferences to the EU level, as well as rivalries with key states such as Germany and Britain over energy and foreign policy choices.

The institutional and ideational context of French European policy-making

French policy-making on Europe is generally held up as a model of tight coordination, with a high measure of core executive control and weak parliamentary oversight (Wright 1996; Menon 2001), though this representation is contested by some (Smith 2005). By comparison with some other leading countries such as Germany, Spain or the post-devolution United Kingdom, however, there is a strong attempt to steer interactions with Brussels. At the level of the core executive, coordination and arbitration is the formal role of the SGAE, which is considered below. French governments have done their best to limit expressions of 'multi-level' governance to their strict minimum. The regional prefects still perform a coordinating role in the management of EU structural funds, except in the Alsace region.[2] Official procedures attempt to ensure that the French state, whether operating at the centre or in the regions, mediates contacts between French local and regional authorities and Brussels.

French governors see the European integration project as vital for the national interest. France likes to be seen to be adopting European solutions. While European integration clearly has the capacity to divide French parties, there is a fairly large measure of cross-partisan *elite* consensus among parties in government over core national values, whether framed in terms of economic policy traditions, paradigms of public service, the social model or the protection of rural communities.[3] Of course, 'France' is not a unitary actor. There are, at any one time, a variety of French positions. There is the official national position as defined in the formal coordinating machinery of the French government (*Secrétariat Général des Affaires Européennes* – SGAE). Then there is the 'Brussels end', including the Permanent Representation (*Représentation permanente*), the role of French representatives in Council committees (the so-called comitology procedure), EU-level policy networks, informal elite contacts, party federations, lobbying on behalf of French cities and regions.[4] How French European policy is developed at the Brussels end falls outside of the scope of this book, but the reader will find it amply developed elsewhere (Lequesne 1993; Menon 2001;

---

[2] The Alsace region has managed EU structural funds since 2005, as an experimental transfer of functions.

[3] In its 2007 report, the Council of State identified three core beliefs that transcend party political rivalries and that ought to guide the actions of France in Europe: 'the preservation of public services in the context of competition law, the development of a more protective European social policy and measures to preserve the rural environment' (Conseil d'État, 2007: 9).

[4] In interviews in the SGAE, my interlocutors were anxious to contrast the French model of coordination and arbitration with that of other countries, which left far more room for manœuvre to diplomatic representation in Brussels. In the case of Spain: 'there is a permanent representation of 300 individuals that tells Madrid what it has to do. In France, we give orders to the permanent representation.'

Balme and Woll 2005). Then there are procedures and understandings within the French core executive: for example the (contested) convention that Europe forms part of the 'reserved domain' of presidential decision-making.[5] The claims made by the national political leadership (whether determined in terms of presidential or prime ministerial authority) are not the same as those of the highest legal and constitutional bodies: the Council of State and the Constitutional Council. Other research has demonstrated the importance of partisan perspectives and arenas of influence, including the European parliament (Hix and Lord 1997), party networks (Ladrech 2000; Cole 2001c) and interest groups (Grossman and Saurugger 2004; Saurugger 2007).

The core argument of this chapter is that the development of the European Union has challenged the policy style and political capacity of existing institutional, administrative, associative and partisan actors, but has also provided strategic opportunities for adaptation and new forms of entrepreneurship. Some elements of misfit are identified, most notably in terms of policy preferences and the role of the state, politico-administrative structures and party politics. But France remains a highly influential EU member state, one determined to influence outcomes in a manner that reflects the country's weight and tradition of exporting its preferences, personnel and prestige. That it does not always succeed in this endeavour allows a realistic appreciation of the nature of contemporary European governance and the inability of any

---

[5] In domestic politics, presidential pre-eminence in European affairs was traditionally so pronounced that Europe was considered to form part of a 'reserved sector' (Howarth 1993). The main history-shaping European decisions have been taken by French presidents. Thus, President de Gaulle launched the Fouchet plan, decreed the 'empty chair' policy and negotiated the Luxembourg compromise. President Pompidou agreed to the accession of Britain, Ireland and Demark to the Community. President Giscard d'Estaing accepted direct elections to the European Parliament and the creation of the European Council. President Mitterrand agreed the reduced British budgetary contribution, and played a major role in negotiating the Single European Act and the Maastricht treaty. President Chirac ensured that France signed the Amsterdam treaty in 1997 and lost the constitutional referendum in 2005. In his first European summit in June 2007, President Sarkozy obtained agreement in favour of a 'simplified treaty' that rescued most of the draft constitutional treaty that had been rejected by the French and Dutch electorates two years earlier. Presidential pre-eminence over history-making decisions, however, does not imply that French presidents are interested in the details of French policy. Most instances of technical arbitration and coordination between ministries concern key officials and – sometimes – ministers.

single state, however powerful, to shape EU policy outcomes in accordance with its preferences.

Europeanisation as the imperfect art of uploading French preferences

The European level has been valued as a site for the export of French ideas, policies and personnel. Traditionally expansive French views of Europe depended upon a vision of Europe as an extension of France; hence the emphasis placed on exporting features of the French model for the benefit of others (Harmsen 1999). Our first understanding of Europeanisation is that of uploading national (French) preferences to the European level. France has been at least as successful in uploading its preferences (and personnel) to the EU level as any other member state. The basic architecture of the European bureaucracy (based around *directions générales* and competitive examinations) is drawn from the experience of the French civil service. Core common policies, such as CAP, were designed with the satisfaction of French domestic interests in mind. French leaders have been influential in steering key institutional reforms, such as the creation of the European Council in 1974, the draft constitutional treaty in 2004 and in launching major policy developments, such as the Single European Act, Economic and Monetary Union and the Common Foreign and Security Policy. The Franco-German 'motor' has, at times, appeared as a credible alternative form of political leadership of the EU (Hendricks and Morgan 2001; Jabko 2004). Through the logic of the *acquis communautaire*, the forces of path dependency within the EU are strong (Pierson 1996). These forces have been consistent with the pursuit of French national interests.

The Common Agricultural Policy provides probably the best exemplar of these powerful path-dependent forces at work, involving a highly successful (from the French perspective) Europeanisation of a national policy preference. President de Gaulle imposed the CAP as the price to pay for France continuing the path of European integration. The CAP was based on a founding Franco-German agreement, whereby France agreed to lift tariff barriers on German industrial goods in return for a system of price support for its farmers (Webber 1999). As the CAP forms part of the initial bargain between France and Germany, the latter usually feels duty-bound to respect France's position. After years of public recriminations, for example, France and Germany came to a bilateral agreement over CAP reform in October 2002 that was subsequently presented to the other member states for ratification (Hayward 2008). The agreement on agriculture was a classic Franco-German bargain. UK Premier Blair was excluded, and had not foreseen this renewed Franco-German strategy. The European Commission was also ignored, neither France nor Germany referring to the conclusions of a report published months before by Agriculture Commissioner Junckler. Agreement on agriculture on French terms was essential to allow enlargement to take place. The example highlights the importance of two-level bargaining, with perceptions of the French national interest and pressure from the domestic farming lobby directly feeding into policy stances pursued at the EU level (Keeler 1987). A reading based on strategic exchange and the promotion of national self-interest is entirely consistent with the history of the CAP. The case of the CAP is also interesting because it provides an example of reversible Europeanisation: France has been unable to prevent a degree of renationalisation of agricultural policy, with Brussels handing back responsibility for expenditure in a range of areas (Smith 2005).

In other areas, attempts to upload French models have proved less convincing. The plural left Jospin government of 1997–2002 provides a good case-study of the capability–expectations gap in French European policy and the weakness of partisan variables in explaining EU-level outcomes. The Jospin government repeatedly insisted upon the need to develop and defend the European social model, perceived to be under attack from neo-liberalism and the invisible forces of globalisation (Ross 1997; Meunier 2004). Under pressure from the French, the Amsterdam summit of June 1997 agreed to hold a special employment summit in Luxembourg a few months later. In its position paper to the Luxembourg conference, the French government called for the creation of 12,000,000 jobs throughout the Union in the next five years. It argued that national economic plans should include precise, quantifiable employment targets. It called for employment policy to be coordinated and regulated at the EU level. In particular, France argued that industrial lay-offs and closures should be approved by the Commission, a move that had echoes of past French practices of requiring the approval of the state for lay-offs (Cole 2001c). In the event, the text approved by the Luxembourg conference was closer to the British Labour government's theses on labour flexibility than the French government's interventionist approach. The Cologne summit (Sauron and Asseraf 1999) adopted a European employment pact that fell far short of French aspirations. Other countries rejected Jospin's demand for an official EU growth target of 3 per cent to absorb unemployment, as well as employment targets with penalties for non-compliance (Sauron and Asseraf 1999). Instead, at the Lisbon summit of March 2000, EU leaders proclaimed that Europe would become the most dynamic economy in the world within ten years and the Open Method of Coordination was born (see below).

The area of the EMU tells a similar story. The French have also been only partially successful in uploading their monetary policy preferences. Since the introduction of the euro, French governments have advocated closer economic policy coordination among the Euroland countries. At times, they have appeared to make progress. Most notably, French pressure lay behind the creation of the Eurogroup of finance ministers. The French view of Eurogroup, as an economic government to which the ECB should be responsible, conflicts with the institutional architecture of the independent central bank and the key economic policy paradigms that prevail therein. If there is some sympathy for the French view of the need for economic government, there has been no serious challenge to the form of independent governance of monetary policy ensured by the ECB. Though political control of interest rates and exchange rate policy remains a demand of most French politicians, it lies beyond the pale in Frankfurt. Moreover, there is no single unified French view on EMU. Economic liberals in the Trésor share a belief in the necessity of independent monetary policy steered by central bankers that is resented by many politicians. President Sarkozy's call for more political control over interest rates has thus far fallen on deaf ears.

The terms of the debate have shifted since the introduction of the euro in 1999. By insisting upon the Stability Pact in 1996 (which became the Growth and Stability Pact (GSP) after the 1997 Amsterdam summit) Germany was able to impose tough convergence criteria accompanying the implementation of the single currency. The criteria outlined in the Maastricht treaty included precise objectives for inflation (within 1.5 per cent of the best performing state), budget deficits (no more than 3 per cent of GDP) and public sector debt (below 60 per cent of GDP). These criteria were designed to ensure a lasting convergence of economic performance once the single currency had been introduced. Neither Germany nor France has been able to respect the criteria written into the Growth and Stability Pact that were intended to ensure the compliance of 'weak' states such as Italy and Greece. France and Germany demonstrated their egoism when they jointly buried the original Growth and Stability Pact in November 2003. Faced with the threat of immediate financial penalties for non-respect of the GSP criteria, France and Germany managed to unite a blocking minority (they were joined by Italy and Portugal) at a crucial ECOFIN meeting, thereby defeating the attempt of the European Commission to levy stiff fines for failure to control their budget deficits. By 2003, the large states – France, Germany, Italy – all argued in favour of flexibility, while the Commission and the smaller states demanded strict compliance. France and Germany now agreed that finance ministers should have a greater role in determining economic policies. Both countries were reluctant to allow the Commission an increased role in defining the strategic orientations that should guide economic policy. In a compromise decision in 2004 that launched a new-style pact, both France and Germany obtained partial satisfaction.[6] As in employment policy, France achieved limited success in uploading its preferences to the EU level.

The example of the Jospin government also revealed the limits of partisan variables in explaining EU outcomes. Though social-democratic parties were in power in eleven of the (then) fifteen member states in the late 1990s, a pan-European social-democratic convergence failed to materialise. The French socialists were unable to achieve more than a symbolic linkage between domestic and European policy or to export their ideas to the EU level. Rather paradoxically, for a government that emphasised the importance of the European level, the most significant reforms of the Jospin government involved highly distinctive national/partisan solutions, such as the thirty-five-hour week, that other countries refused to emulate.

From the above discussion we identify the importance of path-dependent processes, of the comparative advantage enjoyed by France in being able to shape decisions early on in the history of specific policies such as agriculture. As a large country, France is a highly influential EU

---

[6] Germany moved closer to the French position. France argued that public service investments be excluded from the deficit calculations; Germany that measures promoting employment should be excluded.

player and can mobilise a defensive capacity in support of its interests, either through a blocking minority in votes taken under QMV, or through back-door deals with other large countries (as over the GSP).[7] During the Chirac presidency, however, France appeared to adopt an increasingly defensive posture that articulated an unease about the direction of the European construction.

Adapting and adjusting to Europe

In one version of the literature, *adapting* to the requirements of European integration is the strongest form of Europeanisation. The line of causality is clear. Domestic institutions and actors adapt their internal functioning to the logic of European integration. This is close to my own conceptualisation of the operation of Europeanisation as an independent variable, producing identifiable political or policy change (Cole and Drake 2000). *Adjusting* to Europe implies a rather less clear-cut causal dynamic, whereby the requirements of European integration are accommodated within existing institutions. In the ensuing section two rather contrasting examples of adaptation and adjustment are discussed, confirming that the European 'constraint' can produce a variety of strategic responses and repertoires.

Strategic adaptation: the case of the Council of State

The Council of State long resisted the doctrine of the primacy of EU law, affirmed by the European Court of Justice as early as 1964. It finally admitted the principle of EU legal primacy in its Nicolo ruling of 1989 (Mangenot 2005).[8] Transforming constraint into opportunity, the Council of State subsequently acted as a political entrepreneur, seizing the window of opportunity provoked by legal uncertainty and the legitimacy vested by the European treaties to redefine its role within

---

[7] The 2007 Council of State report sets out the various ways in which the French government can make a difference: notably, in organising blocking minorities of 91 votes (under the Nice rules) out of the total of 341, a course recommended by the Council of State when national interests are at stake.

[8] In its Costa/Enel judgement of 1964, the ECJ affirmed that Community laws had precedence over national law, and that judges in member states were obliged to give priority to the EU over national legislation. This was very prescriptive: judges were empowered and obliged to refuse to allow the implementation of any national law/directive that contradicted any European law.

the French polity. As the highest administrative law body in the land, the Council of State has insisted upon its role as the guardian of the EU treaties and their implementation in France, a claim acknowledged by the Constitutional Council.[9] As an institution, the Council of State in particular has gained legitimacy in this exercise of over-adjusting (Mangenot 2005). It has made a strong claim to ideational legitimacy: in the emerging European polity, the law is erected as the absolute principle of legitimacy (Latour 2004). The Council of State has enhanced its prestige within French and European institutions over the past two decades. Members of the Council of State have been appointed in large numbers to the Permanent Representation in Brussels, to the ECJ and in the legal office of the Council (Mangenot 2005).

Most of the work of ensuring legal conformity occurs at a lower level than that of the Council of State. European integration has strengthened the role of the administrative judge as the gatekeeper of legal conformity to EU rules within France. Administrative tribunals have insisted on the legality of EU directives even when they have not been transposed into domestic law by the French government (Stirn and Oberdorff 2004). Both the ECJ and the ECHR look to national judges to implement the laws and norms they edict (Costa 2001; Labayle and Sudre 2004). The administrative judge can deem French laws or regulations to infringe EU law, and refer any matter to the ECJ for arbitration. Some areas where the ECJ has been asked to arbitrate have been genetically modified foods (1998), the remuneration of banking depositions (2002) and over working time (2003).

Adjusting to Europe has also taken place at the level of legal doctrine. The Constitutional Council (10 June 2004) and the Council of State (10 February 2007) have now both declared themselves incompetent to judge whether French laws enacting EU directives are in breach of the French constitution. In practice, this signifies that the EU directive cannot be challenged in the French courts. As the constitution remains the supreme source of law in legal doctrine, and as international treaties have priority over domestic law, there is a need for frequent revisions of the constitution to ensure the two are consistent. In the case of France, there have been five constitutional revisions directly linked to the EU, each allowing France to conform to its own

---

[9] Interview in the Constitutional Council, July 2006.

international agreements.[10] 'Soft' law is not imposed in the same way as 'hard' directives. Thus, the Constitutional Council refused to ratify the European Charter for Minority Languages (15 June 1999), even though it had been agreed by the Jospin government, because the 1958 constitution affirms clearly that 'the language of the Republic is French'.

Strategic adaptation has an anticipatory character. The institutional norms of the EU challenge many traditional understandings of the legitimate role of public authority that, in the French case, is incarnated by the Council of State (Rouban 1997; Chevallier 2003b). There remains tension between French and EU legal traditions. Interviews within the Council of State revealed resentment about some of the directives emanating from the EU.[11] There is not an easy fit, and the concepts used for directives are sometimes difficult to translate into French administrative law.[12] The substance of EU competition policy, for example, in particular the opening up of utilities to competition, went against the grain of French preferences. Insiders were worried about the implications for France's public services of the enforced electricity liberalisation due to be fully operational in July 2007, and even more about the rail directive, which threatened to challenge the SNCF's rail monopoly.[13] These concerns were articulated in detail in the Council's 2007 report on the French administration and the EU (Conseil d'État 2007).

Adjusting (with difficulty) to Europe: the core executive and bureaucratic coordination

Europe has created serious challenges of coordination and cultural adaptation for the French administration (D'Arcy and Rouban 1996; Guyomarch, Machin and Ritchie 1996; Gueldry 2001). In comparative terms, French decision-making on European issues is in theory a model of tight coordination and core executive control. European

---

[10] To ratify the Maastricht treaty (25 June 1992), to apply the Schengen agreement (25 November 1993), to ratify the Amsterdam treaty (25 January 1999), to approve the European arrest warrant (25 March 2003), to approve the European constitution (March 2005).
[11] Interviews, Council of State, January 2006, May 2006.
[12] Interview, Council of State, January 2006.
[13] Interviews, Council of State, January and April 2006.

policy is officially managed by the General Secretariat for European Affairs (SGAE), an inter-ministerial mission formally attached to the prime minister's office (Lequesne 1993, 1996; Harmsen 1999; Eymeri 2003). Officials in the SGAE consider the French model to be the best in Europe. The SGAE not only coordinates French positions before and during EU negotiations, but arbitrates between rival ministerial claims and attempts to police the implementation of decisions taken.[14] Officials contrasted the French model favourably with that of Germany in particular, where multi-level institutional inputs and a lack of chancellor coordination were deemed to produce sub-optimal outcomes. But in its 2007 report, the Council of State recommended the creation of a strategic European cell in the Élysée, argued for a stronger presidential political steering of European issues and implied shortcomings in existing arrangements.[15]

In its 2007 annual report on the French administration and the European Union, the Council of State specifically diagnosed a misfit between the requirements of European law and the prevailing French political and administrative culture. The Council of State report acknowledged that EU law is not sufficiently taken into account when drafting French laws, directives and circulars. There is underlying unease across the French governmental machine about the role of EU actors usurping traditional prerogatives. There remains a weak EU culture within French ministries. Central divisions within individual ministries are imbued with the culture of the decree and are reluctant to engage in impact assessment exercises. As directives are highly technical, delays are commonplace. In terms of directives, the numbers have been increasing, from 70 in 1995 to 130 in 2003 and 111 in 2004

---

[14] Interviews in SGAE, October 2006.

[15] In theory, the French government has a complex and full procedure. The circular of 9 November 1998 from the SGAE (then known as SGCI) sets out in precise detail what ought to happen. It is strongly recommended that the officials in charge of negotiating a directive are also those given responsibility for implementing it. There must be impact assessments for each proposed directive. Transposition must occur as soon as the directive has been adopted. Each ministry must provide a detailed plan within three months of the adoption of a directive for how it proposes to implement it to the General Secretariat of the Government. The SGAE identifies the lead ministry and creates task- and end-groups to implement the directive. Moreover, the SGAE publishes a table giving the state of transposition of directives. In practice, this circular has never been applied.

(Maia 2005). Ministries complain that they lack the expertise to transpose EU directives into national law. In a string of reports, the European Commission has criticised France for its poor record in transcribing directives (Enfert 2005). France has regularly been found guilty by the ECJ, most recently (at the time of writing in December 2006) in relation to its failure to implement correctly the 2001 directive on genetically modified foods. The official representation of a tightly coordinated machine notwithstanding, neither the Council of State, nor the SGAE nor the General Secretariat of the Government is able to bring much influence to bear on individual ministries and their reluctance or their inability to correctly transcribe EU directives.[16]

Efforts at central coordination have also run up against the inherent fragmentation of the EU policy-making process. Smith (2005) argues strongly in favour of a sectoralisation hypothesis. The EU as a system of governance is highly sectorised: a pattern encouraged by the role of individual commissioners as policy entrepreneurs, by the expertise in the main directorates (of the Commission and French government departments) and the weakness of collective responsibility within the Commission itself. Consistent with sectoralisation at the EU level, there is a series of distinct ministerial responses. Most ministries have a European cell and maintain direct relationships with Commission officials. EU networks are multi-layered in character and provide new opportunities for strategic action for political and administrative actors. In spite of attempts by regional prefects to police interactions with sub-national authorities, for example, Commission officials and sub-national actors can develop their own networks.[17] From the perspective of central governors, adjusting to Europe continues to be an arduous task.

From adaptation to inertia

While adaptation requires some demonstration of EU causality, inertia is far more ambivalent about causal relationships between European-level and domestic change (Börzel 2002). Paradigmatic policy change

---

[16] Interviews, SGAE, SGG and Council of State, January, May, August and October 2006.
[17] Interviews in Brittany in 2001 uncovered several examples of such relationships.

or changing relations between the state and non-state actors might originally have had little or nothing to do with EU-level processes, even if they get caught up in subsequent Europeanisation. Institutional responses, actor strategies and diffuse policy processes can each illustrate the argument.

Parliament and the democratic deficit

The existence of a democratic deficit is an established feature among scholars of the EU system of governance (Rozenberg and Surel 2003; Rozenberg 2007). In the case of the French Fifth Republic, the democratic deficit forms part of the 1958 constitution itself, which removes large areas of public policy from parliamentary scrutiny. The French National Assembly has gradually been increasing its involvement in EU affairs. There have been slow – but steady – moves to enhance the influence of parliamentary institutions over EU law and a development of parliamentary capacity to exercise oversight. The Maastricht treaty allowed the vote of resolutions (article 88–4), though the Constitutional Council subsequently ruled that these could not be binding on governments (Ladrech 1994). In 2004, parliament received 310 proposed legislative acts for consideration, these being identified by the Council of State as lying within the domain of the law (Maia 2005). The Amsterdam treaty of 1997 adopted a protocol on the role of national parliaments which increased their rights to be informed of forthcoming EU business. Paving the way for the (failed) referendum on the constitutional treaty, preparations for implementing the subsidiarity protocol of October 2004 (according to which proposed EU framework laws are sent to national parliaments) were put in place by the French National Assembly.[18] The constitutional revision of 1 March 2005 strengthened the French parliament, which obtained the right to consult all EU documents, including those falling within the domain of regulation. The Lisbon Treaty strengthens national parliaments considerably, giving *ex ante* and *ex post* forms of control. But European integration has not really empowered the French parliament. The National Assembly still only gives its opinion and has no binding authority. The French executive has used the

---

[18] Information supplied by Olivier Rozenberg, CEVIPOF, Sciences Po, Paris, June 2007.

'urgency' procedure measures to push through EU legislation by decree. EU directives have either been regrouped into packages and presented to parliament for block approval, or the government has asked parliament for power to approve by ordinances (article 38) (2000, 2001) (Enfert 2005; Sales 2005). If the overall picture is that European integration has strengthened executives in their dealings with parliamentary assemblies, the weakness of the French parliament owes little to the European Union.

Party and partisan actors

In one interpretation, there has been a profound transformation in state–group relations in the light of European integration (Grossman 2003). Europeanisation has redistributed the cards among existing domestic-level actors. It has encouraged an unbundling of the close relations between the state and economic interests that was a core feature of the state-centric model. It has disrupted older models of corporatist co-management, for example in agriculture (Saurugger 2003). It has created new degrees of freedom for French firms, associations, new social movements, even local and regional authorities. It has lessened the dependency of all these actors upon the central state. These themes are developed in more detail in Chapter 6.

It is much less evident that Europeanisation has had an impact in reshaping the French party system. The development of the EU as a quasi-polity has added to the problem of party relevance in European democracies, especially in the economic and monetary sphere, where party political actors appear invisible (Gaffney 1996; Hix and Lord 1997; Ladrech 2000; Marks and Wilson 2000). In most accounts, EU policy is rarely mediated by party, and the party system literature itself is predicated upon the nation-state as the primary operating environment of European political parties. There is a solid body of research on trans-national European parties and European Parliament party groups, however, which points up the agenda-setting role of parties and identifies the emergence of consistent left–right cleavages at the EU level (Marks and Wilson 2000; Hix 2005). As the EU has become more open and more democratic, and as the European Parliament has assumed the role of a quasi-legislature, political parties have begun to perform at the European level their classic domestic role of framing democratic choices and offering competing societal visions.

In the case of France, however, political parties provide another example of a poor fit with the evolution of European integration. The issue of European integration has above all cut across and divided existing parties (Evans 2003). The 2005 referendum on the EU constitutional treaty laid bare the divisions of French parties over Europe, especially the Socialist Party. Since the defeat of the constitutional treaty, both PS and UMP have adopted a more critical tone towards 'Brussels', the issue barely featuring in the 2007 presidential election campaign. The leading French parties have usually been in a minority within the trans-national formations, such as the Party of European Socialists. French parties have not made a great impact at the EU level. European elections are still seen by the main players as second-order elections fought under proportional representation. Paradoxically, Eurosceptical parties such as the CPNT, MPF or MRC tend to do rather well in these elections (especially in 1999), but then use the institution to contest the European Parliament itself (Rozenberg 2007). The strange lack of interest from leading French party figures in the European Parliament has certainly not enhanced French influence in Strasbourg.

Inertia and the causality of policy change

In the Europeanisation literature, inertia signals the absence of clear causal relationships between policy change and European integration. The case of economic and monetary union demonstrates the limits of Europeanisation analysis. EMU is the Europeanised policy domain *par excellence*. But, as I have argued elsewhere, EMU was only possible because the fundamental economic policy paths in France, Germany and elsewhere had narrowed long before the moves to monetary union (Cole 2001b). Monetary union crowned a process of EC economic convergence that was already well engaged. From the 1970s onwards, German norms in economic management were exported across Europe. The 'strong franc' policy pursued in France intermittently from 1976 onwards (and vigorously after 1983) had a domestic political origin. After the 1983 economic U-turn, the main parties were all committed to a monetary policy of shadowing the D-Mark. Quite apart from its contribution to macro-economic stability, 'tying hands' by shadowing the D-Mark performed a valuable domestic politics function; it allowed French policy-makers to identify an external scapegoat for overdue internal reforms (Cole 2001a). French governors also feel trapped by certain aspects of EMU. They have invested considerable political capital in arguing for more political steering over the European economy and more political control over the European Central Bank. Elected president after a campaign in which he repeatedly berated the European Central Bank, Nicolas Sarkozy took the unprecedented step in July 2007 of attending the meeting of eurozone finance ministers and arguing the French case for a delay in reducing its deficit and debt.

The above examples each concern institutions, actors or policy processes whose functioning has been influenced by European integration, but where causalities are ambivalent, and where more convincing narratives are required to identify more fundamental underlying causes of change or stability.

From inertia to rejection

Cole and Drake (2000) argued that Europeanisation operates an independent variable when policies developed by the European Union have produced change that goes against the grain of widely disseminated national traditions. In the case of France the toughest challenges have been in those areas where the French model has been the most distinctive, in public services and industrial policy notably. In most respects, the EU operates as a regulatory, rather than a distributive 'government' (Lowi 1964; Majone 1996). Consistent with the contingent interpretation of Europeanisation presented above, the regulatory policy style of the EU can either conflict with or comfort the policy norms prevalent in member states. These tensions are obvious in the field of competition policy. Whereas Britain has the reputation for being an 'awkward partner', British governments have viewed EU competition policy as an example of best practice, preventing state interventionism and ensuring a level playing-field between firms and countries. In the mainstream French tradition, in contrast, competition policy is criticised as a practice inspired by US anti-trust policies, designed primarily to safeguard the interests of non-European (American and Japanese) trans-national corporations. As it emerged during the 1990s, competition policy threatened cherished French beliefs about the role of public service and economic policy, and forced French governments to abandon key elements of their post-war political and economic model.

The French notion of public service (*service public*) has traditionally gone well beyond that of universalistic welfare to include a high degree of interventionism in the industrial sphere, and the defence of monopoly utility providers such as the former gas and electricity conglomerate EDF-GDF. Traditional French conceptions of public service were based on the delivery of essential services by public sector monopolies (gas, electricity, rail, postal and telecommunication services, air transport), which benefited from protection against domestic or foreign competition, and which were accorded a public service mission in French administrative law (Gugliemi 1994). The implementation of EU competition policy posed a stark challenge to traditional paradigms. As it evolved during the 1980s, this model of delivering public services ran against the grain of EU competition policy. Strengthened by the tough competition regulations of the Single European Act, the Commission developed several mechanisms to break up monopolies, based on the model of US anti-trust legislation backed up by independent regulators. Favoured measures included privatisation, the strict regulation of state subsidies, the opening up of specific industrial sectors to competition and the creation of independent competition agencies (Thatcher 1997; Schmidt 2002). The liberal narrative of opening up monopolies was prevalent within the Commission *and* the Council, excluding broader social considerations.

The process of European integration directly challenged the French public service model. There was a strong belief that this emerging EU regulatory model was incompatible with the French public service mission (Klom 1996; Duperon 2003). Even determined French pressure was unable to prevent the liberalisation of the telecommunications and air-transport markets, traditionally the bastions of French state 'national champions'. At best, France was able to delay opening up the energy, rail and postal sectors to competition. At the Barcelona summit in 2002, the French finally agreed to open up the private domestic energy market by 2007 (the 400 largest energy consumers having been able to choose since 2001). French government responses varied somewhat according to the various services. In the telecoms sector, France could see the technical advantages of increasing competition and expanding markets, and created national-level regulatory agencies early on (ART). But opening up the gas and electricity sectors created great opposition, with French governments oscillating between open resistance and industrial manœuvring to limit any eventual foreign penetration of French markets. The rail service is likely to be the scene for a major battle, and the French government is (at the time of writing) still opposing the opening up of postal markets in 2009.[19]

In most respects, the history of public service reform cast France as a loser. France was unable to defend key domestic interests, in the form of the public sector unions dominating the powerful energy firms. It lost the battle at the level of ideas, unable to convince or persuade its partners of the virtues of its model of public services. French governments did score some victories, however. Under French pressure, article 16 of the Amsterdam treaty entrusted the European Commission with responsibility for 'making sure that general interest services are able to secure their missions'. The Charter of Fundamental Rights appended to the Treaty of Nice (2001) made access to these services a fundamental right of EU citizens. More recently, French politicians from all parties were united in opposing the proposed Bolkestein services directive. France was joined by Germany in its bitter opposition to the services directive, which set out to create a common market in services through the 'country of origin' principle.[20] Faced with German and French resistance, the services directive was shelved in March 2005 and a much-watered-down version agreed in 2006. As they had over the stability pact, France and Germany demonstrated their capacity to resist some of the most unwelcome features of Europeanisation, but this defensive stance revealed considerable unease about the direction of the European construction.

European integration has also affected cognitive assumptions about national and European models, at least among the elites. As the example of EMU demonstrated, member states are influenced by competing models in their midst. If there is no convergence towards a single European social model, there is an important European dimension to social or educational policy (Mandin and Palier 2004; van Zanten 2006). Best practice and a desire to imitate the most successful can produce a type of institutional isomorphism, a practice given a legal

---

[19] Interview, Council of State, January 2006.
[20] Service providers across Europe would be subject to the norms and regulations of their country of origin, rather than the host country. France and Germany feared an influx of professionals from central and eastern European countries, undercutting their national agreements.

base with the OMC, which involves member states agreeing upon trans-national benchmarks, exchanging good practice and publishing targets (Radaelli 1997; Dehousse 2004). 'Soft law' has become an increasingly important instrument of EU governance, especially in the fields of employment, anti-poverty strategies, education and pension reform, where the agenda-setting role has passed from supra-national actors to national governments. While successive French governments have struggled with the hard regulatory EU that emerged from the Single European Act, however, they are not especially at ease with the softer, standard-setting approach of the OMC. French positions are often in a minority, especially since the most recent enlargement of the EU. Under the Nice formula, France has 9% of qualified majority votes, a figure that will eventually increase to 13% under the Lisbon Treaty. Selck and Kaeding (2004) calculate that France is less successful than the UK, Germany or even Italy in transforming its original policy preferences into EU legislative acts.

French perceptions of a loss of influence in the European Commission are very real. The retreat of the French language in EU business since the 1995 enlargement is widely acknowledged.[21] In the European Parliament, while Germany has consistently argued for more powers, France has dragged its feet and has been highly ineffective, on account of the fragmentation of its European representation, the continuing tradition of *cumul des mandats* and the Paris-centric nature of French politics. This perception of a loss of national prestige is closely linked to issues of national and European identity and provokes the question whether Europeanisation itself is in crisis (Cautrès and Dennis 2002).

The 2005 referendum on the draft constitutional treaty

The rejection of the constitutional treaty in the May 2005 referendum sent shockwaves around Europe. There was a 'no' vote of 54.7 per cent (45.3 per cent for 'yes') on a high turnout (69.4 per cent). Thirteen years earlier, the Maastricht referendum of 1992 had offered a narrow

---

[21] English is the only language used in the European Central Bank. And though French remains the principal mode of communication in the European Court of Justice, it is in retreat in the European Parliament, in the Commission and in Council meetings.

victory to the 'yes' camp (51–49), with a similar turnout. The 'no' vote increased by almost 5.72 per cent of electors in comparison with 1992 (Hainsworth 2006). It recruited a majority of electors in all social classes except the liberal professions. The 'no' vote in 2005 brought together the traditional opponents of a more integrated Europe with all those who wanted to oppose the incumbent government. The mainstays of the 'no' camp in the two referendums were the left of the left and the right of the right, with 'no' in 1992 and 2005 supported by the vast bulk of electors identifying with the FN, the PCF and the far left (Perrineau 2005: 239). This traditional alliance represented three-quarters of the 'no' vote in 2005. They were joined by a small majority of PS voters, signifying a major shift since 1992, with 56 per cent of declared PS electors voting 'no' in 2005, against only 22 per cent thirteen years earlier.

There is a convincing argument that the referendum was mainly about domestic French politics. The key to understanding the 'no' vote was a deep-rooted social and political malaise, not a rejection of the EU. It was the latest manifestation of a rejection of the political incumbents. Events during the campaign – such as unemployment rising above 10 per cent in March 2005 – also had an influence. The 'no' vote had become a left vote (55–45), whereas it had been a right vote (67–33) in 1992. If the primary focus was domestic, the referendum campaign revealed deep-seated popular fears about the direction of European integration. The campaign abounded with uncertainties about the new Europe. The proposed Bolkestein services directive mobilised trade unions and anti-globalisation groups such as ATTAC in fierce opposition to the treaty. The centre of gravity of the French debate revolved around a binary opposition between 'social' Europe, presented as consistent with national traditions, and an alien 'liberal' Europe. Defenders of the constitutional treaty were forced onto the defensive, summoned to justify their support for a 'liberal' Europe that reputedly challenged the French social model. More than ever, the 2005 campaign polarised two Frances, one in favour of European cosmopolitanism and neutral towards globalisation; another fearful of change and defensive towards the nation-state. Politically, this division cut across left and right. Sociologically, the new feature in 2005 was that sections of the middle classes joined the camp of popular and populist opposition to 'neo-liberal' Europe, if not to European integration itself (Perrineau 2005). Similar divisions can be mapped in relation to 'globalisation', firmly opposed by around 50 per cent of the French electorate (Meunier 2004; Brouard and Tiberj 2006).

By 2005, Euroscepticism had become a theme that sustained some political parties and caused deep internal divisions in others. Rozenberg (2007) identifies four distinct types of partisan resistance to enhanced European integration that have arisen in the past decade. The far-right Front National has become Europhobic, though this has not always been the case and its anti-EU stance is less central to its core political message than the issues of immigration, insecurity and national identity. The second type of resistance to European integration is in the name of the defence of national sovereignty, ranging from the ultra-conservative Movement for France (*Mouvement pour la France* – MPF) to the left-leaning Republican and Citizens' Movement (*Mouvement Républicain et Citoyen* – MRC). These small but influential parties mobilise support against European integration and unregulated free trade on the grounds of protecting the nation from foreign political and economic influence. The third explicitly Eurosceptical force is the influential rural lobby, articulated in part by the Hunters and Fishers Movement (*Chasse, Pêche, Nature, Traditions* – CPNT). The rural lobby includes a denser network of national politicians (PS and UMP) practising the *cumul des mandats*, who advocate the defence of the French rural way of life. Defending local traditions against the incursions of Brussels is a popular theme, and can explain the reluctance of French governments to transpose EU directives that directly challenge the ruralist lobby. Fourth, anti-globalisation movements such as ATTAC and the European Social Forum have adopted an explicit stance against enhanced European integration, which is taken to be synonymous with the diffusion of a neo-liberal economic philosophy.

These empirical cases demonstrate examples of adaptation, inertia and resistance to change. Adaptation usually involves some form of strategic calculation of the benefits to be gained from advocating European solutions. In the case of the Council of State, this involved over-adapting to Europe as a means of consolidating domestic influence. For a number of social movements and pressure groups, the EU quite simply provided an arena for pursuing group interests and indirectly influencing domestic outcomes. Inertia described institutional responses, actor strategies and diffused policy processes where there was only an indirect causal link with European integration, but where Europeanisation became part of the broader operating principles.

Resistance came from increasingly vocal Eurosceptical parties and movements and from sections of public opinion deeply worried about change and defensive towards the nation-state. Arguably more interesting than the explicitly Eurosceptical movements is the reluctance of the main parties, UMP and especially PS,[22] to engage with European integration. While 'Europe' was largely a positive construction until the early 1990s, the Maastricht referendum of 1992 sharply divided popular opinion, and, at a stroke, reduced the efficacy of using the European argument to justify unpopular domestic reforms or attract electoral support. Europe has a weakening capacity to act as a legitimising device to allow France's governors to modernise the country. The distaste expressed by the popular electorate for the Brussels technocrats is linked to the perception that the French social model is under attack from a neo-liberal 'Brussels', a perception strengthened by the declarations of leading French politicians and consistent with existing discursive frames.

France's European governance

One of the core dimensions of governing as governance lies in the relativity of spatial and temporal boundaries and the multiplication of levels of regulation that impact upon any given 'territory' in this case France. The various governance hypotheses formulated in Chapter 1 would all appear to have some currency in relation to the EU. The description of the EU as a regulatory regime by Majone (1996) in the mid-1990s has had a lasting influence. With few budgetary or administrative means at its disposal, the EU mainly regulates, rather than administers or redistributes. Conscious of criticisms of its own democratic deficit, the EU is also the site where competing versions of participatory governance are tested. Its processes have been described in terms of quasi-pluralism, an institutional set-up that offers a large degree of access and influence to economic interest groups, social movements and think tanks (Mazey and Richardson 2006). EU capacity-building involves developing new forms of interaction between the

---

[22] The 2005 referendum campaign caused a serious division within the Socialist Party, with a minority around Laurent Fabius ignoring the 'yes' vote of the party's internal referendum and openly allying with the PCF, the far left and with anti-globalisation groups such as ATTAC.

state and civil society and elaborating new instruments of coordination. The EU is the original terrain where theories of multi-level governance took root and where they remain the most pertinent. The EU Commission has adopted governance as a framework for its attempts to enhance its own efficiency and transparency and to broaden its capacity by associating a broad range of professional business actors and sources of expertise. It practises multi-actorness better than any national government. Consistent with the functional dynamics hypothesis, moreover, we observe that the European policy process is expert-focused and sector-specific. The description of the EU as a system of networked governance (Kohler-Koch and Eising 1999) exercising functions of coordination and regulation that cut across the traditional competencies of the nation-state appears compelling. In one version of the globalisation literature, the EU is the institutional form for embedding the norms of the international political economy, notably through a mutualisation of currency exchange risk and an institutional embedding of core neo-liberal values (Dyson 2002).

The case of France demonstrates that there is no simple process of translation of EU-level variables to the national context, and that the grammar of Europeanisation is declined in distinct ways in different countries. If, in our first hypothesis, the French state has assumed a regulatory form, then the French regulatory state itself is regulated in most of its fields of activity by the European Commission, the European Court of Justice, the European Central Bank and associated EU-level agencies. The regulatory mode of governance is the prevalent one in the field of competition policy, the environment, technical standards, monetary policy and banking in particular. In at least some of these cases, there appear to be tensions between traditional policy stances and the challenges of European integration. The challenge of competition policy to the survival of French public services is the most obvious case. The resentment felt towards the European Central Bank by successive French leaders is another. The French case is clearly not one of participatory modes of modern governance in so far as the EU is concerned. Rates of participation in European elections are low and French parties do not give a high political saliency to the European Parliament. The evidence for European governance as embedding multi-level dynamics is, in the French case, rather less convincing than that for Spain, the UK, Germany or Italy. Likewise, in relation to multi-actor coordination, France comes closest to sustaining a formal bureaucratic mode of state-led coordination, one that ignores local and regional authorities and downplays the need to lobby actively in defence of French firms and associations.

Is there a misfit between the traditional French state-centric model and this model of EU networked governance? European integration has clearly challenged some core features associated with the traditional state-centric model of French politics and policies (Ladrech 1994; Balme and Woll 2005; Drake 2005; Smith 2005; Grossman and Sauger 2007). But a word of temporal caution is necessary. To the extent that French 'statism' has been reshaped, this is due at least as much to other variables (domestic-level adaptation to global economic pressures) as to European integration itself. The effects of European integration on domestic polities are contingent on underlying events and closely related to the history of the EU itself. The role of the EU in the mid-1980s, before the implementation of the Single European Act, was vastly different from that in the mid-2000s. The number of countries more than doubled across the period and the EU expanded its capacities considerably. The closeness of domestic fit can vary considerably, with overarching developments in European integration appearing closer at some stages of history to national 'models' than at others. Even in countries such as Germany, perceptions of the European construction are not static. As a hybrid quasi-polity, the EU challenges core features of each one of its member states, including France.

The chapter has none the less noted a shift in the way in which Europe is constructed by French elites. Historically, European integration was a powerful discursive register to facilitate change within France, French governors relying on the pro-European sentiment of most French people to push through reform. Such tactics have had diminishing returns. The disastrous dissolution of the National Assembly in 1997, supposedly called to give President Chirac a mandate to allow France to join in the euro, revealed the limits of such appeals. Since the early 2000s, the EU has been routinely blamed by French politicians for national economic ills. To the extent that Europe is seen as part of the domestic problem, it can no longer be used as a legitimising device to justify change. Europe has lost its rhetorical power to persuade. The perception – played out fully in the 2005 referendum campaign – that France no longer counts as much in Europe was always likely to be punished by French electors. The loss of the constructed reality of a Europe designed in French interests is a bitter pill to swallow.

5 | *State capacity and public policy*

While 'government' evokes the sense of the regular exercise of hierarchical power across the whole range of areas of public policy, 'governance' describes a more mediated, context-specific process. The dynamics of public policy vary according to the nature of the policy problem, the characteristics of the policy sector, key historical junctures and path-dependent decisions and the configurations of the actors in play. For those analysts imbued with the concept, policy dynamics can best be understood by fine-grained comparisons of contrasting policy *sectors*. From this perspective, the dynamics in economic development, welfare or education are contingent upon the structural qualities of the sectors concerned, or, in a weaker definition, upon the structural context within which games are played or prevailing ideas or discursive registers diffused. Thus framed, policy sectors can be compared in terms of their ideational structures and discursive coalitions; their institutions, actors and networks; the exogenous or endogenous provenance of change therein; and their capacity for legitimising or resisting change.

Reasoning in terms of policy sectors, the approach adopted here for the sake of comparison, emphasises the contingent nature of power and process. Generalities, whether about power or the nature of the state, require fine-grained, meso-level analysis to be undertaken to provide support for or to falsify general propositions. Comparing distinct areas of public policy is a robust means of testing propositions about governance, as well as revisiting representations of France as a state-centric polity. The three policy sectors investigated in this chapter are the economy, the welfare state and education. The dynamics of governance are mediated and context-specific. The conclusion relates sector-specific analysis to the overarching framework developed in Chapter 1.

The economy and economic development: from *dirigisme* to globalisation

Representations of France as a state-centric polity are strongly rooted in traditions of *dirigisme* in the economic policy sphere. There is an abundant literature dedicated to *dirigisme* in France, one of the key models in the varieties of capitalism literature (Hall 1986, 2001; Hayward 1986, 1997; Schmidt 1996, 2002; Culpepper 2006; McClean 2006). As it operated from 1945 to 1973, *dirigisme* described a particular mode of state economic interventionism, characterised by a mix of indicative planning, administered financing, an active industrial policy aimed at creating national champions and a specific pattern of government–industry relations.

Planning was the most visible element of the *dirigiste* contribution to the French economy, though arguably not the most significant. After the devastation of the Second World War, a set of five-year plans fixed goals for particular industrial sectors and singled out priorities for economic development. Arguably more central to *dirigisme* was the economy of administered financing that Cohen (1996) labelled as 'capitalism without capital'. The French model looked to the state as the main investor in firms, rather than the Paris stock exchange or the international financial markets (Cohen 1996; Kassim 1997). With control over the Bank of France and the banking and insurance systems, by the early 1980s the state controlled the flow of credit. As the private sector depended – by and large – upon the state for capital, governments had the upper hand in their relationships with French firms (Hayward 1997). At the heart of the *dirigiste* model was the construction of the state as entrepreneur and a belief in industrial policy (McClean 2006). In a *dirigiste* sense, governments should be able to direct the market and engineer industrial change in the long-term national strategic interest. The policy of creating national champions assumed a strong (if flexible) state and a high degree of national economic sovereignty. *Dirigisme* also rested upon the close interpenetration of political, administrative and business elites, and hence helped to shape a distinctive pattern of French elitism.

The French model of politics and policy presupposed a rather different equilibrium between state and market than that of its neighbours. There was more *dirigisme*. But there have always been two faces to French economic activity. On the one hand, an interventionist state which actively promoted national champions and engaged in neo-protectionist practices (Schmidt 1996). On the other, French governments in the Fifth Republic pursued a liberal macro-economic policy based on sound money policies and international competitiveness (Dyson and Featherstone 1999). The French economy thus developed under the dual impetus of state capitalism and classical liberalism. What set French post-war capitalism apart was the relative weighting of the state–market mix, being rather more state-driven in the French case than in other comparable countries, but remaining fundamentally a mixed economy.

As classically conceived, *dirigisme* is no longer possible in contemporary France. According to Cohen (1996), the preconditions for *dirigiste* policies were offensive protectionism, public procurement policies, direct state aid and long-term political support (but weak political interference). Contemporary France is embedded in Europeanised economic structures, both in terms of EMU, which imposes strict rules upon domestic economic management and public administration, and the single market, policed by a vigilant European Commission and European Court of Justice, which limits public grants to firms in difficulty and enforces a strict competition policy regime. France is also locked into the global economic order. In economic policy, France has largely played the globalisation game: accepting the end of credit controls in 1990, gradually dismantling the model of state capitalism and Europeanising monetary policy through joining the euro. In the economic arena, global capitalism lessens the reliance of French business on the French state and increases the importance of international capital flows, cross-shareholdings and the international strategies of French groups (themselves very proficient at playing the global card). Inward investment decisions taken by foreign companies can have a major impact on French employment levels, but foreign companies are not usually willing to channel their investment in accordance with French regional policy objectives.

Not only has France become more structurally embedded in the world economy, it has developed a distinctive and successful form of capitalism, built in part upon a thoroughgoing policy of privatisation. Two decades of privatisation since 1986 have transformed the face of

French industry.[1] Around 50 firms and around 1,000,000 workers have been transferred from the public to the private sector. The French state has withdrawn from detailed managerial interference in these privatised firms, though it always attempted to retain influence. French capitalism has been transformed in the process, with large French firms becoming global players with their own strategies. If there is one France that loses from globalisation, there is another one that gains. National champions such as Renault, Carrefour, Bouygues or L'Oréal have all benefited from the opening of global markets. Globalisation has liberated France's captains of industry. Previously under-capitalised groups have now become major players on the world scene. The case of Renault, which has taken over Nissan and become the fourth-largest car-manufacturer in the world, best elucidates the international focus of French business. Socialist Premier Jospin could do nothing in 1997 when Renault chose to close its Vilivoorde factory in Belgium shortly after his arrival in power. French national champions are now able to threaten to delocalise production and move jobs in order to cut costs.

The governance of the leading firms is now much more focused on the international financial markets than the French finance ministry. The Paris *Bourse* has successfully established itself as the leading

---

[1] From the perspective of the French state there have been a number of intended and unintended consequences. The French state has attempted to retain influence. Even after the vast privatisation programme undertaken since 1986, the French state retained in 2006 important minority shareholdings in key groups such as Renault (15.3 per cent), SNECMA (30.8 per cent), Air France-KLM (18.6 per cent), EADS (*c.* 15 per cent), France Télécom (32.5 per cent), as well as majority shares in the former state bastions of EDF (87.3 per cent). But the capacity of the French state to undertake a coherent industrial policy has weakened, as has its ability to intervene in the affairs of leading French firms. Since privatisation a number of the privatised firms have been taken over by foreign groups: Pechiney (Alcan), AGF (Allianz) and the CCF (HSBC). A much larger number of mergers have involved French firms only, such as Paribas (BNP); UAP (Axa); Elf Aquitaine (Total); CIC (Credit Mutuel) and GAN (Groupama). The logic of cross-national alliance-building has sometimes introduced privatisation by the back door, as in the case of Air France (the state had to give up its majority shareholding to allow the merger with KLM) and GDF (the privatisation of GDF being the price of engineering a French merger between GDF and Suez, to prevent a take-over by the Italian ENEL). In the case of GDF and Suez, the politically sensitive, Sarkozy-driven merger resulted in a part-nationalisation of the previously independent Suez, leaving the French state with a blocking minority in the new energy group.

player in the pan-European Euronext alliance. The take-over of Euronext by the NYSE in summer 2006 raised some political objections, but few discordant voices were heard from French firms on grounds of economic patriotism. The counterpart to operating in a more open economy is that overseas interests now control 47 per cent of the capital of the CAC 40 (Clift 2004). The openness of the French economy explains the increase in foreign direct investment, with France second behind the UK in the EU. That Anglo-Saxon pension funds have become the new masters of the French economy is not to everybody's taste (Culpepper 2006).

There is some dispute among specialists about the extent to which French economic policy has been transformed. Levy (2005) contests the belief that nothing much has changed about the direction of French economic policy since the 1983 U-turn. In this 'false narrative', old *dirigiste* instincts remain very much alive. The French economic model still looks to an active industrial policy, to the extent of flouting EU competition and state-aid policy. State activism is directed at encouraging and financing extensive research and training, bringing under-performing regions into national productivity (*aménagement du territoire*), promoting collaboration (rather than competition) between leading French firms and building essential economic infrastructure. There remains much opposition to opening up markets, especially in infrastructure and electricity.[2] There is some evidence to support such a view. French governments have continued to attempt to engineer industrial change, prevent hostile take-overs and practise economic patriotism, with mixed results (Clift 2008). The Raffarin government, for example, rescued a bankrupt France Télécom in 2002 and Alstom, the maker of high-speed trains, in 2003. In 2005, French Premier de Villepin orchestrated a highly public campaign to dissuade the US firm Pepsi Cola from making a bid for French national champion Danone. This episode was followed, in 2006, by de Villepin introducing a policy on industrial patriotism that was immediately criticised by the European Commission: the French government outlined ten areas of strategic national importance in which it would resist foreign take-overs. Many other examples could be given.

And yet, the belief that nothing has changed is ultimately a false narrative. The *dirigiste* instincts displayed by the de Villepin

---

[2] Interviews in Council of State, January 2006.

government (2005–7) ought not to be equated with *dirigiste* capacity. On a number of highly publicised occasions, French governments have been unable either to engineer domestic economic change, or to prevent unwelcome take-overs. In 1999, for example, the Jospin government was unable to cajole the leading French banks (BNP, Societé Générale and Paribas) into merging to form a national banking champion. In 2002, the Raffarin government was powerless to prevent the take-over of former national champion Pechiney by the Canadian Alcan (2002). Most spectacularly, in 2006, after a long struggle, Indian steel-maker Mittal launched a successful take-over of 'European champion' Arcelor in spite of the covert resistance of the French and Luxembourg governments. Though French governments retain influence, they have lost the capacity to direct the strategies of leading French firms. France's global champions, of which there are an impressive number, fear retaliation in return for any protectionist measures adopted in France. The president of the employers' federation MEDEF, Laurence Parisot, harshly criticised the policy of economic patriotism decreed by de Villepin in 2006 as not only unworkable, but also damaging to the interests of French firms trading in global markets.

France and globalisation

If French firms are playing the globalisation game with profit, French politicians from left and right have adopted a more cautious approach and argued in favour of a managed globalisation that protects French interests (*mondialisation maîtrisée*). One source close to the de Villepin government defined *mondialisation maîtrisée* as a demand for rules for international and European economic governance, tougher regulation of the environment, a defence of the cultural exception and support for linguistic diversity.[3] Gordon and Meunier (2001) identify the core features of managed globalisation as: maintaining the state, building a stronger Europe, managing international trade and creating new rules for governing the international system.

Managed globalisation relies above all upon a Europe that is strong enough to regulate international capitalism, and whose social model is

[3] Intervention by a representative of the French trade ministry at a conference on the World Trade Organization Doha round, 15 February 2007, CERI, Sciences Po, Paris.

an inspiration to others. If this theme resonates most strongly with the left, it also formed a central part of President Chirac's discourse from 1995 to 2007. The Jospin government was explicit about strengthening the EU as a tool to manage globalisation (Cole 2001b; McClean and Milner 2001). A managed globalisation would allow Europe to exercise more influence in trade negotiations, foreign policy and monetary policy. Managed globalisation implies a tightly steered trade policy that defends European interests in international trade negotiations (Kresl and Gallais 2002). France fought hard during the 1986–93 Uruguay GATT round to keep services, intellectual property and culture off the international trade agenda (Webber 1999). In the 1994 GATT treaty, the EU obtained the right to exclude education and culture from international trade in goods and services, and France retained the right to subsidise its domestic cinema production. Upon France's insistence, the Treaty of Nice then enshrined the principle of the cultural exception in EU law. France has thus far been able to resist strong pressure from the Commission to introduce QMV to trade in services and intellectual property issues.

France was a strong supporter of creating the World Trade Organization in 1995 as a tougher international trade organisation with binding arbitration mechanisms. She has consistently tried to broaden the scope of trade negotiations to include workers' rights, the environment, health and food safety. Her stance on agriculture and the unconditional defence of farm subsidies brought French governments into conflict with EU trade commissioners during the on–off Doha round launched in 2001. Quite apart from agriculture, France tends to align with the more protectionist wing of the EU, especially in relation to China. Thus, when in 2006 the end of the multi-fibre agreement resulted in free-flowing Chinese textiles imports into Europe, France and Italy headed the resistance and pressurised the Commission into renegotiating a bilateral agreement with China.

To borrow concepts from the Europeanisation chapter, French governments have had mixed success in uploading their understanding of managed globalisation to the EU and global arenas. But such efforts are partly for domestic consumption. Constructing globalisation in terms of multi-polarity, global regulation, the importance of rules and the need for EU-wide responses suits French governors so much more than adapting the hard language of neo-liberal competition and the race to the bottom in welfare. Such a construction confers meaning on the contemporary world in ways that are consistent with powerful domestic discursive registers.

The dynamics of governance

Accounts of post-war economic development generally insisted upon a coherent *référentiel* and an identifiable professional–bureaucratic coalition driving change, especially during the 1945–73 period. Schmidt (1996) identifies the 'independent administrative bureaucracy' as an important actor in driving economic modernisation. For Hayward (1986) state interventionism was able to flourish within the French economy because of a combination of active techno-bureaucratic leadership and passive democratic support. This *dirigiste* model rested upon a pattern of close interlocking relationships between the civil service, political elites and the boards of the leading French firms, often dependent on public procurement policies. Though largely state-driven, this interventionist model came to be appropriated by social partners. Trade unions (especially) and the main employers' association (CNPF) looked traditionally to the state to arbitrate a top-down style of industrial relations, where the state showed the direction to the employers and the trade unions. The traditionally closed policy communities based on interlocking politico-administrative and business elites have weakened somewhat. Today's aspiring members of the French business elite are now likely to add an MBA from a US university to their passage through Polytechnique, X or ENA.

The dynamics of governance in economic development are thus best understood in terms of the changing balance between politics and markets and a weakening state steering capacity. Perceptions of a strong strategic state are deeply embedded in France. The public sector remains larger in France than elsewhere, as does the presence of the state in French economic management and levels of state spending. Yet, as Levy (2005: 170) argues, the French statist model has undoubtedly been weakened since 1983. Planning, industrial policies and *grands projets* belong to the past; most nationalised companies have been privatised; credit, price and capital controls have been lifted; restrictions on lay-offs and temporary and part-time employment have been eased; and 'A macroeconomic orientation emphasizing inflationary growth coupled with large devaluations has given way to one of the lowest inflation rates in Europe and a strong franc, culminating in European Monetary Union (EMU)'(Levy 2005: 170).

Social policy, the welfare state and the French social model

If the *dirigiste* state was irremediably weakened after 1983, Levy (2005) identifies the emergence in the 1980s of the 'social anesthesia state' which undertook a substantial expansion of welfare and labour market measures in order to protect French workers from the harshest effects of the move to the market. Other writers, such as Smith (2004), have similarly emphasised the trade-off between economic liberalisation and social protection. Though unable to direct the economy, the French state has enhanced its intervention in social, welfare and labour market policy in the past two decades. But the overall picture is one of limited state capacity and an inability to steer effectively a policy domain where path dependencies are particularly strong and resistant to change.

It lies beyond the boundaries of the current study to comment in detail on the functioning of social welfare in France, a theme the interested reader will find amply developed elsewhere (Palier 2000, 2006; Smith 2004; Revauger 2006). It is difficult to portray welfare as a single policy sector; rather it encompasses health care, old-age pensions, family policy, unemployment insurance, even education, fields that each have their own dynamics. When the scope is broadened to include the elusive 'French social model', the unit of analysis is still more difficult to define. Some basic definitions do help. In France, social security refers primarily to the contributions-based system of health insurance. There are also separate old-age pensions and family allowance schemes, as well as funds for the unemployed. Health care, family allowances and old-age pensions are managed by insurance funds (*caisses*), which are administered by the social partners (the trade unions and the employers' federations). The principle of social partnership spills over into related areas such as unemployment insurance and training that are also governed on the basis of self-managing funds. Though these funds (*caisses*) enter into contractual agreements with the state, they are managed in a semi-autonomous way. The union Force Ouvrière for long controlled the main health insurance fund, for example, and was renowned for its independent style of management. A priori, the policy style in welfare is that of steering by social partners and the professions and limited state capacity, whether in terms of directing institutions, controlling outcomes or limiting expenditure. Social policy has some key features of a self-regulating network, shaped by strong professional pressures and relatively weak political influence. Though the state aspires to exercise a directive influence, it has proved very difficult to implement reforms.

Political scientists and sociologists have been drawing welfare maps of Europe for the past twenty years. In his seminal study, Esping Anderson (1990) identified the three main welfare models as social-democratic universalistic welfare states (prevalent in Scandinavia), minimal welfare states (the Anglo-Saxon model) and corporatist welfare states, the norm throughout much of western Europe. Subsequent writers have included new categories such as the Mediterranean model. In terms of basic principles, however, there are two main types. The Bismarckian model is a system of social insurance based on contributions and administered by the representatives of the insured (workers and employers). The Beveridge model provides for a system of universal cover, financed mainly by general taxation and only partly by contributions. France falls uneasily within these general typologies, but is closer to the Bismarkian corporatist model than to others. This incremental mix is important for understanding policy dynamics in this sphere.

The French welfare model is an institutional hybrid that emerged in a sedimentary manner in response to social challenges. Post-war social reformers looked closely at the Beveridge report and the model of a universalistic welfare state. As Smith (2004: 32) points out, however, the idea of universalism was rejected by the workforce itself in 1945, as layer upon layer of occupational pension and health schemes had already been established during the inter-war period. French trade unions fought for a large administrative role in managing any social insurance system. The system created in 1945 granted the trade unions and employers' federations a central role in co-managing the social security regime. Though essentially contributions-based, since the late 1980s most new welfare measures – CMU, RMI – have been financed by general taxation (CSG) and have been designed to provide a safety net to prevent the most vulnerable people in society from falling into destitution (Palier 2006). The French welfare state is thus a patchwork, combining contributions, universal benefits and charity, and encompassing a sub-set of distinct policy fields, the two most important of which we now briefly survey.

The French health care system is by and large an insurance-based model, unlike the NHS in Britain. All employees contribute to health funds that are administered by the unions and employers. Health benefits are usually reserved to those who are working: until the introduction of the CMU programme by the Jospin government, there had been no available health care for the non-working poor. The system is complex. There is one general health fund – the CNAM – but there are also many profession-specific ones, which provide top-up benefits. Health care provides a good example of British dogmatism and French pragmatism. There is little trace of the social engineering so prevalent in the case of the National Health Service (NHS) in Britain. The NHS was created against the fierce opposition of the medical profession; in the French case, the system of social security established in 1945 was superimposed upon a set of pre-existing arrangements and compromises, first and foremost with the medical profession. There is little opposition in France to the private management of public goods in health care. Within limits, consumers are free to choose between public and private and are entitled to social security coverage, whoever the provider. The policy style of health care is thus one that appears to go against a 'statist' model of development. The governance of health care has a strongly corporatist flavour. There is a consensus among social partners to retain a high level of health expenditure that escapes in the main from central government control.

The contributions-based system also underpins the French system of old-age pensions. As with health care, there is one overarching state pension scheme and a morass of profession-specific ones. The fundamental principle of the pay-as-you-go (*répartition*) regime is that those in work pay for the pensions of those who have retired. The idea is deeply rooted in the governance structure of old-age pensions and there has been massive hostility to private equity-based pensions within the policy community (from the trade unions in particular). There are a number of problems with pay-as-you-go schemes. First, the principle of intergenerational solidarity is sorely tested by demographic trends (Chauvel 2006). With a ratio of three workers for one pensioner in 1970, the figure is expected to fall to one in 2030. Governments have slowly recognised that the current generous system of pension provision is unsustainable and that employees need to work longer. After a bitter conflict, in 2003 the Raffarin government imposed the principal that the normal working life should be 42 years, to be implemented in phases by 2020. The other feature of the French case is the large number of special regimes effectively underwritten by the public purse. The French state guarantees the delivery of highly advantageous pension benefits to a number of key public sector workers, especially those in the power industry (EDF, GDF), the national railways (SNCF), the Paris Métro (RATP) as well as those with civil servant status working for France Télécom, previously a government department. These pension schemes are heavily in deficit and always rescued by the state. Back in 1995, Juppé ran against tough opposition in his forlorn quest to reform the special regimes. Though the Raffarin government introduced a fairly far-reaching pension reform in 2003, it did not affect the special regimes. President Sarkozy has made the reform of the special regimes a priority, but it remains to be seen whether reformist intent will produce substantive outcomes.

The difficulties of implementing reform in the social policy sector have been repeatedly demonstrated since the mid-1990s and the failure of the Juppé plan (Darnault 1997).[4] The French social model refers to a set of values that are much more deeply embedded than health and old age provision. For one observer, the French have an 'ideological' attachment to public service, with the mobilising myth of social progress by public service coming to form part of modern French political culture (Cohen 1996). The adversary is clearly identified – Anglo-Saxon neo-liberalism – though it is rarely defined in any detail. Mobilisation against the perceived ravages of neo-liberalism is strongest in the field of employment policy, where a dual labour market ensures a high level of social protection for those in work, but offers limited prospects for those outside of contributory social protection networks. The French social model prefers a high level of social protection over the free operation of labour markets and labour flexibility. French governments, especially Socialist-led ones, have

---

[4] The Juppé plan of 1995, which sought to contain spiralling health care and pension costs, provoked massive opposition, leading to reforms being either abandoned or watered down.

favoured state-led employment creation and protection schemes and adopted 'active' employment policies. Active employment policy takes a number of forms: from apprenticeships and work placements, to state-subsidised jobs and employers' social security exemptions.

There is a widely diffused, yet contested belief that government intervention works, the paradigm for which was the Jospin government's state orchestrated shift to a thirty-five-hour week in 1998 (Cournilleau, Heyer and Timbeau 1998; Coutrot 1999). The thirty-five-hour week legislation emphasised job creation through negotiated reductions in the working week (for all firms employing over twenty employees). Implementing the thirty-five-hour week would not only create jobs, but would also further the aims of an egalitarian social-democratic employment policy. In practice, the enforced reduction to a thirty-five-hour week restrained wage growth and was deeply unpopular in the 2002 presidential election with the Socialists' traditional electoral clientele. There were numerous unintended consequences. The branch-level negotiations led to national agreements being signed that allowed for the annual calculation of hours worked ('annualisation') and improved labour flexibility. The effects on employment, however, were deeply controversial and probably impossible to measure. The law assumed that there is a fixed employment total, with any reduction in the working week automatically creating new employment. This 'adequationist' belief was contested by many. The Socialist Employment minister Aubry claimed the legislation had created 600,000 new jobs, a claim challenged not only by political opponents but also by most economists. In ideological terms, the thirty-five-hour week policy was presented by the ruling Socialist party as an attempt to define social democratic employment policies that would combine an activist role for the state with an open economy in a globalising world. The Socialists thus explicitly rejected the 'neo-liberal' interpretation, according to which globalisation requires the structural reform of labour markets. The Socialist Party remained faithful to this approach in its 2006 programme (*projet socialiste*), and its candidate Ségolène Royal proposed to extend the thirty-five-hour obligation to all firms, whatever their size.

When attempting to reform labour markets, French governments come against widely diffused beliefs about the role of work, the search for security and social protection. The mass protests of France's youth against the First Employment Contract (CPE) of 2006

were highly revealing of the ideational context within which governments must operate. The CPE was intended as a bold policy to
respond to the high rate of youth unemployment. After implementing
a new short-term labour contract for the adult unemployed (the New
Employment Contract – CNE) the de Villepin government in early
2006 proposed to create a new labour contract for under-26-year-
olds, introducing a two-year flexible contract that would allow
employers to hire and fire with minimal notice. The measure was
presented as a trade-off between enhanced employment prospects
against a time-limited weakening of labour protection. The terms of
the debate were rejected by the mass protesters. France's student
population made clear its preference for secure, well-paid jobs rather
than flexible short-term contracts, even at the expense of a high rate
of young unemployment.

Dynamics of governance in social policy, the welfare state and the French social model

It is entirely appropriate to narrate the social model in France in terms
of governance. It involves the private management of public goods,
with private and professional actors exercising influence at the levels
of implementation and formulation. Social policy highlights the role of
non-governmental actors in the form of employers and trade unions
and the privileged status of the professions. The issue area of welfare
in particular also elucidates the capacity dimension of French governance: the management of an essential area of public policy escapes
from the tight stewardship of state actors, whatever the intention of
state reformers. The state is unable to control social expenditures and
frequently adds to its own financial burden by introducing short-term,
inflationary 'socially anesthetic' measures (Levy 1999, 2001, 2005).
The role of the state is modest in the administrative circuits that
govern the complex welfare system in France. In practice, the term
'welfare state' is shorthand for a network of interrelated social policy
processes whose dynamics are themselves variable, with the state a
more prominent actor in some sub-sectors – such as family policy –
than others. The prevailing representation characterises the French
welfare state in terms of path-dependent institutions and processes
(Taylor-Goodby 1999; Palier 2006). Change has been incremental
and sedimentary. Though path-dependent structures and expectations

have made major reform very difficult, there have been important incremental changes.[5]

The French social model enjoys broad public support, is embedded in robust institutional structures and mobilises the key social and professional actors. The downside is that corporatist welfare states are remarkably difficult to reform. Palier (2000) famously argued that the French welfare state is frozen. The heavy underlying variables are resistant to change. Welfare operates on the basis of contributory work-based benefits and gives only crumbs to the excluded, such as the non-working poor and the young. The structures of the French social model were designed with a full-employment society in mind. Though France is no longer a full-employment society, expectations of high social protection and well-paid jobs have endured. There is a highly diffused and fragmented authority structure which limits the influence of the state. Social partnership structures, once put into place, are resistant to reform and develop their own inflationary logic. More-over, they sustain social expectations that contribute to the broader problem of state capacity. Though the social protection bill is static – or rising – government revenue is dependent on the economic cycle. Since 1991, there has been a continual social security deficit – even after the Juppé plan. The French state often appears powerless to control social policy.

Education

Arguably no other policy arena is so redolent of the French state tradition as education. In the educational field the French state represents not merely a set of institutions, but also represents a core of beliefs and interests. Habits of centralised thinking in education remain very strong. National education traditions underpin norms and rules, as well as remaining deeply embedded in the consciousness and the behaviour of actors. The heavy variables underpinning the governance of the French education system are traditionally presented in terms of centralisation, uniformity and a neo-corporatist policy style (Archer 1979; Ambler 1985; Duclaud-Williams 1993; Corbett and

---

[5] Notably in terms of the introduction of 'universal' benefits in the form of the minimum revenue, universal means-tested health care or old-age dependency allowances.

Moon 1996; Deer 2002). Mary Archer's classic study provided a particularly influential framework for contrasting centralised and decentralised educational systems. The Archer model set up France as the paradigm of centralisation. In the centralised system, the central state is the leading element and all interactions are centripetal. Small modifications at the centre are felt throughout the system. In this model, a highly regimented Education ministry guarantees the centralised state model. In theory, the Education minister sits at the apex of a hierarchical, regimented organisation, which is coherently organised in its Parisian headquarters (107 rue de Grenelle). The main divisions within the ministry are each directly responsible to the minister, as are the general and administrative inspectorates. The central ministry – *la centrale* – has a powerful outreach to French regions and localities through its regional and departmental field services. At the bottom of the chain are the school heads in the primary, lower secondary (*collège*) and upper secondary (*lycée*) schools, directly responsible to the minister, as well as to their own governing boards. The Archer model explicitly expects lower levels to implement rules and regulations that are defined by the centre.

Education is certainly a field where professional and bureaucratic influences are deeply embedded. Powerful organised interests are central to the management of the sector. Ambler (1985, 2001) diagnosed three neo-corporatist features to French educational management: a mass membership trade union movement (then the FEN, now the SNES); a centralised form of bargaining and access to central policy-makers; and extensive delegated administrative powers to the unions. The civil servants of the main divisions within the Education ministry and the teaching unions have traditionally acted as the gatekeepers of professionalisation. Salaries, pay and promotions are determined by joint committees, composed of trade union representatives and ministry officials. Educational mobility generally remains determined at the national level, and only a small number of annual transfers between schools are allowed on the basis of seniority. Education in France has sometimes been framed as a closed, impenetrable policy community (Duclaud-Williams 1994). In this account, relationships between policy-makers in secondary education have been closed to influences from actors outside of the educational policy community itself (Derouet 1991). Attempts to reform the education system have been resisted by powerful teaching unions. Producers (teachers and officials) and consumers (parents and pupils) are equally attached to a system of national diplomas, a guarantee of social and occupational mobility. The institutions, interests and ideas that underpin the management of French education appear resistant to change. In some accounts, the French education system is totally impervious to change, except when change is forced on it in a crisis such as that of May '68 (Durand-Prinborgne 1990).

This rather static portrayal of continuity in French education overlooks the institutional impacts of important societal changes. There has been a huge expansion in education provision since the late 1960s. In France, as elsewhere, investment in education and training has been one of the principal responses of governments to economic change. While governments have pushed the idea that countries need a highly trained workforce, there has also been a growing demand for education provision from society. These converging pressures have produced a democratisation of education in France during the past two decades. The numbers of pupils attending upper secondary schools (*lycées*) has grown strongly since the 1960s and especially since 1984, when Education Minister Chevènement announced the target that 80 per cent of an age-cohort class should sit the *baccalauréat*. There has been a spillover effect on expansion in higher education. The past four decades have witnessed the emergence of a system of mass higher education in France, with 50 per cent of an age cohort now involved in post-secondary education or training. The growth of educational services has required more schools and universities, better equipment, more focused careers advice. Provision of such varied services has mobilised new actors, such as local and regional authorities, business organisations and voluntary associations. The need for good inter-organisational collaboration has emerged as an important feature of educational governance in France.

The image of bureaucratic inertia must not be overstated. As with any bureaucratic structure, the Education ministry has varied interests within its midst. Our research in 1999–2001 led us to identify two principal ideological coalitions that crosscut formal institutional positions.[6] Modernising officials in the Education ministry engaged in

[6] Interviews in the French Education ministry in Paris from October 1999 to March 2000. Interviews with the schools division, evaluation division, IGEN, IGAEN and higher education division.

deep reflection on the nature of the policy challenges facing French society and the ministry's capacity to learn from past experience (as well as from foreign countries) in order to improve service delivery. There was a strong coalition favouring organisational modernity. Its exponents were to be found in the modernising sectors of the central administration, with support from many school heads, certain trade unionists and the two parents' associations (FCPE, PEEP). While firmly wedded to the idea of education as a public service (rejecting openly neo-liberal solutions in vogue in Britain), the modernising coalition was willing to embrace innovations in educational practice and was open to practices of evaluation and new management techniques. This position was opposed by a traditionalist coalition that equated innovation with an attack on the public service ethos of education. The traditional viewpoint was strongest among the majority of teachers, most teaching unions (especially the SNES) and the traditional inspectors. It had strong political support from within the ruling Socialist Party (PS). These actors were profoundly sceptical about change. They advocated the autonomy of the teaching profession and adopted a traditional view of the role of the teacher as a transmitter of knowledge. This coalition was hostile to cross-disciplinary teaching and suspicious of new teaching methods, such as tutorials and small-group teaching. Above all, this group feared school autonomy and local influence, both of which would be detrimental to an idealised vision of uniformity within the education system.

The dynamics of governance

The centralised model theorised by Archer has been modified in important respects. A series of incremental changes in the governing of French secondary schools (*lycées* and *collèges*) since 1975 have produced rather stronger school heads, slightly more influential governing boards and some budgetary autonomy. School reforms (in 1983, 1985, 1989, 1999, 2003) have attempted to open up schools to their external environment, notably through the creation of school projects (*projets d'établissement*), new teaching methods (team and tutorial teaching) and the involvement of parents, local authorities and local businesses on the governing boards of schools. The obligation (under the 1989 Act) upon schools to produce a school project (*projet d'établissement*) can enhance school autonomy in various ways, and not necessarily in ways imagined by the law-makers. Ambitious heads use school plans to promote rare or elite subjects (such as ancient languages) in order to attract the best pupils from beyond the normal geographical catchment area. Pressures for increased evaluation and for rigorous performance indicators have grown as schools have begun to make use of the greater autonomy that their status as public establishments brings.

The governance of secondary education in France has been influenced in various manners by political decentralisation, in ways considered in Chapter 6. The impact of the decentralisation reforms of the early 1980s went well beyond the provisions for secondary education. There was renewed interest in universities on the part of local authorities, which sought the establishment of branch campuses as a sign of the vitality of their locality.[7] Studies demonstrated that local university campuses were an important factor for economic development: firms were more likely to invest if there was a trained local labour supply. The University 2000 plan, launched by Jospin in the early 1990s, formally brought the local and regional authorities into the loop. Universities were now routinely included in the state–region plans (Baraizé 1996). For their part, local and regional authorities have seen research and development as an area where they can make a difference. They have contributed to research budgets and sought to influence the direction of research.

The emergence of new educational actors has given rise to more interdependent, networked and contractual policy processes at the regional level, a theme explored in Chapters 2 and 6. During the past two decades, the Education ministry itself has become embedded in a complex set of localised partnership agreements and contractual relationships that go beyond the narrow confines of education. The ministry is a stakeholder in various local and regional networks aimed at poverty alleviation and combating social exclusion. The Education ministry is the largest financial contributor to the City Contract programmes, for example, which are multi-agency initiatives aimed at alleviating poverty and improving social inclusion. In 80 per cent of cases City Contracts contain a specific chapter dedicated to education (van Zanten 2004, 2006). The Education ministry is also involved in Local Security Contracts in partnership with the local authorities and

---

[7] Interviews in the Brittany rectorate, 1996 and Brittany regional council, 1995.

the police. Within the ministry itself, there has been a policy of priority assistance to deprived schools (*établissements sensibles*) or schools likely to experience violence (*zones violentes*). Education Priority Zones (*Zones d'Éducation Prioritiare* – ZEP), created by the Socialist government of 1981–6, represent the oldest policy programme intended to direct additional resources (money, teachers) to schools in under-privileged areas, especially in run-down suburbs. Through its partici-pation in these various programmes, the Education ministry has become involved in matters of health policy, economic development, social policy and security. It has been an active player in broadly based partnerships formed to tackle some of the worst problems of urban deprivation. City Contracts and Educational Priority Zones represent a significant departure from the traditional terms of the education debate, centred upon citizenship, equal opportunities and meritocratic selection.

Another significant change in the past twenty years has been the slow, rather stilted emergence of more autonomous universities. There has been a rapid university expansion since the early 1980s. Between 1980 and 1995, universities had to absorb an increase of 82 per cent in their student numbers (Musselin 2003). University-level management has traditionally been poorly developed in France, because functions such as estates, finance and personnel remain with the central govern-ment. Since 1968, however, universities have become more autono-mous actors. The Faure law of 1968 gave universities a measure of freedom to organise their teaching activities. By granting them the status of public corporations (*Établissements Publics à caractère Scientifique et Culturel*), it recognised them as institutions in their own right. On the other hand, universities have had very limited financial autonomy, because they depend upon central government for most of their finance. The constellation of interests opposing increased auto-nomy is a powerful one, comprising most student organisations, the key trade unions and elements of the central administration. Even timid proposals to enhance university autonomy, such as those of Education Minister Ferry in 2003, have had to face fierce resistance from this traditional coalition, particularly students and those professionals fearful of the introduction of 'neo-liberal' competition (Cole 2005). The small size and lack of autonomy of French universities has deprived them of the tools to perform well in international benchmarking exercises, such as the Shanghai table of the top 200 universities.

The higher education sector is one where the parameters of change are the most circumscribed. The May '68 events had a lasting importance in shaping ideas about the acceptable boundaries in French higher education. They created zones of non-decision-making, areas where no government would willingly venture. May '68 embedded the belief that higher education is a public service open to everybody having passed the *baccalauréat*. Formal selection is virtually taboo at the level of university entrance (though it is rife in the higher education system as a whole). When governments have attempted to introduce overt selection, they have faced powerful collective mobilisation by students, as in the case of the failed Devaquet bill in 1986. The rise of the student movement as a social actor has been a corollary of the expansion of the university sector. Governments have been extremely cautious in their dealings with students. There have been repeated bursts of student anger – in 1986, 1993, 1995, 2003 and 2006 for example. Students have shown a remarkable capacity for collective action and for influencing educational policy. The demands articulated by student unions reinforce centralised forms of political action and the centralised structure of educational decision-making.

This context weighed heavily upon the limited university 'autonomy' reform introduced as one of the first laws of the Fillon government in July 2007. The university reform was designed to have a profound impact upon the governance of universities: specifically by strengthening the power of presidents over appointments and by reducing the number of representatives in the governing councils (from sixty to thirty) to facilitate a strategic focus. Enhanced budgetary autonomy would include management of buildings and ancillary staff. After mediation by President Sarkozy, the autonomy law fell short of the initial proposals published by Minister Pécresse. The teaching and student unions obtained assurances that fees would be capped; that the *baccalauréat* would continue to ensure university access; and that the governing councils would still be elected on the basis of trade union lists. Whether this law would fundamentally change the governance of universities was open to some doubt, but the July 2007 reform went in the direction of the slow emergence of more autonomous universities.

Europeanisation is another variable likely to increase the autonomy of universities within their national environment. In France, there has traditionally been little knowledge of other systems. Until the mid-1990s, intra-EU cooperation was limited to the exchange of students under Erasmus schemes. The Europeanisation of higher education has gathered pace rapidly under the 'Bologna process'. In 1998, on the initiative of French Education Minister Allègre, the Education ministers of the four largest EU countries – the UK, Germany, France and Italy – committed themselves to harmonise the architecture of European higher education (Musselin 2003; Belloubet-Frier 2005). French governments have been in the forefront of moves towards European harmonisation, imposing the '3-5-8' (*licence-mastère-doctorat*) reforms on an initially reluctant higher education establishment. These moves have benefited from a cross-partisan political consensus, though there are various sources of resistance within universities (from students and certain academic disciplines). The external 'constraint' has been used to push through a reform of the higher education system in France in record time, something unlikely to have occurred through the normal interplay of domestic interests.[8]

Evaluation of the education sector thus lends itself to rather contrasting and contradictory readings. Habits of centralised thinking in education remain very strong. National education traditions underpin norms and rules, as well as remaining deeply embedded in the consciousness and the behaviour of the actors. On the other hand, important incremental changes have taken place, including internal organisational reforms, the growth of contractual relationships within and beyond the ministry, a degree of political and administrative decentralisation and the development of more autonomous universities (Cole and John 2001; van Zanten 2004, 2006). These changes are consistent with those in comparable areas, such as health management (Griggs 1999), urban policy (Le Galès 2005) and training policy (Berthet and Merle 1999). If the logic of the governance system is internal stability, our survey demonstrated the capacity of external pressures to drive some change. The pattern of governance has modified, but this remains very much a halfway house.

The governance of policy sectors

The sector-specific comparisons in Chapter 5 were explored with a view to developing our overarching framework of analysis. Though all

---

[8] Interviews, higher education division, Education ministry, July 2005.

of our hypotheses claim some support, three axes appear to be the most pertinent in calibrating sectoral dynamics and governance.

First, the sectors considered contain differing mixes of multi-level dynamics and multi-actor coordination. Economic development is a multi-level sector where exogenous pressures (of the global economy and European integration) impact much more directly and visibly than in either welfare or education. Education and welfare are less mobile, more place-specific and more resistant to global economic pressures. In spite of pressing economic arguments for welfare retrenchment, for example, the sector remains dominated by the logic of institutional frameworks and clienteles. The actor configuration has changed most radically in the field of the economy, as France has opened her economy to the European and world markets and as central state steering has been modified to take into account the needs of competitive enterprises. Actor relations have changed less obviously in either education or welfare, though in both sectors incremental reforms have introduced new actors, specifically local and regional authorities and government agencies in both education and health.

Second, the above discussion elucidates the functional dynamics hypothesis, whereby governance appears as a form of functionalism embedded within policy sectors that are highly resistant to political oversight and change. The argument clearly does not hold for the economy, where a powerful argument can be made for a paradigm shift from neo-Keynesianism to global market norms, whether or not this is mediated by the survival of neo-mercantilist tendencies (Clift 2008). In the field of education and welfare, the underlying continuities appear more powerful, with the welfare sector the best for sustaining a path-dependency argument. In all these examples, the policy sector is a useful heuristic. As with governance itself, however, conceptualisation by policy sector imposes a degree of cohesion onto ontologically plural realities. By constructing policy dynamics in terms of regular relationships, policy communities and technical expertise, it tends to underplay change and the power of external and internal drivers of change to reshape sectoral boundaries.

Third, comparing policy sectors also allows questions to be asked about state capacity that are central to the nature of contemporary governance and are germane to the future of the state in France itself. In one version, governance signifies a hollow state, emptied of its substance by globalisation and the international political economy.

This narrative is more convincing in some domains (the economy) than others (education), but even in the economy the French state keeps finding new things to do. Where to place our sectors along the hollow state/state capacity axis depends above all upon their degree of openness to or insulation from the global economy and the relative weight of internal and external variables in explaining the dynamics of governance in each sector. In Chapter 1, it was argued that governance could be understood in part as referring to new mixes of markets, networks and hierarchies. Market mechanisms have had the most impact in the field of the economy, though neither education nor welfare is exempt from pressures on public expenditure. Networks, in the form of self-regulating social partnership modes of management that keep the state at a distance, appear very resistant to change in the field of welfare. Hierarchies have been modified in education, but remain the dominant mode of policy interaction, not least because of the choices of the core actors in favour of a national, state-centric mode of regulation.

6 | State–society relations

Chapter 2 introduced the narrative of French history as that of a coherent central state defining the general will in an objective manner over and above specific professional, territorial or partisan interests. Mainstream French intellectual traditions have been hostile to the interplay of interests (Saurugger and Grossman 2006). In a classic orthodox account, Mény (1986) identified four features in the French policy style that favour the 'general interest' over more pluralist approaches: *élus* are representatives of the nation; deputies are not allowed to defend specific interests within the Assembly; access to the public sector is organised on the basis of merit, rather than quotas; and the Council of State is apt to use jurisprudence to label any decision of the state as being of 'public utility' or the 'general interest'. In Mény's view, the state calls the shots in its relationship with professions and organised groups. The prevailing interpretation, articulated by Mény, is that the French state has historically been less tolerant towards autonomous groups than comparable countries. Organised group activity was forbidden during the French Revolution. Only in 1884, with the repeal of the *Loi le Chapelier*, were professional groups allowed to organise, but they remained weak (Guiliani 1991).

This narrative is historically inaccurate in important respects. The overarching *référentiel* has usually accommodated interests, whether framed in terms of maintaining social equilibrium (before 1939) or modernising society (after 1945). During the parliamentary-centred Third Republic, interests focused their attention on key parliamentary committees with power to distribute resources. The capture of deputies, even parliamentary committees, by specific interests counterbalanced the official discourse valorising the higher role of the neutral state. The influence exercised by interests such as wine growers or North African settlers during the Fourth Republic was well documented by Williams (1964).

Interests are an under-specified but central feature of French politics. The framework for analysis presented in Chapter 1 posited that multi-actor coordination was a core feature of governance, best understood in terms of the social and political coordination of the public, private and hybrid actors involved in modern policy-making. Focusing upon state–society relations, this basic hypothesis gives rise to several lines of enquiry. Is there a specifically French model of corporatism? What do patterns of social partnership inform us about overarching state capacity? Can we identify new forms of networked governance, at the local and regional levels especially? Do state–society relations back up theses of networked or participatory governance? Do multi-level European integration dynamics challenge the French model? This chapter seeks answers to these questions, both empirically and in order better to understand governing and governance in France.

A French style corporatism?

Two ideal-type models of state–group relations have prevailed in the academic literature on interest groups. The pluralist model portrays democracy in terms of the free interplay of competing groups, with the state reduced to an arbitral, night-watchman role. The corporatist model describes a cooperative pattern of state–group relations wherein key decisions are taken jointly by representatives of the state and the professions. Neither of these models fits the French case very convincingly. The pluralist portrayal of politics in terms of a system of groups competing on a relatively level playing field underestimates the role of the state in arbitrating between groups, and deciding which ones are legitimate. The 1901 law on associations finally fully legalised associations, but there was a bias in favour of 'good associations' inclined to work with the state in the pursuit of the general interest (Barthélemy 2000). The state occupies a powerful position because it is able to decide which groups are 'representative' of a particular sector, which groups are 'good' and which are narrow and self-serving (Baumgartner 1998). For its part, the corporatist model overestimates the degree of organisation into cohesive professional groups and the unity of purpose within professions. If the corporatist ideal-type comes closer to describing the orthodox model of French public policy-making, the pluralist mantra of multi-actor interaction is closer to the model of governing as governance.

There is a strong argument that a state-flavoured version of (neo-) corporatism best describes the orthodox model of policy-making in France (Jobert and Muller 1987; Mény and Thœig 1989). This model does not refer to organic corporatism, which was given its fullest expression during the Vichy regime (1940–4) in the context of Pétain's National Revolution (Paxton 1972). Rather, the neo-corporatist model draws inspiration from the institutionalised forms of interdependence between state and society that characterise most modern EU states. Schmitter and Lehmbruch (1979) defined neo-corporatism in terms of a number of principles: non-competition between groups, recognition of groups by the state, the representational monopoly of the single group and compulsory membership of professional groups. The neo-corporatist model, as defined by Schmitter and Lehmbruch, captures *some* important elements of the French model, though it more accurately describes the German, Austrian or Scandinavian experiences. But the metaphor of state corporatism is in many senses a more accurate descriptor.

Whether of the state- or neo- variety, a number of core corporatist features can be identified. The state's recognition of 'representative' groups and its *de facto* accreditation of certain associations (at the expense of others) represents a strongly corporatist feature of modern French politics. This area is highly ambiguous. The state sets itself above special interests, but it recognises the need for dialogue with social partners. Through subsidising voluntary associations, trade unions and professional associations, public authorities (central and sub-national government) bring social organisations into their public policy orbit. Baumgartner (1998) refers to these groups as being colonised by the state. This relationship has many positive sum qualities. Associations value the recognition conferred by the state, fight hard to keep it and to exclude others from consideration. Through using mechanisms of co-management public authorities mobilise the expertise that professional groups possess, in return for granting influence over details of policy implementation. This model of institutionalised social partnership is especially prevalent in the social welfare sector, briefly surveyed in Chapter 5. The power of employers and trade unions lies in their management of the social security and labour disputes machinery. The social partners make decisions that affect almost all French citizens (in health, for example) and manage colossal budgets that have a direct impact on people's lives. Critical observers argue that these incentives encourage rent-seeking behaviour by union leaders, most of whom are fierce defenders of this public service model (Smith 2004). Others regard the institutional incorporation of the main social partners (employers and trade unions) as a guarantee of social peace.

The trade unions benefit most from these arrangements. The 'official' trade union federations are guaranteed an institutional presence, control over financial resources, access to information and influence at the formulation and implementation stages. The French trade unions occupy a paradoxical position. They are undermined by weak organisation, low membership and internal divisions, but they occupy strong institutional positions. If the MEDEF, the main employers' organisation, is unrepresentative of the business world,[1] the French unions are less representative still, with under 10 per cent of the working population members of a trade union. In national elections to works councils and arbitration committees the five national trade union federations barely manage to obtain 50 per cent between them (Parsons 2005; Andolfatto and Labbé 2006). But the national federations – CGT, CFDT, FO, CGC and CFTC – still dominate top-level negotiations over labour relations, social welfare and training. Collective agreements (usually national, branch-specific agreements) are signed by employers and at least one accredited 'social partner'. Unlike pure corporatist countries, the representative basis for trade union agreement for collective conventions is weak. Making agreements stick can be difficult, as the professional groups are often too divided to articulate a single voice. Even when collective bargaining agreements are signed, they no longer commit all firms within a given branch. By and large, labour relations have been decentralised to the firm level and plant agreements are now the norm (Lalliement 2006).

Empirical work across sectors reveals a far less one-sided relationship than the state–corporatist metaphor implies. The state relies on the cooperation of key professional organisations for the delivery of public services and for the self-regulation of the professions. State agencies have sometimes appeared to be captured by core professional interests: the role performed by the farmers' union, the FNSEA, was traditionally offered as evidence of this, though FNSEA influence is in decline (Keeler 1987). A lesser-known example is that of the professional association of

---

[1] The membership of MEDEF is 60 per cent industrial employers, though most new job creation takes place in the service sector.

champagne producers (*Comité Interprofessionnel des Vins de Champagne* – CIVC). In the case of champagne, the French state encouraged wine producers from the 1940s onwards to organise themselves into a cohesive inter-professional structure in order to implement decisions determined jointly with the state. According to one account, the role of the producers goes well beyond one of self-regulation to encompass price-fixing, the organisation of resistance to EU competition law and the drafting of directives on behalf of the Agriculture ministry (Diart-Boucher 2007). This example illustrates that the boundary between what is public and what is private is porous. Sometimes the public and the private simply blend into each other. Thus, one national agency, *Institut National des Appellations d'Origine* (INAO), has authority for all matters concerning the protection of place names (*appellations d'origine*). Though it is a public corporation (*établissement public administratif*), it is dominated by representatives of the wine-growing professions. Through the *délégation de service public*, this mixed body issues regulations that can be contested in the administrative tribunals. In this case, a professional body exercises power that goes well beyond self-regulation. There are few better examples of co-management between the state and the professions, a situation criticised by the European Commission and the European Court of Justice.

A central aspect of the French corporatist model is the role of the *corps* and of the professional orders. The role of the technical *grands corps* surfaces in numerous public policy studies. Separate studies have highlighted the importance of engineers from the Bridges and Highways *corps* in urban policy in the 1960s and 1970s (Thœnig 1973), of mining engineers in energy policy (Cohen 1988) and of arms engineers in civil aviation (Muller 1989). The advantage of such studies is that they highlight the role of powerful actors within the state, as much as the incorporation of outside interests into the decision-making machinery. A sense of *corps* identity is not limited to the upper reaches of the administration, but is present throughout the public sector. There are similarities between the administrative *corps* and the professional bodies, membership of which is compulsory for the professions concerned. The *Ordre des médecins* or the *Ordre des pharmaciens*, which regulate membership of the medical and pharmaceutical professions, are the most notorious. The system of professional bodies strengthens the role of the professions in determining conditions for new entrants and in regulating professional practice.

The fourth dimension of the French model is what Jobert and Muller characterise as the model of republican corporatism. The management by professionals of public services lies at the heart of the French model. Various diverse influences converged in the late nineteenth century to provide the foundations of the modern French welfare state: the ascendancy of republican political institutions in the 1880s, the diffusion of ideas of solidarity under the influence of political radicalism, the development of the legal doctrine of public service, the first moves to municipal and state intervention in welfare and the emergence of coherent professional organisations. For Muller, the development of the professions formed part of the process of raising national identity and safeguarding republican institutions. Republicans looked to the independent professions as a support for the state against the church. Consistent with prevailing ideas about the limited state, the belief was widespread that social services were best administered by professionals vested with a sense of public service. The professions would ensure a scientific management of social problems and remove the temptation for politicians to indulge in pork-barrel politics. The logical corollary was a form of professional management, with state oversight through contractual relations.

The French state is divided around two poles: the social state and the technical state. In the social state, the core actor is the professional: the teacher in education; the doctor in the health sector. The social state, run by service producers, is closer to the classic corporatist model. In education, the unions occupy key institutional positions of influence and no reform can be managed without prior consultation with them. In health, the medical profession has been able to manage and steer change. In neither health nor education are the professionals completely coherent, however. In education there are divisions between primary and secondary school teachers, as well as between public and contracted-in schools. In health, the general practitioners are divided and are looked down upon by the specialists in the university hospitals. In their classic work, Jobert and Muller (1987) argued that the power of the professions is to some extent dependent upon the weakness of prestige of the lead department. The Social Affairs and Education ministries are not among the most prestigious. The technical state, on the other hand, is driven by the influence of the *grands corps* that are brought into the state machinery. Thus, in the orthodox model, engineers in the telecoms *corps* dominated policy within the telecommunications directorate; the mining *corps* drove energy policy, the Highways and Bridges *corps* were central to urban policy. State corporatism is strongest in the technical state, and it is this model that has been subject to the most serious challenges.

These elements add up to a powerful picture of a specific form of corporatism. The concept of corporatism captures some aspects of the French model better than others. Unlike in the ideal-type of neo-corporatism or the practice in some northern European countries, for example, professional groups in France are often deeply divided and weakly representative. Some features that institutionalise professional influences are in practice forms of private government from which the state is excluded. Thus, in a paradoxical way, the model of social part-nership that will now be considered, must be regarded as quite distinct from state corporatism, though it borrows certain features from it.

Social partnership in action: the case of workplace training

Most writing on social partnership concerns industrial relations, health or social welfare. One under-investigated area is that of adult training and life-long learning. The field is a good one for elucidating broader themes of inter-organisational dynamics. The question is no longer whether the state dominates groups or groups have captured the state, but whether self-regulating networks have captured control of the policy process.

Social partnership forms the cornerstone of public discourse about training and employment. The belief that social partners (employers and trade unions) are the key stakeholders in determining priorities for increasing skills in the workforce is widely disseminated. The 1971 law made it a legal obligation for all firms employing over ten workers to develop a training plan. It also introduced the training levy, a legal requirement for firms to spend a proportion of their wage costs on training.[2] The French state has retained a powerful background and

[2] Around forty interviews with members of the training policy community were carried out in the Brittany region from 2001 to 2003. A smaller number were also carried out in the National Education Ministry in Paris and in the Nord/Pas-de-Calais region (in 1999 and 2000) as part of a project funded by the Nuffield Foundation on the 'Local Governance of Education in Britain and France'.
I thank the Nuffield Foundation for its support. Firms with over ten employees must spend 1.5 per cent of their gross wage costs on training. They either

regulatory presence, but most work-based training issues are left to negotiations between employers and their workforce. The trade unions and employers' associations are the key partners in this pattern of social partnership. Unions and employers determine national branch-level agreements that are then worked out in detail at the level of the firm. The social partners, in tripartite discussions with the state, also determine the number of day-release schemes for young people (*contrats d'alternance*) that will be financed on an annual basis (Reverchon 2003). The social partnership model functions imperfectly, but it remains the keystone of work-based adult training. Though trade unions and national employers' associations often disagree about the mechanics of training (whether, as in 2003, to favour branches (MEDEF) or the inter-professional (unions) level, or whether to permit training in working time), they form part of the same national network of influence. There are strong underpinnings binding unions and employers together. Social partners (employers' associations and unions) have favoured in-house qualifications specific to particular branches, upon which salary scales can be agreed. The MEDEF has generally opposed moves towards validating work-based experience through formal diplomas, preferring to emphasise the importance of in-house training and the certification of skills (Perucca 2000). Formal diplomas bring an actor into play – the Education ministry – that both the MEDEF and the unions would rather remained outside of the firm. Trade unions and employers both oppose a more open intervention of the Education ministry in validating workplace experience or regulating training. Each seeks to keep the state at a safe distance from operational decision-making. Above all, each is anxious to retain a share of the vast sums of money that are generated by the training levy.

There are strong organisational imperatives for employers' associations and trade unions to maintain a tight control of training. Small and larger firms are represented by different professional organisations, the

organise training themselves, contract the training out to non-profit-making organisations (the OPCA), or simply pay over 1.5 per cent to the Treasury in the form of a tax. In addition, firms with ten or more employees must pay the apprenticeship tax, representing 0.5 per cent of the total wage bill. A range of approved organisations can collect the apprenticeship tax: apprentice training centres, schools with sixth forms, chambers of commerce and various other training providers. The effect of these levies is debatable. Large firms spend much more than 1.5 per cent on training. For small companies, the levy is 0.15 per cent of the total wage costs and most pay it without bothering to organise training.

UPA/CGPME and the MEDEF, each with their own nationally based mutual insurance funds (AGEFOS-PME and OPCAREG).[3] These mutual insurance funds, the OPCA (*Organismes Paritaires de Collecte Agrée*), perform an obscure, but vitally important role in organising training. The OPCA are opaque bodies can best be described as training mutual insurance funds, of which there are two main types. First, the main inter-professional employers' associations – MEDEF, CGPME – have created their OPCA, charged with collecting the training levy from firms and organising training in return. Second, specific economic branches have created OPCA, often jointly managed by the employers and trade unions: the agri-business sector is a good example.[4] These bodies have been harshly criticised by some observers. The MEDEF, the CGPME and the trade unions are allowed to claim a commission from their OPCA for organising training. The OPCA collect funds, but they do not have to spend these monies on training. There are few instruments for controlling either the good use of public money, or evaluating the quality of training undertaken. In their defence, the OPCA claim to organise high-quality training courses for firms that do not have the expertise to do so. Moreover, they are experts in negotiating European Union grants, which contribute to the overall training spend in their areas.

Rather like the examples of social welfare and policy instruments in previous chapters, the training field demonstrates how social partnership arrangements can develop an autonomous rationale, removed from public accountability and only very loosely regulated by the state. The role of networks provides another interesting case.

Horizontal coordination: networks and networking

At the heart of the governance approach is the need to capture inter-organisational relationships, rather than to focus on organisations *per se*. Corporatist analysis represents one attempt to systematise interdependent relationships. Another effort at conceptualisation that explicitly

---

[3] Interviews, AGEFOS-PME and OPCAREG, March and July 2001.

[4] In the case of agri-business, the national OPCA is AGEFAFORIA. It is run as a joint MEDEF–Union enterprise, with a rotating chair. In spite of the importance of agri-business in Brittany, AGEFAFORIA does not exist on a specifically Breton basis. Its regional delegate is responsible for twelve separate *départements* (covering the Brittany, Pays de la Loire and Lower Normandy regions). Interview, March 2001.

shares the diagnostic of state restructuring is that of the policy networks school, which has gained ground in European political science in recent years. Its advocates (Richardson and Jordan 1979; Benson 1982; Rhodes 1988, 1997; Marsh and Smith 2000) claim that it provides a framework for operationalising and observing the interdependent relationships identified as lying at the heart of modern governance. The concept has some supporters in France, where Jouve (1995) interprets networks as signifying that there is 'a growing recognition that the state is composed of differentiated institutions, and actors with their own logics'. State actors are constrained to cooperate with non-state decision-makers in a growing number of policy sectors, such as education, housing, social policy and the environment.

Upon a close reading of the literature, four principal themes emerge from policy network analysis that have a general applicability. First, a network is a regularised pattern of relationships between individuals or across institutions. Second, policy networks consist of a cluster or complex of organisations connected to each other by resource dependencies: organisations form networks because they are dependent upon each other. Network theory can be interpreted as a refinement of the pluralist analysis of the political process, whereby decision-making systems are responsive to fragmented groups. Third, the policy networks literature emphasises the importance of policy sectors that structure interactions. This dimension of network analysis is strongly emphasised by Marsh and Rhodes (1992), for example, who contrast the open interactions involved in economic policy-making with the closed technical world of civil engineering. There are similarities with the orthodox model of public policy as conceptualised by Jobert and Muller (1987) in France, for whom the emergence of cohesive policy sectors is the organisational response to the division of labour in the classic model of government. Sector is taken by Jobert and Muller to be synonymous with profession, and professional influences figure prominently in the Marsh and Rhodes model as well. Finally, several writers operate a distinction between tightly organised professional policy communities and much looser issue networks. While policy communities are tight self-regulating networks, issue networks are much looser ideational coalitions which seek to influence the agenda.

Policy networks are rarely explicitly evoked in the French literature. The most influential school of organisational sociology – the CSO – preferred alternative concepts. Common to the works of Crozier,

Friedberg and others was the role of social and political elites, whether top-ranking civil servants, or, at a lower level, prefects and political *notables*. In this research tradition, the network is used to characterise policy-making within these rather closed politico-administrative systems, rather than across organisations. In Friedberg's 1974 study of the Industry ministry, for instance, networks consisted of individual interactions between high-ranking members of the civil service to iron out dysfunctions within the bureaucratic system (Friedberg 1974). Friedberg's networks were by definition elitist: they involved inter-actions between members of the *corps des mines*, who dominated both the Industry ministry and the main industrial groups. The French system of *grands corps* thus shaped the types of interaction within the French state and between the state and industrial groups. Such inter-personal links were perfectly compatible with hierarchical modes of organisation, since contacts were limited to similarly ranking state officials, or to members of the same *corps*. At a different level of analysis, Gatto and Thœnig (1993) discovered 'inter-individual net-works' among 'friends' occupying similar positions in different ministries involved in public security issues. Such bureaucratic networks enabled communication between services, counteracting their tendency to auto-nomisation. These networks were a means of regulating dysfunctions in complex administrative systems.

As organisational sociology gained in maturity, it integrated new inter-organisational realities. The 'action system' (*système d'action concrète*), conceptualised by Crozier and Friedberg (1977), appeared in some important respects as a precursor of the policy networks approach. Both concepts describe how interdependent actors invent new forms of cross-organisational collaboration. However, the French sociologists placed much more importance upon the role of individuals in mediating the complex relations between local and national state, quasi-state and group actors in making policy. This approach takes agency seriously, in marked contrast to the more structural version of policy networks described by Marsh and Rhodes (Rhodes 1988; Marsh and Rhodes 1992). The concept of 'networking' invests networks with a more active dimension (Raab 1992; Lazega 1994). Organisations form networks because they are dependent upon each other, but the nature of inter-organisational relations is mediated by the relationships between the individual actors involved. Actors will deploy their avail-able resources to attempt to achieve their aims. These resources can be varied: for instance, financial, legal, organisational, professional or personal. Social interactions constitute a framework or structure which can be studied and analysed in its own right.

Who governs urban governance? Economic development in Lille and Rennes

The network metaphor captures well the complex relationships governing modern cities. The network is a useful device for identifying the range of actors from central, local, semi-public and private sector organisations involved in local governance. Extensive investigation in two French cities in 1994–6 allowed some partial answers to be given to the question of who 'governs' urban governance in the field of economic development. In the tradition of the US community power studies, the research set out to map relationships in two British and two French cities. Full findings are available elsewhere (John 1998; John and Cole 2000). The findings presented below are subject to caution. They are valid only for the cities concerned, the period covered and the policy field under investigation. The method used – of sociometric network mapping – is subject to the usual precautions of usage. The standard building block for formal network analysis is the *frequency* of interaction between actors (for summaries of the vast literature, see Scott 1991; Wasserman and Faust 1994; Wasserman and Galaskiewicz 1994; John 1998). Frequency of interaction is a rather crude measure; it does not inform us about the quality of relationships or about trust and reciprocity. By identifying those individuals who have high centrality scores in a policy network, however, the researcher can deduce what kind of network it is, who forms part of the network and whether the network is dominated by bureaucratic, political or private actors (John 1998).[5]

The evidence uncovered in our two French cities supports a more pluralistic interpretation than the old model of cross-regulation between political and administrative actors discussed in Chapter 3. In two very different cities – Lille and Rennes – we identified a very large

[5] Among other objectives, the research set to map the frequency of interactions between key actors (how often did they see each other?), their degree of centrality within the network (did they occupy a central location?) and their degree of 'betweenness' (did they act as intermediaries to bring other actors into contact with each other?).

Table 6.1. *Lille's economic policy network: selected centrality scores (top 10 by degree)*

Actor	nDegree	nBetweenness
[1]	202.78	15.15
[2]	180.56	5.87
[3]	179.39	13.45
[4]	154.17	6.13
[5]	138.11	4.42
[6]	131.94	4.13
[7]	119.94	2.20
[8]	111.11	3.67
[9]	106.94	3.70
[10]	106.94	1.38

Key: [1] President of the Lille-Roubaix-Tourcoing Chamber of Commerce; [2] Economic Affairs *adjoint*, Lille town hall; [3] Mayor of Roubaix; [4] General Secretary for Regional Affairs (prefecture); [5] Associate General Secretary, Lille town hall; [6] Mayor of Lille; [7] Mayor of Tourcoing; [8] Director of the Urban Development Agency; [9] Regional Prefect; [10] Mayor of Villeneuve d'Ascq.
Technical note: 'nDegree' refers to the degree centrality measure. This was calculated by counting the number of adjacent links between one actor and the others. This offers a crude measure of network centrality: the higher the score, the more central an actor is in the network.

'nBetweenness': betweenness measures the extent to which actors fall between pairs of other actors, showing the extent to which they are intermediate between others within the network. The higher the score, the more the actor mediates networks.

The research team ascertained the network by personally interviewing the key actors and mapping the relationships between them. The research period in each city was about six months. In Lille the period was from August 1994 to January 1995; in Rennes from February to August 1995. Using the snowball sampling approach, we identified seventy-eight economic policy actors in Lille and sixty in Rennes. As an opening question, the interviewers asked each respondent: 'Who are you in regular contact with on economic development policy issues and how frequent are your contacts?' The interviewer explained that contacts could be discussions or decisions about policy issues and that contacts included meetings, telephone conversations, personalised letters or emails. Responses were coded as follows: 5 – daily or every other day; 4 – weekly or every two weeks; 3 – monthly; 2 – every two or three months; 1 – every six months or more. The interviewers gave respondents a questionnaire to complete and send back to the research team after the interview. In the questionnaire, respondents were asked to specify their contacts on policy on the scale of 1–5 and the results were cross-checked with the responses in the interview. Where actors' contacts were not consistent, we averaged the scores. The team imported these scores into a DOS text editor and imported them as a value graph into a network analysis programme – UCINET IV – which gave the degree centrality and betweenness scores reported in Tables 6.1 and 6.2. A similar exercise was carried out in relation to the British cities and results published as John (1998).

Table 6.2. *Rennes' economic policy network: selected centrality scores (top 10 by degree)*

Actor	nDegree	nBetweenness
[1]	220.34	12.68
[2]	186.44	10.12
[3]	177.66	10.91
[4]	162.71	5.67
[5]	144.07	6.51
[6]	138.98	8.25
[7]	128.81	3.99
[8]	127.12	1.67
[9]	108.47	8.25
[10]	101.60	1.98

Key: [1] Mayor of Rennes; [2] President of the Brittany Employers' Federation; [3] Economic Affairs *adjoint*, Rennes commune; [4] President of the Rennes Chamber of Commerce; [5] Economic Development vice-President, Brittany regional council; [6] General Secretary for Regional Affairs (prefecture); [7] Economic Development vice-President, Ille-et-Vilaine departmental council; [8] Mayor of St. Jacques; [9] Director-General, Ille-et-Vilaine departmental council; [10] General Secretary, Rennes commune.

See Technical note, Table 6.1.

number of actors who have some sort of influence on economic development, and a core of 'deciders' who were in permanent contact with each other. In each city, the policy core involved in economic development comprised three groups: the main local politicians (the mayor, his assistants and expert advisors, officials whose brief included economic development and urban planning); the business community (as represented by the Chambers of Commerce and, to a lesser extent, the leaders of the employers' associations); and representatives of the territorial state (the SGAR and officials involved in the regional prefecture). Regional actors were marginal in the city networks, though more present in Rennes, the capital of the Brittany region, than in Lille. Central government and EU actors were important in both countries because they controlled substantial funds, but only regional state actors appeared in the networks.

These findings also produced interesting contrasts between the two cities. Lille had a highly diffuse network because of the complex political geography of the area, especially the large number of

communes (there were eighty-five in the metropolitan area). During
the period of fieldwork (1994–6) Lille had managed to attract big
development projects, such as the Channel tunnel rail link and the
Euralille commercial development. In response to enduring economic
crisis in the 1980s, traditionally hostile political and economic elites
moved closer together and invented novel forms of public–private
collaboration (not only via mixed economy societies but also using
private capital to part-finance major infrastructure projects) (Cole and
John 2001). The Chamber of Commerce, and its president, performed
the pivotal mediating role between business interests and the PS-run
town hall. This finding is captured not just in the number of total links
maintained ('degree centrality'), but also in the high 'betweenness'
score, the best measure of how actors mediate between other actors.
Political and economic decision-makers cooperated to devise solutions
based on exploiting the city's favourable location in the new Europe.
This instrumental form of cooperation could not have been predicted
on the basis of a simple path-dependency hypothesis. In Rennes, the
reverse happened. In the post-war period, Rennes had developed a
sophisticated mode of urban governance, based on close collaboration
between the town hall and local civil society organised into associations. At the time of observing the networks, in 1995, this mode of
cooperative governance was under severe stress, with local businesses
fiercely opposed to the mayor's proposed new underground transport
system. As surveyed in 1995, the economic network centred around
the mayor of Rennes and his close municipal associates, with fairly
weak relationships with the local business community and other
elected local authorities. This pattern of governance might well have
been a feature of exceptional circumstances in the city's local history
(Le Galès 1993). The limitations of formal network analysis are that it
can provide only a snapshot of relations at a given point in time.

A number of conclusions emerge from this process of mapping the
structure of local networks. First, big cities have more complicated
networks and require stronger, more innovative forms of local political
leadership. Second, centrality within networks matters: actors occupying a central location within networks are the most powerful. Third,
the greater the number of individuals and organisations within a network, the more difficult formal coordination becomes. On the other
hand, broadly based networks facilitate social interaction and can help
to embed trust.

Regional circuits and competitive interdependencies

Most network analysis does not attempt to map out interactions between individuals, but to investigate new forms of interaction between organisations. The gradual development of local and regional public spheres has been the consequence of administrative and political decentralisation since the 1960s. By regional public sphere is meant an arena within which a plurality of organisations interact: local and regional authorities, regional prefectures, the field services of central ministries, associations organised on a regional basis, social partners. The state–region plans, considered in Chapter 2, helped to legitimise the idea of a regional public sphere, though their future has been called into question. The gradual emergence of a regional public sphere should not be exaggerated. Social partners – employers and trade unions – generally look either to national-level negotiations (in training or employment policy, for example), or to more localised agreements. Even regional-level negotiations might bypass the regional council, for instance by the regional employers' association (MEDEF) dealing directly with the regional prefecture and side-stepping the region. That there are competing tensions and trends within local and regional public spaces is not in doubt.

These conflicting pressures require more fine-grained empirical analysis. The role performed by the regional councils was the object of detailed empirical analysis in 1994–6, and 2001–3, with a view to uncovering the extent to which the regions have built their institutional capacity, as well as to chart the relationships they maintain in regional public spheres.[6] The related fields of education and training reveal how regions have become central actors in some sub-fields, but also how they are excluded from powerful circuits of influence, especially those that involve the professions (teachers and trainers) or the social partners (unions and employers). Both education and training are crowded spaces; as newcomers, the regional councils have had to develop relationships with existing organisations and attempt either to make a

---

[6] Interviews were carried out in two main stages. From 1994–6, a total of 156 interviews were conducted in the Nord/Pas-de-Calais and Brittany regions. From 2001–3, seventy-eight interviews were carried out in the Brittany region. All interviewees were guaranteed anonymity. Interviews were taped and transcribed. The 2001–3 interviews are deposited with the Essex data archive: 'Devolution and Decentralisation in Wales and Brittany, 2001–2003', UK Data Archive, www.data-archive.ac.uk, study number 4802.

space within existing networks, or substitute alternative circuits of influence. The well-documented policy field of education mobilises strong professional interests (teachers, educational administrators) to the extent it has sometimes been considered a closed, impenetrable policy community (Duclaud-Williams 1994). The issue area of training and life-long learning has similarities with, but is distinct from that of education. Training is best understood as a generic definition to cover various related (but distinctive) processes, namely: school-based forms of professional education and work placement; work-based youth training; work-based adult training (or life-long learning) and individual learning (Shackleton 1995; Brown, Green and Lauder 2001). The French regions have control over some aspects of secondary education (school buildings and equipment) and training (apprenticeships and planning provisions for 16–25-year-olds). But in both fields their legitimacy is contested by professionals. In education, there was a bitter dispute from 2003–4 driven in part by the opposition of public sector ancillary workers in secondary schools to being transferred to regional council control. But incremental reform efforts finally won the day, with the TOS gradually being transferred to the regional councils. Likewise, in training, there was stiff opposition from workers employed in the training centres controlled by the Labour ministry (AFPA) to being transferred to the regions.

Education and training demonstrate both the importance and the limitations of incremental change and the need to adopt a broad temporal perspective. As a result of successive incremental reforms, the regions have become involved at various levels of the education and training supply-chain. Since 1987, the regions have had the sole regulatory authority over apprenticeships, which they organise and fund. Since 1993, the regions have been given the main responsibility for planning post-school 16- to 25-year-old training and are required to draft an overall plan (the PRDF – *Plan Régional du Développement et de la Formation des Jeunes*) to this effect (Cabanes and Bouygard 1997; Berthet and Merle 1999). Schooling is obligatory until the age of 16 years, but the regions claim an influence in school-level planning, as choices made at 14 years will have an influence on the training and apprenticeship programmes that the regions must organise from 16 years onwards. The regions also have various programmes designed to foster life-long learning and continuing education and they contributed massively to the University 2000 scheme. In practice, the regions exercise a good deal of direct and indirect influence, especially in the field of vocational education. Their influence spills over into the management of upper secondary schools, especially the vocational schools (*lycées professionnelles*). The head of the Education ministry regional field service, the rector, would not dream of opening a new vocational school (or even a general *lycée*) unless she had guarantees from the regional council that the appropriate level of equipment would be provided. Likewise, no school would open a post-baccalauréat technical class (*Section Technique Specialisée* – STS) without consulting with the region and the professional branches. The regions have contributed to expensive investments in the vocational schools and the technical streams within general schools.

There have been unintended consequences of these incremental reforms. In the education decentralisation laws of 1983 and 1985, local and regional authorities were given control over new buildings, extensions and renovations to existing buildings, and provision of equipment.[7] The departmental and regional authorities have definitely made an impact, way beyond their contribution to the total proportion of educational expenditure. They have renovated school buildings, built new schools and modernised the equipment used within schools. Certain councils have been ambitious in relation to educational content and have funded programmes of intensive language training, given small-group teaching grants or funded additional teacher training (Dutercq 2003). The regional policy community has an influence on all decisions affecting vocational education and training. In this field, elected regions and state field service officials interact with regional lobbies such as the employers' federation (MEDEF and its constituent elements), firms, chambers of commerce, trade unions and associations. The smooth functioning of the system necessitates the cooperation of the state, the regions and – increasingly – the professional branches (Cole 2001a).

Some examples from fieldwork carried out in 1994–5 and 2001–3 illustrate the unintended consequences of incremental change, but also the persistence of the heavy variables that govern the education and training systems.

---

[7] Within these narrow limits, the regions were to have responsibility for the *lycées* (upper secondary schools), the departments would control the *collèges* (lower secondary schools) and the communes would – where applicable – continue to administer the nursery and primary schools.

The relationship between the main sub-national actors in French secondary education is best described as one of competitive interdependency. In spite of embedded institutional rivalries, actors are bound to each other by a tight pattern of resource dependencies and, in most cases, by a shared commitment to raising educational standards. In the words of one interviewee 'Without cooperation from all sides, one could well imagine a complete blockage of the system.'[8] A regional council might decide to build a school, but the implementation of this decision depends upon the rector (the lead state education official) agreeing to provide the teaching posts, and the regional prefect consenting to place the proposed school on the 'annual list of operations', the financial probity of which is controlled by the field office of the Finance ministry. The rectorates determine teaching needs, but in practice they depend upon the cooperation of the regions to build schools and finance equipment. The state and the region usually have to agree before a new school can be built, or a new academic stream opened. Where to locate a new *lycée* or open a new section is the object of a complex bargaining game between actors with different territorial, administrative and professional interests. The key state official, the rector, sometimes has the last word, since he can refuse to provide new schools (or new sections) with the teachers that the regional and local authorities are not allowed to provide.[9] But twenty years after the decentralisation laws became operational, the regional councils have excelled in building, maintaining and renovating school buildings across France. By 2003, there had been a 250 per cent increase in expenditure by local and regional authorities on education (*Le Monde*, 5 June 2003). New *lycées* provide visible reminders of the existence of the regional councils across the country.

The record in training is more mixed. The regionalisation of training policy has steadily gathered momentum. However, to conclude that the regions 'govern' training would be highly misleading. Training is the interdependent policy domain *par excellence*; there are many policy stakeholders involved. The region is in charge of youth training – of 16- to 26-year-olds – and has some influence in continuing and adult

---

[8] Interview, rectorate of Rennes, May 1995.
[9] Fieldwork in the Lille academy revealed the case of at least four *lycées* proposed by the Nord/Pas-de-Calais regional council that the rector vetoed by refusing to supply teachers.

education. But the French state retains control over many training programmes and specific populations (such as prisoners), and has increased its influence to insist on new training opportunities for recipients of welfare benefits. The European Union is determined to push its own agenda in this domain. Above all, social partners (trade unions and employers) are very important players, circumscribing the policy space for regional authorities and creating strong path-dependencies. The 2003–4 decentralisation reforms had initially promised to transfer *all* responsibility for training and life-long learning to the regions, but this provoked powerful resistance from embedded interests such as careers advisors, state field agencies and training suppliers.

The ability of the regions to 'govern' training is strictly circumscribed. Existing players have proved obstructive. In the field of adult training in particular, the social partners are reluctant to recognise local and regional authorities as key stakeholders. The 1993 Training Act created a real tension between regional training policies and the leadership of the regional councils, on the one hand, and the strengthening of the social partners on the other. There was a major contradiction in the 1993 law. The law increased the responsibilities of the regional councils for planning training, but it also concentrated resources in the branches, by creating the OPCA considered briefly above.

The empirical analysis of these two sectors reveals contrasting findings. The effect of successive incremental reforms (in 1983, 1985, 1987, 1993, 2002 and 2004) has been to confer precise legal rights and duties on regional councils in secondary education, youth training and apprenticeships. In none of these sub-fields are the regions the sole players, however, and maximising regional capacity has depended upon effective strategic action. On the other hand, some regional councils have adopted an expansive view of their role, including areas where they have no statutory responsibility such as higher education. They have not hesitated to use the weapon of finance to influence curriculum decisions in the secondary and higher education sectors, especially by investing in sophisticated technologies that impose certain curricula choices or by making research contracts conditional on pursuing research relevant to regional concerns. The conquest of every region in mainland France except Alsace in 2004 provided fertile terrain for attempting new forms of regional experimentation, most spectacularly using the regional councils to reintroduce a version of the *emplois-jeunes*, the flagship policy of the 1997–2002 government repealed by the Raffarin government in 2002.

The evidence presented thus far can be read as a powerful argument to support the emergence of more networked forms of local and regional governance, specifically linked to the creation of new institutions, the development of forms of institutional learning and, above all, the strengthening of political capacity as a result of inter-organisational dynamics. In other areas, the governance argument is much more difficult to make.

Associations, new social movements and the public sphere

The third lens for understanding intermediary institutions is the more classic one of state–society relations. There are rival narratives about state–society relations that each capture a part of reality and each serve an instrumental purpose. First, there is the portrayal of state–society relations in terms of a static and frozen republican model, incapable of mediating change. Second, there is the paradoxical picture of a vibrant new citizenship, based in part on contesting the existing social order. Third, there exists an untidy reality where practice and principles are most often at odds with each other, and where republican principles are consistent with the emergence of a more differentiated pluralistic polity.

The classic interpretation is that of a republican model that is deeply resistant to change. In the republican conception, all citizens are created equal and are members of a national political community. They owe their allegiance to the nation as a whole, rather than to regions, ethnic groups or intermediary associations. The public sphere ought to be neutral (François and Neveu 1999). Matters of personal and especially religious belief are guaranteed by the constitution, but they are expected to be confined to the private sphere. If the French political community is open to all, regardless of ethnicity or origin, central to becoming 'French' is socialisation into French values, including a respect for the neutrality of the public sphere (Schnapper 1994). The republican frame of reference has a powerful appeal. The efforts of republicans to inculcate a universal model of French citizenship were broadly inspired by ideals of the enlightenment, by the legacy of the French Revolution and by the church–state conflict of the late nineteenth century. A demand for equal treatment underpins the French republican model, the glue that binds the rich diversity of territories that together constitute contemporary France.

On the other hand, the core intellectual arguments of republicanism find it difficult to account for, explain or recognise societal change. Specifically, the French model of republican citizenship has great difficulties in accepting diversity and hence in adapting to the reality of a multi-ethnic, regionally differentiated society (Wieviorka 1997; Cole and Raymond 2006; Kiwan 2006). The myth of republican equality has presented formidable obstacles to designing policies to help those who are substantively disadvantaged. State and local authorities have been extremely resistant to allowing any public displays of faith by France's sizable Muslim community, in particular by blocking the construction of mosques and refusing (until recently) to recognise the status of Islamic religious institutions. Most important was the passing of a law in 2004 barring the wearing of 'ostentatious religious symbols' in public schools, a reform clearly aimed at headscarves worn by Muslim girls. As Duchesne (2005) observes, the headscarf affair attests to an enduring resistance to pluralism, where diversity is seen as threatening republican egalitarianism and equality is confused with uniformity. More than any of its neighbours, France demands respect for 'thin universalist' republican principles as a condition of citizenship.

A second version of the state–society debate concerns the paradox of a new citizenship, based on contesting the existing social order. France is a pluralistic society which contains a broad range of political orientations and cultural practices within its midst. The robust health of voluntary associations and community activism counters evidence of civic anomie. All associations are a means of linking the individual and society and they provide a form of social counterbalance to state control. In their loosest definition as '1901 associations', groups in France have proliferated during the post-war period. Up to 20,000,000 French people are active in associations of one form or another. By way of comparison, the UMP can boast 200,000 active party members; the PS 100,000. The number of associations created in France doubled between 1975 and 1990. Waters (2003) refers to the emergence of a new citizenship to describe the growth in associations since the 1980s.

The paradox of a new citizenship based on contesting the existing social order is exemplified by new social movements. French sociologists conceptualise social movements much more than they do groups (Neveu 2002). For Alain Touraine, social movements are structures between the individual and the state that seek to change society (Touraine 1994). The labour movement is the original social movement and most associations during the early twentieth century were created as part of this broader class-based movement. The most spectacular new associations that have emerged since the 1980s are explicitly focused on issues of citizenship, democracy and participation or alternative visions of society (*altermondialisme*). They are suspicious of the state and of traditional political parties, and see themselves as actors of social change. New social movement activity since the 1980s has centred on anti-racism, human rights, defending the unemployed, the rights of immigrants, gay rights, the defence of the homeless, the environment or women's rights.[10] Most of these social movements are focused upon access to French society for previously excluded groups, such as the homeless, the socially excluded or immigrants. Some movements contest the underlying foundations of global capitalist society as it currently functions. The anti-globalisation (*alter-mondialiste*) movement in particular has become a major force in Europe, including France. From a constructivist perspective, the success of groups such as ATTAC or individuals such as José Bové derives from a combination of accepted collective action registers on the French left and clever strategic positioning. Direct action tactics (such as destroying fields of genetically modified crops) are easily understood, as are discursive registers that play on a broader fear of economic globalisation and international free trade. These anti-globalisation groups have undoubtedly influenced the climate within which French politics is carried out and have created a major headache for the main left-wing party, the Socialist Party.

The rise of these various new social movements illustrates the weakening of the mediating role of political parties (Haegel 2007). Unlike Britain and Germany, where environmental and anti-nuclear movements wreaked havoc on the parties of the left, the French party system long remained impermeable to the disruptions of the new social movement politics of the 1970s and early 1980s. Until 1981, aspirations of social change rested firmly upon the mainstream left-wing parties, especially the Socialist Party, which partly resurrected itself in

[10] Groups such as SOS Racisme, SCALP, Ras l'Front, Agir Chômage, Sans Papiers, Act-Up, Don Quichiotte, ATTAC and many others.

the 1970s by voicing the demands of new social movements. The latter were so disappointed with the Mitterrand presidency (1981–95) that they turned to more independent forms of activity. Today's new social movements usually present themselves as rivals to political parties, though a number have strong links with the resurgent far left (for example *Agir Chômage* with the Revolutionary Communist League (LCR) (Wolfreys 2003)). The division between new social movements and the mainstream left has been deepened by the success of the anti-globalisation (*altermondialiste*) movement and charismatic personal-ities such as José Bové. The *altermondialiste* universe is much closer to Bové or to the LCR than to traditional parties of the left such as the PCF or PS (Agrikoliansky, Fillieule and Mayer 2005).

The third version of the state–society relationship is the 'untidy reality', somewhere between a stilted republicanism and a resurgent citizenship. A more pluralistic polity has emerged. There has been a somewhat more open attitude towards the needs of disadvantaged groups, notably immigrants and women. Traditionally, group-based claims have been viewed unfavourably under the republican ethos, as fomenting ethnic particularism and threatening the principle of equal treatment of all citizens. French authorities have found a way around these constraints through a 'politics of stealth' that buries integration policies within territorial policies. Government policies to assist dis-advantaged urban areas (*politique de la ville*) or educational commu-nities (ZEPs) have provided significant benefits to immigrants, who are heavily over-represented in these communities. Likewise, youth employment measures (such as the *emplois-jeunes* programme of the Jospin government) have enrolled large numbers of immigrants. With regard to gender, the extent of reform has led Mazur (2005: 229) to suggest that France has experienced a 'sea change in the way gender equality issues are discussed and addressed in public policy'. The untidy reality illustrates itself also by the gap between discourse and behav-iour. The French model of republican citizenship has been a dichot-omous construction from its inception. In theory, there is a strict republican dichotomy between public and private spheres. In practice, there has been a long tradition of formal rules and negotiating excep-tions to rules. While formal rules stress uniformity, exceptions to rules have allowed a state-centric polity to adapt to territorial, social and religious pressures. While public schools are seen to embody republican citizenship, for example, ever since the Debré law of 1959 there has been a *de facto* compromise between church and state. The Republic has shown itself to be much more flexible in practice than in theory to its various religious groups, demonstrated by public support for mosque-building programmes or by the practice of 'contracted-in' Catholic schools.

The untidy reality metaphor can also be used to qualify the new citizenship argument. The increase in the number of associations is not merely the logical corollary of a rise in participation and/or dissatisfaction with parties. The organisational incentives of the '1901 association' status are attractive. According to French law, voluntary associations or clubs must be registered under a law dating from 1901 as 'non-profit-making' associations if they are to be assured legal protection. '1901 associations' are required to adopt certain organisational characteristics (such as having written statutes and a management board) and to register their existence with the prefecture. In return, these '1901 associations' can expect to receive public subsidies. The '1901 association' format conveniently blurs the boundaries between what is public and what is private. It has become a cover to enable public funds to be directed to organisations serving private interests. The main economic interest groups – such as the MEDEF or the CGT – have created pseudo-'1901' organisations, in order to receive public subsidies. Under the Jospin government, the '1901 association' statute also allowed organisations to recruit heavily subsidised young workers (*emplois-jeunes*), a source of labour considered vital for the survival of many of these organisations.[11] Even government departments have on occasion created '1901 associations' in order to overcome particular legal restrictions on their activity as public sector authorities. The system of local authorities providing financial support for local voluntary associations means that even groups bitterly opposed to the local authority often depend upon grants for their continued existence (McAna 2003). In practice, funded associations are *de facto* implementing agencies for municipal authorities across a very wide range of areas, confirming the porous boundaries between public and private.

Given the responsibilities devolved upon them, when associations fail the consequences can be very damaging. There is evidence of weakening integrative capacity on the margins of French society. The

---

[11] This finding emerged from interviews with Breton cultural and language associations in 2001.

urban riots of November 2005 were highly revealing of the crisis in relations between young people of immigrant origin and republican institutions such as the police. Traditional republican institutions (the police, the army, public schools) are less able to ensure integration because they were designed for another age ... or at least for another society. As well as highlighting the limitations of the formal institutions of the Republic, the urban disturbances signalled a breakdown in the informal institutions that had helped to ensure integration two decades previously. Urban riots since the early 1980s have revealed the weak capacity of low-level institutions. The 2005 crisis laid bare the weakness of social capital in the suburbs of France's conurbations, the absence of networks, parties, voluntary associations, schools or religious organisations that could provide social stability. The unrest was particularly acute in the areas of the Paris Red Belt, whose cohesion was previously assured by a powerful Communist Party representing a skilled working class (Kiwan 2006; Raymond 2006). The PCF is today far too weak to perform its tribune role as voice of the industrial proletariat, and the proletariat itself has largely disappeared (Lavabre and Platone 2003). There has been no reconstruction of alternative networks or forms of associative or partisan activity. On the other hand, the November 2005 crisis also showed how French mayors were in the forefront of daily contact, the limited resources at their disposal notwithstanding. Mayors coordinated attempts to mediate between the state and civil society and to draw the attention of public authorities and opinion to the difficulties in the *cités*.

Multi-level dynamics and challenges to the French model

The state-centric model developed in Chapter 2 insisted upon the focal role of the state, a strong centre being the focus of state–society interactions. The French models of elitism, of stato-corporatism and of territorial administration were all predicated upon a strong centre that ordered interactions in a hierarchical manner. Within this model, formal rules were less important than informal interactions, typified by informal mechanisms of inner-elite bargaining and, above all, by a model of *corps*-based solidarity that cross-cut formal legal and administrative responsibilities. According to Schmidt (1996, 2002), the traditional *dirigiste* model was one based upon the state defining policy in a unilateral manner, with social interests intervening only in the implementation phase. French economic interests looked mainly, if not exclusively, to the state to promote their aims and protect their interests. Until the mid-1990s, the typical reaction of a leading member of the MEDEF was to lobby the French government to adopt a more protectionist stance in Brussels, rather than to make the journey to the European capital.[12] Grossman and Saurugger (2004) argue that there is a poor fit between the orthodox French model of interest intermediation and the policy style required to succeed in Brussels. There is a weaker tradition of lobbying, and French groups feel themselves disadvantaged when faced with British, German or American rivals. French economic interest groups have sought to play catch-up and there is an increasing tendency to join pan-European and international organisations (Quittkat 2002; Woll 2006). The main employers' federation, the MEDEF, has set up specialist European and international structures within its own organisation and forms part of UNICE, the European employers' federation.

In one interpretation, there has been a profound transformation in state–group relations in the light of European integration. Europeanisation has redistributed the cards among existing domestic-level actors. It has encouraged an unbundling of the close relations between the state and economic interests that was a core feature of the state-centric model. It has disrupted older models of corporatist co-management, for example in agriculture (Saurugger 2003) It has created new degrees of freedom for French firms, associations, new social movements, even local and regional authorities. It has lessened the dependency of all these actors upon the central state. After a slow start, French interest groups have become more proficient at professional lobbying, and have learnt how to defend their interests in Brussels (Grossman and Saurugger 2004).

Two rather contrasting case-study examples lend support to the thesis of institutional learning. Grossman's (2003) study of the banking sector provides the first example. In the banking sector, established traditions of national state control were gradually undermined as a result of incremental changes brought by the Single European Act, the White Paper on financial services and a series of EU directives. Though national banking associations were initially state-centric in their

---

[12] Interview with the *Union des industries textiles*, Nord/Pas-de-Calais, November 1995.

responses, the sector began to organise itself on an EU-level once the Europeanisation of financial services became firmly established. The creeping Europeanisation of banking associations thus reflects changing institutional incentives at the EU level. Another recent case-study demonstrates how expertise acquired at the EU level can be used by a group in a sector whose regulation remains mainly national. Michel (2002)'s case study of the UNPI (*Union National de la Propriété de la Immobilière*) reveals how a nationally organised group can mobilise European arguments to back up its cause. Within France, the UNPI had to face stiff competition from an active social housing lobby which was itself not afraid to use the European argument in its own interests. The UNPI invoked the European Charter of Fundamental Rights, a charter that embeds the right to property ownership, but does not consider social housing to be a fundamental right. European law was used to bolster the group's domestic bargaining position. These two rather contrasting examples both demonstrate the benefits of thinking of the EU level as providing strategic opportunities, even when, as in the case of property ownership, the focus of group activity remained mainly national.

The metaphor of multi-level governance captures these pluralistic tendencies well. It is virtually impossible for any group to 'capture' the EU institutional machinery. The EU provides a set of institutional arenas that can provide a focus for strategic action, but can rarely produce static rental situations. The institutional fragmentation of the EU polity fits well with governance accounts and bears some striking similarities to accounts of US public policy (Baumgartner and Jones 2002). Lobbying in the EU is, in part, a process of venue shopping: focusing upon the right institutional venue at the right time in the complex policy process. As well as being a multi-level institutional venue, the EU is a regulatory regime and a multi-level legal order of a new sort (Majone 1996). In so far as it presides over a regulatory regime (rather than engaging in costly distributive politics) the European Commission interacts directly with leading economic interests that operate within the Union. Complex negotiations typically precede the publication of proposed directives in sensitive economic and commercial areas. Its role as guardian of the treaties, and as competition policy overlord in particular, brings the Commission directly into contact with business interests. In this technocratic world, scientific technical expertise is the key resource, and the use of a scientific register is essential if a group is to have influence (Saurugger 2003). In the case of nuclear energy, for example, the Commission has little expertise, and technical expertise is highly valued. At another level, criticisms of the democratic deficit have led the Commission to favour the pluralist confrontation between interest groups as a surrogate for a more democratic Euro-polity, as well as a means of strengthening its own capacity. New actors – firms, civic associations, new trade unions – have emerged in the public sphere. There has been a growth in the number of associations and social movements, many of which are active in trans-national networks and feel empowered by their dealings with Brussels.

On the other hand, the impact of Europeanisation is rarely clear-cut. Downloading EU incentives is not the only side of the story. Consistent with models of two-level bargaining (Putnam 1993), French governments have used domestic-level resistance to proposed reforms as a powerful bargaining chip at the Brussels end. The decision to shelve the Bolkestein services directive in advance of the 2005 EU referendum is one obvious example, but there are many others. Powerfully organised domestic interests can provide support for the resistance of French governments to the 'neo-liberal' stances finding favour within the college of commissioners. At a broader level of abstraction, the ability of domestic farming, film, audiovisual and theatrical (even educational) interests to weigh on French positions towards GATT/WTO negotiations played itself out in the EU negotiation of a cultural exception in the 1994 Uruguay round (Webber 1999). French resistance to stiff cuts in farm subsidies was one contributory factor leading to the suspension of the Doha round in 2006. These tactics can be highly effective. Since the French defeat of the constitutional treaty in 2005, a number of highly sensitive dossiers for France have been put on the backburner.

The governance of state–society relations

In this chapter, alternative understandings of state–society relations were presented in terms of state corporatism, social partnership, networked governance, new citizenship and multi-level governance. Each of these models corresponds to one or more important facets of contemporary French governance. There was some evidence of new citizenship and participatory governance, based in part on the rise of movements and associations contesting the existing order. More generally, republican principles are consistent with the emergence of a more differentiated, pluralistic polity.

The other four cases all demonstrated the reality of governing as a multi-actor process. The French model of state corporatism has been weakened in some important respects, most notably where the state is faced with the pressures of European integration and decentralisation and the changing role of the *grands corps*. This movement challenges one dimension of state capacity, understood in terms of the traditional one-sided relationships maintained by the state with professional and business groups. The chapter also uncovered the emergence of forms of social partnership (in training notably) that can assume the form of self-governing networks that keep the local and national state at a distance. The institutionalisation of such networks might be interpreted as another challenge to state capacity, but equally valid is the argument that social partnership is an exercise in central state steering at a distance. The state has delegated control of non-core functions to social partners and local authorities, but reserves the right to intervene as and when it sees fit. To borrow a metaphor from rational choice, the state remains the 'principal', but in practice the 'agents' develop an autonomous governing capacity that resists attempts at central state control. In education and training as in welfare, the chapter uncovered evidence of 'layering', of creating new institutions, agencies and programmes on top of old ones, adding to complexity and uncertainty without improving the central state's steering capacity.

Social partnership networks could also conflict with the new forms of local and regional governance. The evidence presented in France's cities and regions can in some respects be read as a powerful argument to support the emergence of more networked forms of local and regional governance. But our survey also underlined the persistence of the heavy variables that govern the education and training systems, variables that circumscribe local and regional experimentation. The emergence of the EU as a multi-layered polity, finally, presents some groups, firms and professions with new strategic opportunities to exercise influence and bypass the state. These findings confirm the contingent character of French governance, as well as the need felt by governors and the scientific community to adopt concepts and discursive concepts that make sense of politics, public service and policy, the core theme of the next chapter.

7 | *Making sense of the state*

Governing as governance challenges core understandings of the traditional state-centric model, as the argument of the previous chapters has shown. Complex legal orders and interdependent relationships lay bare traditional beliefs about the supremacy of the state and the viability of a system of public law. Some interest groups have begun to shift the focus of their lobbying away from central government. The state itself now emphasises its own productivity as the key to future prosperity. Multi-level dynamics and the requirements of multi-actor coordination create new challenges for actors vested with public authority. The operation of the international political economy has produced metaphors of a hollow state that go to the very heart of the French statist model.

These various pressures are not simply accepted in a passive manner. This chapter shows how French academics and policy analysts have sought to understand and make sense of the changing environment in a way that is consistent with or builds upon accepted frameworks. It then argues that state officials view new management practices and organisational reforms through their own lenses as public servants and their own belief in the appropriate behaviour their professional status implies. Above all, the chapter suggests that the main national political parties and politicians attempt to make sense of their own activity and accord a pre-eminent role to politics and the state.

Making sense of the state: the cognitive and normative school

Ideas and ideational approaches have been very influential among sociologists, political scientists and policy analysts in France. Various key schools can be identified. The action sociology school emphasises the importance of strategic action within and across organisations and assumes that ideas serve primarily instrumental purposes (Crozier 1963; Crozier and Friedberg 1977; Friedberg 1993). The constructivist

168

school emphasises the importance of mediation, representation and social interaction in shaping preferences and perceptions of reality (Christiansen 2001). The disciples of influential sociologists such as Bourdieu or Foucault focus on power and domination within society as a whole. The cognitive and normative school of public policy analysis is arguably the most relevant in terms of investigating government and governance in France. The cognitive and normative approach emphasises the centrality of social interaction in the production of ideas, common values and beliefs. While recognising the importance of socially constructed visions of the world, it also claims to be based upon observable empirical realities and to account for post-war policy-making in France better than any other theory.

In France, the cognitive and normative approach was first theorised by Jobert and Muller (1987) in *L'État en action*. Jobert and Muller present an analytical framework according to which policies appear not as programmes (in the Anglo-Saxon tradition), but as forms of social mediation, carried out by the central (and local) state. This framework is marked above all by the portrayal of a powerful state determined to shape French society in accordance with its wishes. The objective of public policy is: 'to modify the cultural, social or economic environment within which social actors (imbued with their own sectoral logic) operate' (Muller 1990b: 26). This French model is one characterised by a strong state-making policy in collaboration with powerful professions. The interpenetration of the state and the professions produces, in Muller's expression, a model of sectoral corporatism, a form of co-management of public policy. According to this model, public policies are the product of a rather one-sided interaction between societal norms and beliefs and the particular values, norms and images prevalent in different policy sectors. Though others are identified with the cognitive school (such as Bruno Jobert and Yves Surel), Pierre Muller is the standard writer against whom all others define themselves and this section will mainly focus on his work.

Muller makes substantial theoretical claims, setting out to develop a theory of public policy that understands and explains the nature of public policy in France and in Europe. There are three main dimensions to the cognitive-normative model as defined by Jobert and Muller: the importance of the ideational environment (in the form of the *référentiel* or paradigm), the socially constructed status of meaning (*sens*) and the importance of the mediators, elites whose role is to interpret reality.

The ideational basis of public policy is embodied in the *référentiel*, which can loosely be translated as a societal paradigm. The *référentiel*, Muller's most original contribution, is a set of beliefs comprising the basic values of society as interpreted by the elite. Through the *référentiel*, the elite defines the norms that describe acceptable behaviour for society as a whole. Muller insists that the *référentiel* is not an ideology. It refers to norms and cognition. The normative element is prescriptive, involving broad principles and visions about what the content of public policy ought to be. The cognitive element is drawn from these prescriptive principles; it consists of scientific arguments that follow from normative preferences. There is a close link between prescription and expertise. The literature emphasises how normative and cognitive factors are brought together in the same frame: deep values determine the principles for action and the preferred instruments for policy implementation (Surel 2000a).

Muller identifies three successive societal paradigms (*référentiels*) in the twentieth century. The balanced paradigm (*référentiel d'équilibre*) of the first third of the twentieth century rested on ideas of a limited state. As guardian of liberal economic policy traditions, the state was deeply reluctant to intervene openly in economic management, except in periods of war. Domestically, the main function of public authority during this period was to guarantee social equilibrium and to build upon the central role occupied by the rural and farming communities. Overseas, the state engaged in an active colonial policy. In the immediate post-war period, new norms of modernisation and economic growth prevailed over older concerns with social equilibrium. The modernising framework (*référentiel modernisateur*) that prevailed from 1945 to 1965 was closely associated with the role of the new Planning Commissariat. The post-war paradigm shift challenged all those policies that had been developed in the inter-war period based on social compromise. The modernising state swept aside existing policy priorities, leading to harsh social conflicts with peasants, miners and other social groups. From the 1970s onwards, the modernising set of beliefs of the immediate post-war period gave way to a new paradigm based on adapting to economic crisis (*référentiel du marché*). The emphasis now was upon limiting public expenditure, modernising the state, embracing the firm, accepting the primacy of the market and harnessing European integration to assist domestic reform (Muller 1990b; Jobert 1994; Muller and Surel 2002). Beliefs about policy diagnosis and solutions can change, sometimes rapidly, but the *référentiel* signifies that polices are developed within an overarching ideational framework.

If the emphasis is on the state as embodying legitimacy, policy sectors and policy communities also occupy an important position within the Muller schema. Public policy is closely linked to the notion of sector: sectors allow representations of the role of actors within society. Muller defines the policy sector as a 'set of social roles structured in general by a professional logic'. The sector organises professional roles and develops specific professional norms and values. In any sector there are recognisable professional roles. The medical sector, for example, contains roles relating to the exercise of distinct medical functions, such as doctor, nurse, health worker or patient. The professions matter much more than local or regional loyalties, and sectors have replaced territory as the key form of sub-state organisation (Muller 1990b, 1992). While territory (local or regional loyalties) had a horizontal logic, the professions are best organised in a vertical manner, thereby strengthening the state-centric focus of public policy-making. During the *trentes glorieuses*, public policies emerged as the result of interactions within stable policy communities of actors at the summit of the state, mainly civil servants and representatives of the professions. The policy sectors studied by Muller – agriculture, civil aerospace and nuclear power – had stable policy communities over long periods of time. The bureaucratic-professional elite that drove policy shared a system of common values, one that celebrated the culture of the *grand projet* and heroic state action.

The *référentiel* is thus the fruit of conflict and compromise between varied interests within society; it is not a perfectly coherent representation of the world and will contain its own inconsistencies. But it represents the accepted framework within which new conflicts and compromises must take place. In addition to the overarching, or global *référentiel*, Muller identifies a set of lesser frameworks, which consist of beliefs shared by members of a profession or sector. There is always a 'global-sectoral relationship': the specific profession or sector has to ensure its own professional beliefs are consistent with those of society as a whole. This formulation is rather similar to the classic political culture hypothesis of Almond and Verba (1963), whereby underlying cognitive beliefs constrain political and policy choices. This relationship is a hierarchical one: societal norms impose themselves upon the professions, which have little possibility in the short term of changing the overarching framework. The *référentiel* draws upon its roots in European sociology. Influenced by Durkheim, Muller insists upon the division of labour in modern industrial societies and the importance of sub-systems (sectors) as guides that give meaning to human actions. The *référentiel* consists of overarching values, perceptions of issue saliency and causal relations, as well as the hierarchy between sectors.

The cognitive model also emphasises public policy in terms of socially constructed meaning (Faure, Pollet and Warin 1995). As societies become more complex, so they become more reflexive. They develop the capacity to give a meaning to their own interactions. Cognitive and normative frames allow actors to make sense of their world. They help to produce identity and to instil a sense of collective unity amongst elites at the heart of the state. This dimension of Muller's thought has attracted a lot of criticism, not least for its imprecision. Rather than identifying the overarching meaning of an issue, or policy, it is more logical, his critics argue, to identify the alternative prisms that can be brought to bear on a subject. There is rarely one conceptual lens, but alternative constructions of the nature of the social problem (Palier and Surel 2005; Palier 2004).

The third dimension of the cognitive-normative approach is that of the *médiateurs*, loosely translated as mediators or power-brokers. The concept of the mediator introduces an element of agency into what appears often as a holistic, structural representation. Muller's mediators are strategic actors, key intermediaries between state, society and sector. They 'define and construct the world' and elucidate the truth, rather like Gramsci's intellectuals. Socio-economic situations do not 'produce' solutions; they need to be interpreted. The mediators derive their power from their conceptualisation of the dominant frames that are accepted by most actors and by outside society. They interpret the *référentiel* and redefine it in terms that can produce norms and policy outputs. *Médiateurs* thus perform a cognitive function (helping to understand the world) as well as a normative one (setting out the objectives of different policies).

Identifying who the mediators are is a key concern of the policy analysts. The *médiateur* is understood by Muller as a collective actor, rather than an identifiable individual. In the case of agriculture in the 1960s, the *médiateur* was in reality a tightly defined coalition of prime ministerial advisors, the planning commissariat and the young

Christian farmers' organisation (*Jeunesse Agricole Chrétienne* – JAC). In health policy, Griggs (1999) argued that young doctors were influential in defining the 1958 hospital reform that shaped the sector thereafter. Jobert and Muller (1987) emphasised the role of the young farmers' organisations in redefining the agricultural *référentiel* in the 1950s and 1960s. Thœnig (1973) identified the engineers in the Highways and Bridges *corps* as the professional group performing the roles of mediation and interpretation in the post-war modernisation in urban policy. These examples notwithstanding, one of the key criticisms levelled against Muller's model is that the *médiateur* is an abstraction, rather than an individual actor. Empirical research has found it difficult to identify the elusive mediators (Palier and Surel 2005). It is uncertain what observers are supposed to be looking for: individual actors, small cohesive elites or more diffuse intermediaries? Muller (2005) responds that identifying who the mediators are is less important than understanding the various forms that mediation takes.

The above discussion on mediation has important consequences for the governance of French democracy. The French cognitive model brings the state back into public policy analysis. The model allows for a strong centre and for strong policy sectors, defined as organised professions. The sector is important, but subordinate. The overarching *référentiel* sets the parameters within which the concerns of specific sectors can be accommodated, as well as allowing choices to be made between competing professional claims. In this design, sectors are not self-governing networks, in the British policy networks tradition. Their identity is constructed in the relationship they maintain with the overarching values and norms of society. Central decision-makers will arbitrate conflicting or rival claims. Sector-specific norms must be consistent with and subordinate to those defined at the centre. There is a hierarchy between sectors as well, which will develop their own framework according to the importance placed upon their activity by the national community.

Claims and counter-claims

Throughout the years, a number of criticisms have been made of the Jobert and Muller approach, as outlined classically in *L'État en action*. The French cognitive policy-making model has been criticised for its statist centre of gravity, while developments have revealed the complexity of French public policy-making (Gaudin 1995; Fontaine 1996). The *référentiel* has been dismissed as too general a concept, one that is impossible to operationalise or falsify (Palier and Surel 2005; Hassenteufel and Smith 2005). The *référentiel*, the critics argue, assumes a degree of coherence that does not exist in reality, either at the level of society as a whole or in relation to specific policy sectors. It also assumes a homogenous ruling elite, whose existence is doubtful. Muller's notion of policy sector has been challenged by a number of writers. Laborier (2003) argues that there ought to be no assumption of ideational coherence within a sector. She contests the belief, articulated by Muller, that all actors will progressively rally to a common understanding of their sector. Actors do not need to share the same viewpoints to come to an agreement. Within policy sectors, there are likely to be rival coalitions, as with the advocacy coalition framework in the US, which embraces the notion of competing policy narratives advocated by rival coalitions (Sabatier and Jenkins-Smith 1993).

The theme of operationalisation is addressed squarely by Bruno Jobert (1994) in *Le tournant néo-libéral*, another of the key works in French public policy analysis. In this later work, Jobert rejected the earlier ambition of *L'État en action* to build a model of analysis that is valid for all public policy. Muller's co-author now advocated a more parsimonious research strategy, one based on middle-level analysis. In *Le tournant néo-libéral*, Jobert and colleagues investigated the policy communities involved in advocating or legitimising economic policy choices. He identified three distinctive discourses and representations in three separate economic policy fora: the scientific community of economists; the political community; and the relevant policy networks. Jobert compares across policy forums, as well as cross-nationally. There is a differential receptivity to change across these three fora. In France, the UK, Germany and Italy, the economists were the most receptive to neo-liberal ideas, the epistemic community being dominated by American economists. Within the political community, in contrast, there was initially a marked rejection of the neo-liberal approach for fear of its electoral consequences. In the 1970s and 1980s, there remained a powerful belief in Keynesian ideas across Europe, but everywhere there was a gradual shift towards accepting the market. The policy networks involved in the welfare state were the most difficult to convince, but neo-liberal ideas finally penetrated even these policy networks. The Jobert approach now placed more importance on interaction and advocacy. Exchange occurs between advocates of rival positions; eventually, a new coalition will emerge which challenges the existing orthodoxy. Jobert also engaged in cross-national comparison. The market *référentiel* will take distinctive forms in different countries. In the UK, the driving force was the government, which looked to private institutions for inspiration. In France, Germany and Italy, on the other hand, there was no such global paradigm shift, rather an incremental process of adapting to changing realities.

In articles in 2000 and 2005, Muller defended his approach against its critics. He justified the French cognitive approach by the argument that public policy is normative *and* cognitive. For Muller, the *référentiel* is not an ideology disconnected from reality. It refers to moral preferences (norms) and evidence-based solutions and algorithms (cognition). It has a precise vision of what the content of public policy ought to be, as well as preferred policy instruments for tackling identified problems. The market *référentiel*, for example, is not just an ideological preference in favour of neo-liberalism, but also a set of precise beliefs about policy instruments and design. Muller refers to the normative/cognitive matrix to describe this mix of preferences and solutions. In the Muller model, social forces (interests) cannot be understood without reference to the ideas they convey and vice versa. The key argument lies elsewhere. Though ideas are shaped by interaction between actors, they tend to develop an autonomous capacity, which Muller refers to as the 'autonomisation of the cognitive and normative matrix'. Strongly influenced by Gramsci, Muller's *référentiel* thus has a hegemonic quality: it expresses the worldview of the ruling classes that comes to be accepted naturally by other social groups.

Muller has been criticised for ignoring human agency, a claim he rejects (2000, 2005). Muller's cognitive approach is one based on interaction between actors: hence, he claims, it is rooted in empirical sociology. The main thrust of Muller's argument, however, is that interaction is not designed to resolve policy problems; actors engage in public debate to express their perceptions of reality, how they see their place in the world, how the world should be. Interests only exist in so far as they express their own views of the world and what it should be like. Likewise, policy sectors are important primarily because they exist in the minds of their agents.

From global to globalisation

Initially proposing a state-centric model, by 2000 Muller was empha-sising how the global had been relocated from the national to the supra-national level. In the classic schema, the government 'produced' meaning. Governments could also control systems of social partnership and political regulation. But now a form of global governance has emerged, where the nation-state no longer controls the instruments of political regulation (Muller 2000). In modern European societies, Muller argues, the articulation between the global and the sectoral occurs at the level of the EU and international organisations. The EU is the only level where there is the possibility of creating a new political order. Other writers in the cognitive school have been very cautious before applying their models to EU processes. Surel (2000a, b) concedes that the traditional French cognitive approach has limited answers for European integration. The French cognitive model, which relies on an overarching *référentiel* and coherent sector-specific norms, appears ill suited to explain European integration. The EU is not a classic polity and it is certainly not formed on the basis of a homogenous model. The EU is a hybrid of competing territorial and sectoral interests, of hard competition between rival centres of power (Commission, Council, Parliament) and rival ideological constructions that render concepts such as the European social model empty signifiers. The EU is far too complex to be described in terms of its overarching *référentiel*. While common policies might rest upon the emergence of common norms and shared beliefs, a number of alternative prisms can be used to explain any EU decision. On the other hand, a strong case must be made for integrating cognitive variables in our understanding of Europeanisa-tion, notably through the increasing use of soft law and instruments such as the Open Method of Coordination (Lequesne and Surel 2004).

France's complex relationship with globalisation can also be eluci-dated by the contribution of the cognitive and normative school. Most definitions of globalisation identify a series of objective material shifts. Thus, for Gordon and Meunier (2001: 5) 'globalisation refers to the increasing speed, ease, and extent with which capital, goods, services, technologies, people, cultures, information and ideas now cross bor-ders'. The concept is commonly used to refer to the spread of neo-liberal policy norms and the retreat from the Keynesian welfare state and social democracy (Rosamond 2001). This version of globalisation makes powerful truth claims, requiring neo-liberal responses and taking as read the belief that there is no alternative. Thus defined, globalisation goes to the heart of the state-centric model identified in Chapter 2. It challenges republican discourse by disempowering the state. It runs counter to French economic policy traditions by 'handing power to the market' (Gordon and Meunier 2001). It sets up an alternative cultural framework to theorise the global that celebrates individualism, free trade and American English. But the French case can also support an alternative reading of globalisation. Heavily influenced in their own behaviour by constructivist traditions, some French politicians construct visions of a global future that rest upon a rejection of the Other, defined as the Americanisation of culture and the hegemonic role of the US in the post-Cold-War period. By the start of the new century, globalisation was being represented by writers such as Forrester (1996) as a powerful threat to French culture and national identity, a representation that found a strong echo in public opinion. According to polls conducted in late 2006 and early 2007, a majority of French considered that globalisation threatened their national identity (Brouard and Tiberj 2006).

Though obviously challenging some key features of the French orthodox model, globalisation has also provided French governors with an opportunity to redefine a French model that is broadly consistent with past traditions. On the French left, there is a strong cultural attachment to denunciations of Anglo-Saxon capitalism, unregulated international free markets and social dumping. Even beyond the left, there is little appetite for the 'neo-liberalism' that is associated with the past two decades of European integration and the growing influence of global economic norms. Except for a brief period in the 1980s, Gaullism has eschewed any reference to economic liberalism, while the centre-right has at most advocated social liberalism. Even UMP candidate Sarkozy backed away from embracing economic liberalism during the 2007 presidential campaign. One of the few social movements to have experienced real growth in the past few years is the anti-globalisation movement, symbolised by ATTAC and by José Bové, each interpreted as a defence of a particular vision of the French model (Agrikoliansky, Fillieule and Mayer 2005). Irrespective of the degree of integration into world markets, it remains important to theorise French distinctiveness, to conceptualise a coherent mode of political regulation and to make a claim for a specific form of competitive advantage on that basis.

Making sense of the state: appropriate behaviour and public officials

Making sense of the state also refers to perceptions of professional duty and representations of what constitutes appropriate behaviour by those who are directly employed as civil servants. As developed by March and Olsen (1989), sociological institutionalism places emphasis not only on the importance of rules, procedures, strategies and conventions, but also upon the beliefs, paradigms, codes, cultures and knowledge that give meaning to these rules. Through operating within institutions, actors are imbued with symbols and belief systems. Public officials act upon their perceptions of what is the correct code of behaviour. Sociological institutionalism thus frames institutions in terms of the belief systems of actors, considered as members of a profession, *corps* or grade, rather than as utility-maximising individuals, as in rational choice theory. Its underlying assumption is that individuals within organisations are conservative, fearful of change and resolute in defence of their interests.

In a number of accounts, civil servants in particular are portrayed as being prone to rule-driven behaviour and strongly influenced by a legalistic culture (Grémion 1979; Padioleau 1982; Wright 2000; Knapp and Wright 2001; Stevens 2003). Vested with a belief in their public service mission and their role as guardians of the rules, French officials will only 'break the rules' in order to provide better services for citizens (Dupuy and Thœnig 1985) or to increase their bargaining resources within an organisation (Crozier and Friedberg 1977). The bureaucracy sometimes functions efficiently only because rules are not enforced, but maintaining the fiction of rule-based treatment for everybody is a core belief.

Notions of appropriate behaviour provide important insights into the resistance to change demonstrated by public sector workers and at the middle levels of the bureaucracy. Changes in terms and working conditions have run up against stiff opposition from agents. There have been many examples of unsuccessful reform attempts by ambitious ministers. Premier Juppé's attempts to reform the employment statutes of public sector workers provoked mass strikes in November and December 1995 that brought the country to a standstill. More recently, Premier Raffarin's attempt in 2003 to equalise pension provision between public and private sectors provoked a furious backlash from the public sector trade unions. In between these two examples, the Jospin government (1997–2002) provided some excellent illustrations, both of the scope of reformist ambition and the meagre results achieved.

If the implementation literature in public policy tells us anything, it is that mid-ranking civil servants, professionals or public sector workers are strategically well positioned to block reforms of which they disapprove. One example is particularly illustrative of the difficulties in reforming the public sector in France: the case of the failure of the Finance ministry to reform itself in 2000. France has a particularly costly and inefficient system of tax collection. One bureaucratic unit (DGCP – the public finance directorate) is responsible for assessing tax liabilities, another (DGI – the general directorate for taxes) for collecting taxes. This separation between tax assessment and tax collection dates back to Napoleon. In 2000, Finance Minister Sautter announced his decision to merge the two divisions, with the aim of simplifying France's costly system of tax administration. He encountered determined resistance from both divisions, each with its own distinctive culture, its *corps* identity and its specific pattern of union strength. Faced with mobilisation from the public sector unions (*Force Ouvrière* in particular), Sautter abandoned his reform. The Education ministry provides an equally cogent example, where reforms that threaten the core interests of the teaching profession encounter the determined and usually effective opposition of the teaching unions (Corbett and Moon 1996; Ambler 2001; Cole 2005).

The key to understanding this resistance to change might lie in penetrating the cognitive worlds of specific professional groups. Rouban (2003) argues that public sector workers in France have reacted against what they perceive to be challenges to their professional ethic, based on a history of self-regulation. Successful reforms need to be compatible with the prevailing self-representations of professionals. The most successful changes in behaviour have occurred when reforms were perceived to be consistent with existing professional practices, which was the case for the *Armées 2000* programme within the Defence ministry (Rouban 2003). But, as a general proposition, there is little appetite for change and no social demand for the reform of the state. The politicisation of public sector workers has accompanied attempts to change working conditions, symbolised by the rise of radical unions such as SUD, or the high incidence of strikes in the SNCF. Public sector

workers were attracted in large numbers to candidates of the extreme
left in the 2002 and 2007 elections and featured overwhelmingly in the
'no' camp in the 2005 referendum on the draft constitutional treaty
(Perrineau 2005; Hainsworth 2006). The capacity for resistance of
public sector workers has been greatly weakened, not least as a result
of the part-privatisation of former public firms such as France-Télécom,
EDF and GDF. Public sector unions are no longer the powerful veto
players they once were. But union opposition constitutes a formidable
reminder of the contested nature of state reform and the deep opposition
to the withdrawal of the state from mobilised groups of workers. And the
appeal of public service goes well beyond the ranks of the public sector
workers, explaining the high level of public support for what appears on
the surface as rent-seeking behaviour by public sector unions.

The case-study of public service reform undertaken by Jones (2003) is
suggestive not only of the resistance of some officials to processes of
state reform, but also of the need to engage in fine-grained empirical
comparisons to be able to generalise. The terms and conditions of
service of public officials are enshrined in the civil service code, *Statut
général de la Fonction publique*, created in 1946 (Clark 2000; Jones
2003). The code outlines the process by which an individual can
become a public official, as well as stipulating the terms and conditions
of service once that status has been acquired. The civil service code
embodies a logic of appropriateness for the organisational behaviour of
officials in discharging their responsibilities. It provides a codified
charter that, in theory, protects civil servants and requires governments
to proceed cautiously when considering proposals to revise the terms
and conditions of service of public officials (Claisse 1993; Siwek-
Pouydesseau 1996; Chevallier 2003b).

On the other hand, the French administrative system is so fractured
into rival *corps*, divisions and ministries that it is unlikely that French
civil servants as a group are imbued with a single 'logic of appropriateness' (Bézès 2000, 2006). One of the key criticisms of sociological
institutionalism is that it is difficult, if not impossible, to falsify. An
alternative approach is to test when the argument of 'appropriate
behaviour' is used to frustrate change and when it is not. The key to
understanding how to do this lies with another strand of the new
institutionalist literature, which identifies the degree of penetrability
of organisations to their external environment as the key variable
(Clark 1998). Appropriate behaviour itself is not static. The behaviour

of public officials might be influenced by perceptions of professional duty, but other variables might prove more important in shaping their thinking. Uncovering causalities is in part a matter of empirical investigation.

Recent research into managerial reforms in three separate government departments and their field services – Infrastructure, Education and Agriculture – provided one such example of detailed investigation (Cole and Jones 2005). The research developed the hypothesis that capacity of field officials to accept reform might depend more upon their degree of *institutional receptivity to change* than the conceptions of appropriate behaviour of individuals or groups (Jones 2003; Cole and Jones 2005). The measure of institutional receptivity to change is a compound one that encompasses several dimensions. In addition to conceptions of appropriate behaviour, the key variables are the attitude of the central services to field service autonomy, the openness of the field service to the outside world, the type of service delivery involved and the extent of involvement of field officials in local networks. This hypothesis was tested in surveys conducted by Jones (2003) and Cole (Cole and Jones 2005).[1] The field services are gradually becoming accustomed to exercising greater managerial autonomy and applying managerial practices to their operations. They are engaged in policy orientated at learning. There was, however, a variable receptivity to change across different parts of the French administrative system. In response to the 1982–3 decentralisation reforms, several ministries

[1] Jones carried out thirteen interviews in the regional field services of the Infrastructure, Agriculture and Education ministries in the Champagne-Ardennes region during May 1996 and January and February 1997. In the Reims rectorate, interviews were conducted with the secretary general, heads from the financial affairs and examinations sections, staff in the division for inspectors and administrative staff. For the regional directorate of the Agriculture ministry, the regional director and his deputy were interviewed, as well as administrative staff in the directorate. At the regional directorate of the Infrastructure ministry, interviews were carried out with the regional director, a technician from the unit for technical policy and assistance to businesses and an official seconded to the directorate from the National Institute for Statistics. All interviewees were asked about their experiences of the administrative reform process and its impact on their respective field service. Cole carried out twenty interviews with officials in the Education and Infrastructure ministries in 1999, 2000 and 2004. Most were conducted in the Parisian headquarters of the Education ministry and dealt specifically with contractualisation, evaluation, political and administrative decentralisation and management reform.

undertook modernisation programmes at field service level (de Montricher 2006). Field service managers in the Infrastructure ministry, for instance, were delegated greater managerial autonomy in budgetary and human resource management from 1983, within the framework of a contractual agreement with the central ministry (Pavé 1992; Duran 1993).[2] Similarly, the Education ministry delegated increased budgetary autonomy, more flexible human resource management and greater control over pedagogical direction to its regional field services, the rectorates (Cole 1997, 2001a). In the new institutionalist tradition, these organisational inheritances are important variables. Those ministries that had engaged in reform processes early on found it much easier to implement change than others. Infrastructure was the most dynamic, followed by Education and Agriculture.

This variation was due in part to the attitude of central ministries. While Infrastructure had a long tradition of innovation, the Agriculture and Education ministries provided ample evidence of the resilience of traditional institutional features. Clark (1998) argues that the field services of those ministries engaged in business-type activities are more susceptible to managerial reforms than those ministries involved in purely administrative functions. Infrastructure has always had close relationships with the private sector and local government, bringing its agents into contact with decision-makers beyond central government. Education has by far the most sizeable field services, making it the most similar to a classic bureaucratic organisation. While size reduces proximity, the type of service delivery – curriculum design, teacher mobility, demography, inspection – ensures that the Education ministry operates in an interdependent policy space. The Agricultural ministry stands apart from the others. Its ability to develop a specifically regional policy is limited by the nature of the policy sector (agriculture being a Europeanised domain), by the EU, by the national and departmental focus of farm pressure-group activity and by the relative weakness of agriculture as a territorial department.

Closely related to issues of central attitudes and service delivery, the proximity to local or regional policy networks is another important variable. The development of a regional public sphere is an essential feature of sub-central French governance. The influence of field services depends not only upon the vertical relationships they maintain

---

[2] Interviews, July 2004.

within their ministries, but also upon the degree to which they are embedded within local (especially city) and regional communities. This degree of embeddedness is more important for certain ministries than others. Infrastructure, Education and Agriculture each maintain distinctive relationships with their client groups and there is some evidence that these vary in different places. Good inter-organisational relationships can determine whether the local authorities involve the field services as partners (essential for the Infrastructure ministry) or seek alternative sources of expertise. Some field services have made considerable efforts to establish themselves as legitimate actors in the eyes of local actors (Duran and Thœnig 1996).

These examples from the field describe a process of incremental change that is context specific and driven by sometimes contradictory pressures. Sociological institutionalist arguments based on the appropriate behaviour of officials capture only part of this process. The differential receptivity to change by the field services was also a function of internal organisational dynamics, the attitude of the central services to field service autonomy, the degree of openness to the market, the type of service delivery involved (more or less market focused), and the extent of penetration in local networks. The Infrastructure ministry was more receptive to management change than either Education or Agriculture. Though innovation was weaker in the field services of the Education and Agriculture ministries, there was evidence of change within both ministries. Reform of the state programmes from 1989 onwards provided these field services with experience of having greater control in their operational management, especially in financial and human resource matters, a development strengthened in some respects by the new budgetary procedure known as the LOLF.

Making sense of the state through parties and political leadership

Making sense of the state is the core business of political parties and political leadership. In the Muller model considered above, the political sphere is above all important in its ideological function, much more so than its role in public order. It is through politics that fundamental choices are made and hierarchies are established and acted upon. France's political parties generally equate politics and the political sphere with national political institutions and the national political

community. They have resisted the doctrine of *adapting* to Europeanisation in part because they remain imbued with the republican culture
of national sovereignty, which comforts their belief that they can make
a difference, if not necessarily direct change. In the mainstream
republican discourse, politics regulates economics, rather than merely
adapting to markets. On the mainstream French left in particular, there
is a strong cultural attachment to the primacy of the political, and a
belief in the legitimacy of politics to shape markets. Even beyond the
left, there is little explicit endorsement of the neo-liberalism that is
associated with the past two decades of European integration and the
growing influence of global economic norms.

  To a degree, the parties of the mainstream left and right share a
renewed reference to the Republic as the overarching national political
community. On the left, the reference to republican values has become
all-encompassing, reverting in many senses to the positivistic, ration-
alist culture characteristic of the republican left in the late nineteenth
century (the emphasis on progress, *laïcité* and citizenship). For its part,
the right has rediscovered the Republic as a means of marking its
difference from the far right. There are a number of common themes
underpinning the new republican consensus. Both left and right share
a common (though not identical) perception of the role of France
within European institutions and international organisations.

  Neither left nor right has embraced the doctrines of neo-liberalism (as
opposed to classical liberalism), except for short and exceptional
periods in recent history (the RPR in 1986). Both left and right have
looked to safeguard the state as a means of preserving a French way of
life faced with globalisation. Most fundamentally, as the 2003–4 debate
on *laïcité* demonstrated, left and right are closer to each other in relation to defining the conditions of French citizenship than either is to the
domestic far left or the far right, or, indeed, to rival Anglo-Saxon or
Germanic notions of citizenship.

  A belief in the efficacy of state action characterises the Socialist Party
(*Parti socialiste* – PS) in particular. The Jospin government (1997–
2002) delivered a distinctive political programme that bore some
similarity to the 1981–6 period of Socialist rule (Cole 1994, 2002b;
Ross 1997). As the French Socialist Party returned to office shortly after
the election of the Blair government in the UK, comparisons were
inevitable. Consistent with its own traditions of discursive radicalism
and the enduring influence of French Marxism, the French Socialists

rejected most of the precepts of New Labour. In response to Blair's 'third way' between the old left and the new right, Jospin pointedly refused to define a new orientation between social democracy and liberalism, preferring the former to the latter and declaring 'yes to a market economy, no to a market society'. While Blair advocated reforming the policy environment to adapt to globalisation, Jospin stressed the importance of EU and state-level public policy intervention to control globalisation. While Blair assiduously courted business during the first New Labour term, the landmark reforms of the Jospin government, especially the thirty-five-hour week, were implemented in the face of fierce business opposition.

State intervention in the labour market through the thirty-five-hour working week lay at the centre of the Jospin government's reform programme, which also employed an activist employment policy symbolised by the *emplois-jeunes*, the creation of 350,000 temporary jobs for young workers. Far from accepting that adapting to European integration and the global economy meant abandoning traditional policy preferences, Jospin believed the left should use the state to fight unemployment, promote growth and reform society. The Jospin period thus represented a powerful attempt to renew the statist traditions of the French left, to build state capacity and to identify new problems that were appropriate for state activity. The state still figures in a prominent position in the Socialist construction of reform. The French left continues to celebrate key symbolic staging points such as the forty-hour week and paid holidays of 1936, the French welfare state and social security system in the early post-war period, or the 'social conquests' of the 1981–6 and 1997–2002 governments.

This specific party context is key to understanding the failed candidacy of Ségolène Royal in 2006–7. Royal's breakthrough was initially spectacular. Elected as president of the Poitou-Charentes region in the 2004 regional elections, she developed an increasing political profile in 2005–6 and secured a large victory in internal PS primaries in November 2006, appearing briefly as the only Socialist likely to defeat Sarkozy in 2007. Within the context of the French left, Royal represented innovation. In important respects, Royal's strategy was rooted in an associative enterprise parallel to the PS. The successful capture of the nomination combined elements of an external appeal (she was by far the most popular Socialist from 2004 onwards), a parallel organisation (through her association *Désirs d'avenir*) and a powerful strategic location within the PS (as president of the Poitou-Charentes region). For associations and supporters, choosing a woman to represent the PS was a sign of renewal. Of key interest in terms of the model of participatory governance, Royal advocated the need to reinvent new democratic fora, such as citizens' juries and local referenda. She defined her own campaign platform through an exercise in democratic 'participation', based on listening to the 'people' as she toured the country from November 2006 to January 2007. Her platform promised to introduce more decentralisation and to strengthen the regions in particular. She called for institutional innovation and democracy, through strengthening parliament and limiting the powers of the presidency. And, in a rather different register, she pledged to attack conservative interests in French society; whether teachers in education, workers benefiting from special pension regimes or other protected interests.

Royal's Achilles heel was her own party. Her victory in the internal PS primary was prepared by the careful cultivation of key figures within the Socialist Party organisation, by her participation in face-to-face debates with rival contenders Dominique Strauss-Kahn and Laurent Fabius and by her promise to campaign on the basis of the party's Socialist Project of 2006. There was a tension between this commitment to respect the party's programme and procedures and the call for a participatory, elector-focused campaign. This fundamental ambiguity was unresolved. Royal's campaign oscillated rather chaotically between the promise of programmatic and political renewal and the declarations of orthodoxy drawn from the Socialist Project of 2006, upon which her own presidential platform was based. Royal made the classic 1970s-style promise to create 500,000 public sector jobs and to penalise companies that delocalise their economic activity. While she had criticised the thirty-five-hour week in the PS primary campaign, she defended it stoutly during the presidential election. In exit polls after the first and second electoral rounds, Royal lacked credibility on issues of presidential stature and policy credibility and her relationship with the party was never fully resolved.[3]

---

[3] In the *Baromètre Politique Français* surveys carried out for the CEVIPOF from April 2006 to February 2007, Royal trailed Sarkozy consistently in terms of 'presidential stature', but Sarkozy appeared to represent more of a 'danger' for the future.

Nicolas Sarkozy appeared much better organised and politically coherent than Royal. His election as sixth President of the French Republic on 6 May 2007 was clear and unambiguous. During the 2007 campaign, Sarkozy demonstrated his ability to appeal to a broad cross-class electorate, to mix a distinct ideological message based on values with policies designed to cater for specific electoral clienteles, all the while presenting a holistic and fairly coherent appreciation of the changing nature of French society. Sarkozy's election as president provoked a good deal of analysis about his political persona. Is he an economic liberal in the tradition of Margaret Thatcher in the UK or Ronald Reagan in the US? Or a moderniser in the tradition of former British premier Tony Blair? Indeed, is he a populist in the tradition of Silvio Berlusconi, the former Italian premier? Or ought he be best situated with reference to past French leaders, most especially those in the Gaullist tradition? Here is not the place to engage in a detailed analysis of the Sarkozy presidency. Comparing the style and substance of Sarkozy with comparable core executive leaders makes sense, however. Not only does comparison elucidate our understanding of the incumbent president, but it helps in identifying the public policy repertoires that continue to accord a primordial role to politics, the political sphere as regulation and the centrality of the state.

The image of Sarkozy as a neo-liberal, a gallic version of Margaret Thatcher overwhelmingly predominated in the Anglo-Saxon press in the aftermath of the French election. Sarkozy was portrayed as a new type of French politician, a man of the modern right, socially conservative and economically neo-liberal. Sarkozy shares with Thatcher the same discourse on the need to liberate business from excessive burdens, to make labour markets more flexible, to control the trade unions. Both leaders condemned excessive taxation as a burden on individual and corporate initiative and set out to reduce taxation for the highest earners (40 per cent top rate in the UK, *bouclier fiscal* at 50 per cent in France). Rather like Thatcher, Sarkozy emphasises the value of work and the responsibility of the individual to find work. Like the Iron Lady, Sarkozy advocates the importance of individual material incentives over collective goods (*travailler plus pour gagner plus*) and the need to reduce regulatory and fiscal burdens on employment. Both Thatcher and Sarkozy have identified specific interests as internal enemies, be they special retirement regimes or self-seeking trade unions. Both Thatcher and Sarkozy start from a perception that economic performance is more important than social protection, that the welfare state presents a structure of opportunities that can be individually abused, that the poor are to some extent responsible for their fate.

Yet the reading of Sarkozy as an economic liberal is fraught with difficulty. The French president is much more interventionist, less neo-liberal, less likely to allow the free interplay of markets and less likely to adopt a discourse of adapting to globalisation than former British premier Thatcher. Sarkozy was an interventionist Finance minister from June to November 2004, using his resources to create national champions and scare off foreign investors.[4] During the 2007 campaign, he made it clear that he would have sought to frustrate the Mittal take-over of Arcelor had he been president.[5] Immediately after his election, he intervened in the management of the EADS consortium and continued to attempt to steer the course of industrial mergers thereafter.[6] His tough-talking stance on the need for enhanced EU economic protection brought Sarkozy into conflict with the UK and other liberal-minded countries during the June 2007 Brussels summit that agreed to relaunch discussions on a simplified treaty. His attack during this summit on the 1957 Rome treaty's commitment to free trade and competition caused a rift with the Commission and a number of member states. These actions were not those of a neo-liberal determined to roll back the state.

While the comparisons in the British press were mainly with Thatcher, some observers preferred the comparison with Blair. Thus, Garton Ash (2007) defines Blairism in general terms to refer to a 'post-ideological and pragmatic conception' of politics, mixing themes associated with left and right, more concerned with what works than with ideological coherence. In this construction, Blairism marries social justice, individual enterprise and full employment, with a residual role for the welfare state. There are some obvious similarities between

---

[4] In the pharmaceuticals sector, he openly intervened to prevent the Swiss Novartis from interfering with the Sanofi-Aventis merger that he engineered. With respect to Alstom, he intervened to prevent the 'national champion' from going under.

[5] In 2006, Indian steel-maker Mittal fought a bitter and ultimately successful take-over battle for control of Arcelor, the Luxembourg-based steel firm in which French interests were paramount.

[6] After months of hesitation, President Sarkozy engineered a merger between former state bastion GDF and the private sector energy supplier Suez. The creation of this 'national champion' resulted in the part-nationalisation of Suez, justified by the need to retain France's energy independence.

Sarkozy and Blair: the emphasis on the importance of reforming the social model, the value of work, the discourse centred upon individual responsibility, the emphasis on responsibilities before rights, the respect for diversity and for forms of positive discrimination as a pragmatic response to an increasingly multi-ethnic society.

A number of the reforms introduced by President Sarkozy were directly inspired by Blair: for example, adopting tougher criteria for obtaining welfare benefits, new obligations on the unemployed to undergo training and the granting of tax credits to facilitate employment for the low paid. Other early measures were presented in terms of bringing France up to international best practice: the 'modern' approach to public administration and service delivery through target-setting and monitoring and the provisions for university autonomy are two obvious cases. Sarkozy's reforms can be interpreted in terms of accepting broad European norms of enhancing the productivity and efficiency of the state. The role of the state ought to be to introduce market-supporting policies, to improve the efficiency of its own operation, to improve levels of education and training, to improve productivity and open access for all the talents. By calling for a performance culture with the apparatus of the machinery of state, Sarkozy is consciously addressing broader European norms of best practice. The state remains a powerful reference. And the role of the captain is to steer the ship of state.

Sarkozy's political leadership

Président, chef du gouvernement, de la majorité, du parti, de l'administration, des armées, leader, patron, numéro un, il veut être tout cela à la fois.
(*Le Point*, 24 May 2007).

Sarkozy built the Union for a Popular Majority (*Union pour une Majorité Populaire* – UMP) as a modern conservative party that explicitly set out to distance itself from Gaullism (Haegel 2007). Yet the Gaullist lineage is clearly appropriate in some respects. Like de Gaulle, Sarkozy stands for restoring strong political leadership at the centre of the state. But while de Gaulle sought ostensibly to remain above the fray, Sarkozy has developed a more directive political style that seeks openly to assume the mantle of leadership. There has been a marked presidentialisation of the core executive and personalisation of inner-executive relations since May 2007. Under Sarkozy, the presidency 'governs' in a more overt way than at any other stage of the Fifth Republic. Sarkozy inherited an institutional set-up that is propitious to strong personalised leadership around the presidency. The presidential election is more than ever the 'decisive' one since the reform of the *quinquennat* in 2000 and the reversal of the order of elections so that the parliamentary elections have followed the presidential contest since 2002.[7] But institutional variables do not dictate behaviour. While Royal proclaimed her support for the Sixth Republic and interpreted this in terms of restoring parliamentary authority and inventing new forms of participation, Sarkozy has made explicit a leadership vision where a president with a popular mandate exercises executive authority[8] but where counterweights are also openly assumed.[9]

Strengthening the Élysée as the centre of operations has been a core preoccupation. The Élysée staff has been vested with new responsibilities. Through press conferences and missions for the president, the General Secretary of the Élysée, Claude Guéant, has performed a more public role than any of his predecessors. Other presidential advisors (special advisor Guiano, spokesperson Martinon) have also occupied the public limelight. President Sarkozy has created new agencies within the Élysée for homeland security and defence, testament to his determination to centralise control over internal and external security. He has promised to the two internal intelligence forces (RG and DST)

---

[7] In 2000, Lionel Jospin changed the order of the elections due for 2002 so that the parliamentary election would follow the presidential contest, strengthening the claim of the latter to constitute the most important or 'decisive' election. The term of the presidential office was reduced from seven to five years in 2002, bringing presidential and parliamentary elections into line and making the latter more than ever dependent on the former.

[8] Sarkozy announced a commission on the future of the institutions to consider whether articles 20 and 21 of the 1958 constitution (which vest executive authority in the prime minister) ought to be changed or abolished to reflect the pre-eminence of the president.

[9] But Sarkozy also promised an official statute for the main opposition party and intervened to ensure that the presidency of the Finance Commission was in the hands of the PS. The president pledged that parliamentary committees would have a larger say in approving nominations in the future, and held out the prospect that the most restrictive clauses in the 1958 constitution might be revised.

into one, and named close advisors to key positions in the police and security apparatus. In the first and second Fillon governments, Sarkozy broke up powerful ministries that might constitute alternative centres of influence to the Élysée. The creation of the ministry for Public Accounts and the Budget, alongside the Finance ministry, is the best example of this. Suspicious of the influence of Bercy, Sarkozy announced his major tax reform (*paquet fiscal*) as a presidential initiative, not a decision co-managed with the Finance ministry. Directly taking his inspiration from Blair and Number 10, Sarkozy announced that the Élysée must approve all public statements of ministers to avoid dissent, enforce collective responsibility and coordinate governmental activity.

President Sarkozy involved himself in a very detailed manner in the selection of government ministers and advisory staff. The division of labour between president and prime minister was agreed long in advance of his election, with Premier François Fillon accepting the president's predilection to *govern* and his own role as that of faithful lieutenant. Fillon has been influential in a number of respects, not least in embodying a method of social negotiation that provided an inspiration for Sarkozy in his first few months. But during the first nine months of his presidency the role of coordination and governmental leadership that is, in theory, that of the prime minister in the 1958 constitution was vested in Sarkozy, who maintained a close relationship with his advisors and 'his' ministers. Sarkozy personally determined the composition of the first two Fillon governments. The policy of opening up the presidential majority to include prominent figures from the Socialist opposition (notably Bernard Kouchner as Foreign Affairs minister) was a political gamble,[10] destabilising the PS, keeping the UMP at a distance and strengthening the claim to govern in the name of

[10] The first Fillon government excluded classic *Sarkozystes* such as Patrick Devidjian, yet reached out to include political 'opponents' such as Hervé Morin (Defence minister, head of the New Centre Party), Bernard Kouchner (PS, Foreign Affairs), Jean-Pierre Jouyet (secretary of state for Europe, Socialist and former head of Jacques Delors's office in the European Commission). Besides Brice Hortefeux, Immigration and National Identity minister, the first two Fillon governments were noticeable for the absence of core Sarkozy supporters. In addition, Socialist personalities such as Jack Lang, Claude Allègre and Jacques Attali all accepted missions for the president, who supported former PS Finance minister Strauss-Kahn as head of the International Monetary Fund.

all of the French. Opening up the majority was not limited to political opponents, but also to representatives of civil society, to businessmen and recognised experts in their own domain.[11] In his first few months in office, Sarkozy inaugurated a new political style and pattern of elite accommodation. A lawyer himself, the new president marked his distance from France's traditional elite (fewer *énarques*, or *inspecteurs des finances*), to provide a reflection of the diversity of French society, to open out to civil society and to ensure parity (*Le Monde*, 21 June 2007).[12] The motivation of the incumbent president is less important than the public expression of the need to reconcile France with her own diversity, talent and plural political traditions.

Sarkozy's presidential leadership is neither of the modest nor the restrained kind. He has made it clear that there is no reserved domain; he has the capacity and thirst to intervene in all aspects of policy. When the proposals for university autonomy aroused powerful opposition, Sarkozy personally intervened to smooth out objections. He has exercised a ubiquitous presence and during the first nine months intervened in the smallest details of policy; over higher education reform, Airbus, industrial mergers, taxation, immigration, the armed forces, minimal service in transport or the social dialogue. In 2007, Sarkozy had a high quotient of personal resources (skill, energy, popular support) and an unassailable political base: the presidency, a majority to support the president, a supportive Senate. Whether this highly favourable structure of resources would endure was another question. Key challenges lay ahead in employment, public debt, intergenerational solidarity, living standards, France in Europe and, on the world stage, global trade, energy and the environment. How Sarkozy would respond to these challenges was uncertain at the time of writing (early 2008), but the first months placed a personalised form of presidential political leadership at the centre of interactions.

---

[11] Such as Martin Hirsch (of the charity Emmaüs), Fadela Amara (creator of the association *Ni Putes, Ni Soumises*) and Bertrand Laporte, the manager of the French rubgy team.

[12] The France of all the talents was symbolised by the rise of the *beure* Rachida Dati to the key post of Justice minister, and by the nomination of Rama Yade, of Senegalese origin, as a secretary of state in the Foreign Affairs ministry. Male–female parity was respected more faithfully than in previous governments, notably by naming Michèle Alliot-Marie as Interior minister.

Making sense of the state

Making sense of the state, and of the role of the political sphere, more generally remains a core concern of policy analysts, public officials and party politicians in France. Paradigms conceiving of public policy in terms of state-centric action, hierarchy and overarching coherence have been challenged to the core, but the attempt to uncover meaning, to assert the need for *hyperchoix*, to look for new 'centres' of regulation and modern forms of state activity continues. Notions of appropriate behaviour are important for understanding the resistance of middle-ranking officials to organisational changes that threaten terms, conditions and a tradition of self-regulation. More fine-grained analysis allows comparisons to be drawn that situate actors at the intersection of contradictory and incompatible pressures. In all cases, however, reference to professional duty and to the ethos of serving the state remain powerful, acting as a lens to interpret these rather contradictory pressures.

In the case of France's political parties, finally, discourse remains centred on state capacity-building, on the possibility of making a difference. Politicians and parties have sought to make sense of the state. If the 1980s was the decade of responding to external 'constraints', in the sphere of European integration notably, the 1990s and 2000s saw a powerful reaction against threats to an imagined national community. Politicians from the left (such as Jospin or Chevènement) or from the centre-right (such as Chirac or Villepin) made a strongly defensive political appeal in favour of the French model, phrased in terms of defending French capitalism, protecting the social welfare model and supporting the integrative model of citizenship. This defensive political discourse was the real legacy of the two Chirac presidencies (1995–2007), which left few achievements.

Both candidates in the 2007 presidential campaign deliberately distanced themselves from the Chirac years and positioned themselves as representing a break with the past. The 2007 electoral series openly addressed the core issues raised throughout *Governing and Governance in France*. Both Royal and Sarkozy shared a certain diagnosis of France as an underperforming nation given her natural talents and resources, a nation that could recover with far-sighted political leadership. Both candidates pledged to improve the efficiency of the state (though both also made commitments that were costed as unrealistic by independent experts). Both Royal and Sarkozy diagnosed a number of core problems with the functioning of democratic institutions and each posed solutions they deemed most apt. Ségolène Royal proposed a coherent version of the participatory mode of governance developed in Chapter 1. Participatory governance had to confront the resistance of existing institutions, notably political parties, whose role as representative intermediaries is threatened by experiments in direct democracy. Sarkozy had fewer problems with the UMP than Royal with the PS, as he had made the conquest of the party created to support Jacques Chirac the centrepiece of his presidential strategy. But Sarkozy also acknowledged the difficulties of France's traditional republican model of representative democracy in accommodating diversity and managing a multi-ethnic society. The representation of diversity within the Fillon government was genuinely innovative. The 2007 election held the promise of a new direction; the victor, Nicolas Sarkozy, has adopted a much more active interpretation of his role than his predecessor, but only time will allow us to make sense of his enterprise.

8 | *Governing and governance in France*

France's governors face key challenges in an age of state transformation and changing patterns of state–society relations. This book has embraced a critical version of the governance paradigm. Governance is best understood as a middle-range concept, rather than an overarching meta-narrative such as power or domination. Governance imposes a model on a complex reality. It identifies objects that are ontologically plural, and hence finds it difficult to identify precise dependent variables. Any framework for analysis must accommodate the contingent nature of governance itself, as well as its application to specific cases. This final chapter offers a series of concluding judgments about France's version of governance. Though the processes described throughout this book add up to very substantive change, there are countervailing and contradictory forces at play. The theme of governance is better at explaining change than continuity, but even change does not occur on a *tabula rasa*. It is processed, at least in part, by existing political institutions. It is interpreted by reference to sets of ingrained ideas and referential frames. It must brave the reaction of established interests. If the metaphor of governing as governance is central to the argument, governing can also take the form of resisting change. The second half of the book has presented much evidence of institutions, interests and ideas resisting the pressures for change that have been labelled collectively as governance.

Governing as governance in France

The framework of analysis presented in Chapter 1 started from two fundamental premises: that the state is embedded in a complex system of multiple legal orders and interdependent relationships; that domestic institutions, ideational traditions and interests mediate the style of governance in France. Several distinct axes were identified along which the empirical cases could be classified. These axes were those of new modes of participation and regulation; multi-level/multi-actor dynamics; the hollow state and state capacity; and sector-specific and cross-sectoral dynamics. These axes provide an analytical grid to compare the various cases that have been investigated empirically throughout the book, to place France in comparative context and to theorise about the internal consistencies and priorities of French-style governance.

New modes of participation and regulation

Along with all other member states of the EU, France is caught between the conflicting participatory and regulatory modes of modern governance. From the evidence presented, it is possible to identify two prevailing narratives about France's version of governance. The first narrative emphasises the participatory pluralist version of governance. In contemporary society, the principle of sovereignty has been eroded. There is less likely to be a sole centre of power. There has been an increase in the numbers of actors associated with decision-making processes. Both internally and externally, the state is forced to associate new actors with the decisions it makes. There is a weaker distinction between public and private, and power is dispersed across several levels. Governance falls clearly within the pluralist frame. No actor can control decision-making processes alone. In this pluralistic governance, government remains a central figure, but the capacity of the state has been limited to such an extent that it cannot control the consequences of the interactions it has put into place. Whatever the intentions of central governors, there is a loosening of ties between the state and civil society and a weakened capacity to direct or steer interactions.

The pluralist narrative is compelling when considering changes to the traditional French models of territorial administration and state corporatism. In Chapter 3, the findings from France's cities and regions were interpreted as a powerful argument to support the emergence of more networked, multi-actor forms of local and regional governance. In Chapter 7, the state corporatist model has, it was argued, been weakened in core respects. There is a degree of misfit between the functioning of traditional state-centred power networks and the operation of European integration and, to a lesser degree, decentralisation. Social movements and professional associations have discovered new degrees of freedom and arenas for influence. The emergence of the EU as a multi-layered polity presents groups with clear strategic opportunities for promoting their causes within France by mobilising supranational and sub-national avenues of influence. But it is at the local level that new democratic experiments – citizens' juries, local referenda, *conseils de quartiers* – make the most sense.

On the other hand, experiments with new democratic tools such as citizens' juries or local referenda have encountered scepticism from the public and resistance from most political parties (Rui 2004; Roger 2007). Ségolène Royal's 2007 campaign did little to dispel such attitudes. The accepted modes of collective action remain mainly focused on the French state, especially if broadly defined to include local and regional authorities. The role of the street in French politics paradoxically reinforces this centralisation, both functional and geographical, as it is physically concentrated in Paris and focused on forcing French central government to back down from announced reforms. Collective action registers based on contesting central authority, rather than participation and deliberation, remain deeply embedded.

A second narrative emphasises the strategic adaptation of the central state to new policy challenges, in the shape of the emergence of the regulatory state that attempts to steer at a distance. Governing in contemporary France involves a more or less conscious attempt to redefine a strategically powerful and focused state. In the case of state reform, senior civil servants sought to offload non-strategic functions in order to focus on their core tasks. When so much policy-making escapes the control of national governors, those areas that remain within the preserve of the nation-state are jealously guarded. While the state has lost some functions, it has gained others and developed more efficient ways of central steering. The complexity of policy challenges has forced the French administration to imagine innovative responses. The central state has attempted to strengthen its indirect capacities to govern at a distance, by inventing new instruments to facilitate central regulation, specifically agencies, performance indicators, new forms of monitoring and budgetary reform (Lascoumes and Le Galès 2004; Borraz 2007). In the French regulatory state, as elsewhere, the choice of specific instruments can provide a means of sidestepping established interests and introducing new organisational and management ideas that are unlikely to be embraced by established networks. Such was the case for the numerous semi-autonomous agencies that were created during the

2002–7 period. Even older instruments such as contractualisation appeared as an attempt by central actors to strengthen their oversight role in a complex multi-actor policy field. The state reform programmes studied in Chapter 2 each involved an attempt to reassert central state identity, faced with exogenous challenges, inter-ministerial rivalries within the state, the rise of territorial politics and players and the importance of private and semi-public actors.

If both these narratives describe well certain features investigated in the book, contemporary France has moved closer to the regulatory than the participatory mode. But neither pluralism nor regulation fits easily into the prevailing realm of discourse, a theme to be developed further below.

Multi-level and multi-actor dynamics

Our second axis combined multi-level dynamics and multi-actorness. In truth, there is a much less clear dichotomy than in relation to our other three axes. One might imagine a clustering of multi-level dynamics and multi-actorness towards the same end of any scale, as for example in the multi-level governance framework. Governance is best understood as involving multi-level dynamics across a broad range of policy fields *and* multi-actor coordination. One of the core dimensions of governing as governance lies in the relativity of spatial and temporal boundaries and the multiplication of levels of regulation that impact upon any given territory, in this case France. If the French state has assumed a regulatory form, then the French regulatory state itself is regulated in most of its fields of activity by the European Commission, the European Court of Justice, the European Central Bank and associated EU-level agencies. Though it is capable of acting as a strategic entrepreneur, the French Council of State perfectly articulates these fears of a 'hollow state' that run against the grain of French history and traditions.

The argument that European governance embeds multi-level dynamics is weaker in France than in the case of Spain, the UK, Germany or Italy. French governments have done their best to limit expressions of 'multi-level' governance to their strict minimum. The regional prefects still perform a coordinating role in the management of EU structural funds, except in the Alsace region. Official procedures attempt to ensure that the French state, whether operating at the centre or in the regions, mediates contacts between French local and regional authorities and

Brussels. But the formal narrative of coordination in the name of the general interest sits uneasily with the sectoralised networking that characterises much EU policy-making and that escapes from the tight control of the French state. Whatever their intention, French governments are unable to control interactions by French business interests, or even local and regional authorities (Grossman 2003).

Likewise, whatever the formal discourse about the strict separation between public and private, French governments accept the need for multi-actor coordination at all levels of policy development. This book has uncovered three forms of multi-actor coordination: public–private interactions in the governance of France's cities and localities (Chapters 3 and 7), new modes of economic coordination in the post-*dirigiste* state (Chapter 5) and new arenas for the promotion of private interests (Chapter 7).

France is more apt, *in relative terms*, to look to the state as a mechanism for economic coordination than either the UK or Germany. But the difference is one of degree. French governments often lack the capacity to achieve state-led coordination in economic policy, even though the state remains highly active in market-supporting activities. The governance of the leading firms is now much more focused on the international financial markets than the French Finance ministry. As observed in Chapter 7, French business interests have their own sophisticated lobbying strategies in the EU and world trade arenas.

The multi-level/multi-actor axis is a reality of EU politics. The governments of other large EU countries have been more proactive in supporting multi-level and multi-actor interactions, less focused on preserving a state-centric mode of coordination. The representation of France's cities and regions in Brussels falls well behind that of Germany or the UK, whose governments actively lend their support to place promotion. The partnership dimension of governing as governance is more in evidence at local and regional levels. Local networks have become much broader, to encompass mayors and their *adjoints*, representatives of local economic power (chambers, employers associations, individual business people), voluntary associations and public–private partnerships (mixed economy societies) combining to engage in new forms of political and economic entrepreneurship. Network analysis in Rennes and Lille (Chapter 7) uncovered networks of public, semi-public and private actors in the governance of French cities.

State capacity and the hollow state

The third axis identified was that of state capacity and the hollow state. Drawn from the international political economy school, the hollow state metaphor constructs governance as the residue of the political sphere, the state emptied of its substance by the international political economy. From a political economy approach, Jessop (2007) identifies a transition from the Keynesian welfare state to the Schumpeterian workfare state as the principal consequence of the shift to a post-Fordist economy since the 1970s. The function of the Schumpeterian workfare state is to support the market and to create the conditions for innovation and enterprise in relatively open and competitive economies.

The metaphor of the hollow state underplays the efforts undertaken by central governors to build *state capacity*, to invent new forms of political steering and to discover new activities. The issue of state capacity is best framed in terms of three core questions. Do 'strong' actors located at the centre of the state direct public policy? Have central state actors adopted strategies designed to exercise a tighter overall supervision of the direction of public policy? How capable is the state in terms of its ability to achieve its own public targets (for example in relation to welfare spending or economic and monetary union)?

In response to the first question, we perceive a diminished capacity for core state actors (politicians, senior civil servants) to exercise a directive influence and observe the gradual appearance of new levels of regulation (local, regional, European, global). These developments all undermine the capacity of state-centric political and administrative actors to envisage government as a hierarchical chain of command. The evidence presented across a range of policy sectors in Chapter 5 pointed to a weakening overall ability to shape outcomes. In economic development, the French state has a weakening capacity to direct economic policy, though it has not lost all of its interventionist instincts. In education, the state has been forced to broaden the scope of participation in the expensive delivery of education services. In welfare and social policy, on the other hand, there has been a stronger pattern of state intervention since the late 1980s, with the creation of the minimum income (RMI) and universal health care (CMU) in particular. But social solidarity remains a domain of weak state capacity.

In response to the second question, the state has adapted to new, uncertain circumstances in an attempt to steer policy as best it can.

One of the paradoxes of the debates about governance is that the capacity of the state has been challenged at the same time as government, understood in its broadest sense, has never performed so many functions. Even a minimal market-supporting state has new responsibilities in social policy, education and training, raising the skills level of the workforce (Levy 2006). Rather than a weakening of the state, *per se*, it is as legitimate to argue that the type of state activity has changed. Arguably, states can be more effective as regulators than they ever were as distributors of services. The new policy instruments adopted by governments since 2002 have been designed in part with state productivity in mind. The LOLF in particular (the new budgetary procedure) is designed to enhance productivity through target setting, monitoring and performance indicators. These innovations are consistent with developments at the EU level, where technical agencies have grown exponentially.

The response to the third question (how capable is the state in terms of its ability to achieve its own public targets?) is, to a degree, context-specific. In the case of welfare, Chapter 5 identified limited state capacity, whether in terms of directing institutions, controlling outcomes or limiting expenditure. The policy style in welfare, one of steering by networks of social partners and the professions, limited state oversight. In the case of controlling public expenditure, France was unable for several years (2002–6) to respect the criteria on deficit and debt reduction written into the Growth and Stability Pact that were intended to ensure the compliance of 'weak' states such as Italy and Greece. On the other hand, the theme of state productivity progressed even in areas, such as welfare, that have resisted central steering. New organisations such as the regional hospital agencies exercise core steering functions in health care.

The counter argument to state capacity-building is that processes of automatic government (Weaver 1988), by their very essence, limit the capacity of governments to implement change. Rose (1993) argues strongly that policy choices are limited by past choices. Incumbent governments cannot ignore past commitments that are given substance by complex legal systems and pre-existing institutions and actor configurations. Policy programmes pursue their autonomous development irrespective of the activities of governments in power. Important areas of public policy are defined in technical terms, as neutral and beyond the legitimate sphere of public intervention. This can enhance overall steering capacity in some respects, as it allows central government (or the EU) to define technical norms over and above the interplay of interests. But it can also remove whole areas of public policy from the oversight of politicians and ministerial civil servants altogether, a trend that goes against powerful traditions of political oversight.

Sector-specific dynamics

Our fourth axis was that of sector specific versus cross-sectoral dynamics. At one end of the spectrum, governance is envisaged as a form of functionalism, embedded within policy sectors that are highly resistant to political oversight. Powerful networks are able to resist governance as state capacity-building through developing sector-specific forms of private government. The contrary position conceives of policy-making not in sectoral terms, but as involving the pooling of expertise across strict professional boundaries, the democratisation of expertise and new cross-sectoral interactions between associations, professional bodies and political authorities.

In Chapter 5 the dynamics of governance were compared in economic policy, welfare and education. In these fields of investigation, the actor configuration has changed most obviously in the field of economic development, less so in education and welfare, which are less mobile and more place-specific. In economic development, the interventionist state has ceded ground, though it has not lost all of its old reflexes (Clift 2004; McClean 2006). What remains of the interventionist state operates in a narrowly confined and restricted space. Government–industry relations have been transformed, with French businesses often in the first rank of global effectiveness, but French governments are still tempted by the discourse of economic patriotism and protection (Culpepper 2006). France's leading trans-national corporations are much less state-centric in their focus than they once were (Grossman 2003). Older patterns of domination, such as that of the *grands corps*, are weakening even when they persist. Economic development is a multi-level sector where exogenous pressures impact more directly and visibly than in either welfare or education.

In the field of education, underlying continuities appear more powerful. The mainstays of the 'governance system' are civil servants, professionals and students, who often interact in a mutually reinforcing way in favour of the status quo. But there have been important innovations on the periphery and the gradual development of more unpredictable outcomes (van Zanten 2004, 2006). If the logic of a governance system is internal stability, our survey demonstrated the capacity of external pressures to drive some change, including pan-European pressures and a gradual awareness of the importance of global competition in higher education.

The field of welfare is the one where change has proved the most difficult and the path-dependent narrative is the strongest.[1] In terms of its governing principles, France comes closer to the Bismarckian contributions-based model of social insurance than the Beveridge model of universal cover.[2] This incremental mix is important for understanding policy dynamics in this sphere. The French 'social model' is an institutional and normative hybrid, managed in the main by social partners (the trade unions and employers' associations), regulated by the medical, pharmaceutical and health professions and overseen by the state. French social policy has some key features of a self-regulating network, shaped by strong professional pressures, regular political influence, but weak state capacity.

The very concept of policy sector has been challenged by a number of writers, for whom the characteristic of contemporary governance is that it lies beyond sector (Laborier 2003; Pasquier and Weisbein 2007). Governance challenges all existing institutional forms, not only the state but the professions as well. The weakening of the French model of sectoral corporatism, investigated in Chapter 6, lends some support to this hypothesis; depicting French policy-making in terms of tight stato-corporatist policy communities from which outsiders are

---

[1] The concept of path dependency lies at the very core of historical institutionalism. According to this concept, initial decisions are crucial because they tie in future decisions. In a colourful image, Pierson (2000) introduces the notion of 'increasing returns' to describe this process. Past experiences are predictable, whereas change is unpredictable. There are strong incentives not to change direction once decisions have been taken at critical junctures. Policy communities develop expertise and experience and with time there are always many insiders who benefit from existing arrangements. Decision-making involves a process of sedimentation, as successive layers of decisions are made. Though sub-optimal in some senses, such decision-making reduces uncertainty, hence is acceptable to most actors. Policy networks embrace stability rather than change.

[2] The Bismarckian model is a system of social insurance based on contributions and administered by the representatives of the insured (workers and employers). The Beveridge model provides for a system of universal cover, financed mainly by general taxation and only partly by contributions.

excluded is not supported by the evidence presented thus far. Explicitly cross-sectoral governance is most in evidence in France's localities and regions. Recent studies have uncovered the democratisation of expertise and new cross-sectoral interactions between associations, professional bodies and political authorities (Cadiou 2007; Catlla 2007; Taiclet 2007). On the other hand, the EU policy process is highly sectoralised, reconfiguring professional policy communities at the supra-national level and so making them less easy for any one nation-state to control.

Comparing policy sectors allows questions to be asked about state capacity and change that are central to the nature of contemporary governance and germane to the future of the state in France itself. Arguments based essentially on the reluctant adaptation to external pressures carry more weight in economic policy than in education or welfare. But, as Chapter 5 demonstrated, the state has not simply vanished from economic policy. Nor is education or welfare immune from trans-national economic and cultural pressures. Public spending targets force governments to attempt to control domestic education and welfare spending.

Thus, sectors are more or less open to external influences, which can empower some actors at the expense of others. They are more or less well placed to resist global economic pressures and in none is there a single hegemonic *référentiel*. Laborier (2003) contests the belief, articulated by Muller (2000), that all actors will progressively rally to a common understanding of their sector. Within policy sectors, there are likely to be rival coalitions, as the advocacy coalition framework contends (Sabatier and Schlager 2000). These rival coalitions advocate policies that are more or less credible depending upon internal and external circumstances. In the field of the economy and economic development, for example, there was competition between sound money conservatives in the Finance ministry and more *dirigiste*-inclined planners in the technical *grands corps*. In education the dominant discourse centred upon the constitutive role of the state in education, but this discourse was challenged in part by a reform-minded coalition that emerged in the late 1990s. In the area of welfare, there was also a dominant discourse, a powerful rhetorical commitment to the French social model by most actors within the 'system'. The dominant discourse of social solidarity served to occult the conflict of interests between protected insiders and socially excluded outsiders (Chauvel 2006).

From the above, we deduce that France's governance comes closer to the pole of the regulatory state than the participatory or pluralist democracy; that multi-level dynamics must compete with the ambitions of a state-centric mode of coordination; that there is a complex relationship between perceptions of state puissance and loss of capacity; and that the dynamics of governance in economic policy, welfare and education are mediated and context-specific. Comparing France with similar countries adds weight to these conclusions.

France in comparative perspective

Understanding governing as governance in France is no different in many respects from observing interactions in comparable European countries. Everywhere there have been challenges to orthodox models of government and patterns of state economic interventionism. All governments have had to adapt to processes of Europeanisation and abandon some traditional policy instruments (for example, control of interest rates) and modify others (state aids to industry) in the light of increased economic interdependence and, for members of the eurozone, monetary union. All governments have had to acknowledge new levels of policy action, if only to respond to EU funding regimes; the creation of NUTS regions in the countries of central and eastern Europe is a case in point.[3] All governments have had to respond to new global challenges, though the evidence presented here suggests that responses can vary considerably according to national traditions. Most European governments have undertaken reforms in public administration designed to increase productivity and monitor performance.

Comparing French-style governance with that of similar countries thus involves conceptualising *degrees of (discursive) difference*. There are dangers in attributing mechanical effects to movements such as Europeanisation, globalisation or even decentralisation; these constructions are interpreted and mediated in different ways in specific contexts, whether that context be organisational, sectoral or the form of the state. Policy-making takes place within a realm of discourse,

---

[3] The NUTS 'regions' are administrative constituencies designed through negotiation between member-state governments and the Commission to allow states to receive EU structural and cohesion funds.

a system of ideas and representations that is comprehensible to the actors involved. A number of core features of governance uncovered in the book face obstacles in resonating with the realm of accepted discourse and achieving discursive legitimisation. It is not suggested that there is one hegemonic discourse or global referential. The proposition is more modest: borrowing from the constructivist literature, new ideas need to resonate with existing identity constructions, as they are embedded in national institutions and political cultures, if they are to be fully legitimised. Changes need to be domesticated before they enter into the domestic *acquis*. Even radical changes can be accepted, so long as they are justified in terms of reference that are comprehensible and acceptable to French society.

French politics has often required conceptualising a coherent centre, a global *référentiel*, a sense of direction, of scalar hierarchy, of equal treatment, of inalienable rights guaranteed by the state acting in the general interest. In comparative terms, the model is well defined and coherent. The French model appears robust and distinctive in relation to models of citizenship, ideas about the state and public service, the separation of public and private spheres, the doctrine of equality, the refusal of ethnic differentiation. The state-centred republican model, developed in Chapter 2, is defective in important senses, but it provides a framework for making sense of a complex modern society when other frameworks (for example Anglo-Saxon economic liberalism or 'communitarianism') run against the grain of domestic political traditions.

Referring back to our four axes, comparison provides another means of calibrating where France lies in relation to its main European partners. Along with all other member states of the EU, France is caught between the conflicting participatory and regulatory modes of modern governance, our first axis. Seen from a comparative politics perspective, both the participatory/pluralist and the regulatory poles have some difficulty in entering into the French 'realm of discourse'. The pluralist vision, represented by open competition of interests and the minimal state, is quite foreign to prevailing French frames, though organisational sociologists and scholars of public administration have rightly identified the plurality of interests within the state itself, divided into bureaux and *corps* with competing concerns. There are some strongly neo-corporatist features to the modern French polity, even though the social partners are too weak to sustain the genuine neo-corporatist patterns of interest intermediation at work in Germany, Austria or the

Scandinavian countries. Likewise, collective bargaining practices have weakened in industrial relations, where plant-level agreements are now the norm. Though the modern state has adopted a more regulatory form, French governors are not particularly at ease with regulatory governance either, whether driven by the EU or bodies such as the WTO. Adapting to regulatory norms is in part imposed, in part purely formal. The French state can appear to adopt a regulatory form, through agencies, performance indicators, targets, etc. But in practice agencies are rarely autonomous, performance indicators are usually voluntary and failure to meet targets is seldom penalised. There remains a distrust of core features of markets that underpin the regulatory model. Other states, such as the UK (with its belief in markets) or Germany (imbued with a legal culture), are much more at ease with the modern regulatory state. In the case of France, there is a governance misfit, or at least the makings of one. Neither the regulatory state nor the participatory polity sits easily within the realm of discourse.

In comparative terms, the metaphor of a governance misfit also elucidates the difficulty faced by France's governors in adapting to multi-level dynamics. The French state-building enterprise has, historically speaking, been remarkably successful in inculcating deeply rooted beliefs linking the national territory with social progress. French sub-national authorities have traditionally operated within a central-ising state tradition, which emphasises the indivisible nature of political legitimacy and the organisational pre-eminence and legitimacy of the state. In practice, this tradition has not prevented the development of forms of local and regional capacity, territorial variation, public–private partnerships or experimental transfer of functions. But the doctrine of equal treatment remains deeply pervasive, as illustrated by the case of the experimental transfer of functions in the 2004 Decentralisation Act.[4]

Comparison with other EU states reveals the persistence of this belief in equality as uniformity. In comparative perspective, France appears to be the only one of the five major European nations determined to resist

[4] Though any sub-national authority can bid to run services on an experimental basis, this decision needs to be approved by parliament. Moreover, after a five-year period, the French parliament will then have to decide whether the transfer of functions should be made permanent. If so, the new policy responsibility will be transferred to all cognate sub-national authorities throughout France, thereby ensuring equal treatment.

a form of asymmetrical territorial development on its mainland. Germany, Spain, the UK and Italy have each undergone developments that can in some senses be labelled as federal, quasi-federal or asymmetrical.[5] In the case of France, a distinctive form of sub-national governance has evolved. But there are no equivalents to strong regions with fiscal and/or legislative powers, such as Scotland, the Belgian and Italian regions, the Spanish autonomous communities or the German Länder. France's twenty-two regions have a shared general competency and some tax-varying powers but no hierarchical control over other layers of local government. Governance might challenge the state, but not the unitary state form.

The tensions within our third axis (hollow state versus state capacity) are also elucidated by comparison. Whether in terms of citizenship, state–group relations or territorial administration, France has been seen to represent a statist pole among European states. In central–local relations, Page (1991) distinguishes countries with Napoleonic traditions like France, Spain and Italy, with their strong states and weak local government, from the functionally stronger local governments in states like Sweden and the UK (Page 1991). Comparing state–group relations, Grossman (2007) also places France in the statist camp, opposed to the neo-corporatist northern states and the pluralistic UK. Writers such as Schnapper (1994) celebrate the egalitarian ethos of the French Republic, guaranteed by a benevolent state and a strict dichotomy between public and private, while registering alarm at the dangers of the Anglo-Saxon communitarian model. Such distinctions are useful in so far as they provide a representation of France, in comparative terms, as a state-centred model. Part of the problem of state capacity relates to the capability–expectations gap that such a traditional conception carries with it. The state can no longer deliver the promises that the language of leadership and aggregation implies. Making sense of the state remains a core part of the activity of politicians, parties, pressure groups and public officials, but the capacity of the state to direct or achieve its own objectives is open to doubt. This gap is at the root of France's governance misfit.

In terms of our fourth axis, sectoral dynamics can also benefit from a comparative focus. From the evidence presented in Chapter 5, certain

---

[5] Asymmetrical, in the sense that different parts of the 'national' territory develop more or less advanced forms of autonomy.

policy sectors (the economy) appear much more amenable to global policy norms than others (welfare). But the process of mediation and translation into the legitimate realm of discourse does not necessarily follow a straightforward path. The case will be illustrated by concentrating on the example of economic policy-making. Legitimate political discourses vary according to context. Though Jobert (1994) identified the emergence of a global neo-liberal paradigm from the 1980s, he also demonstrated that neo-liberalism has not had the same meaning in countries such as the UK, France, Italy and Germany. Neo-liberal norms have not been mediated in the same way in each country, nor have they been equally germane to the legitimate political discourse that is needed to justify change. If, in the US and the UK, the neo-liberal frame was espoused as an opportunity in an age of globalisation, such was not the case in France (especially) or Germany, where domestic interest and discursive structures put up stiffer resistance.

The mechanisms of diffusion of trans-national paradigms such as neo-liberalism are likely to vary across country, sector and policy community. In one political economy interpretation, EMU has been interpreted as a means of anchoring globalisation within the European Union and forcing European economies to adapt to new global realities (Dyson 2002). But EMU is not just pure neo-liberalism. It is mediated in distinctive ways in different national contexts. In France, during the Maastricht negotiations EMU was framed in terms of strengthening European sovereignty in international money markets, of replacing the dollar as the international reserve currency and of offering the possibility for a European economic government that would defend the European economic and social model against globalisation. The terms of the debate have not shifted that much. The institutional architecture of a European Central Bank immune to political influence is not to the taste of most French politicians, Sarkozy and Royal included. Pierson (1996) argued strongly in favour of historical path-dependency to explain why and how global pressures will be 'translated' into national norms. The justification for EMU in France could not simply be one of adapting to globalisation or of making Europe the most competitive space in the world. To resonate with 'previously embedded and institutionalized values, symbols and myths' (Marcussen *et al.* 2001: 101) EMU had to be framed in terms that had meaning in domestic discourse, such as economic sovereignty, European power or competition with the United States. The belief among French governors that the state matters, though *dirigisme* belongs to the past, still resonates strongly in the case of economic policy.

It was argued in Chapter 5 that governance could be understood in part as referring to new mixes of markets, networks and hierarchies. In the French case, market mechanisms have had the most impact in the field of the economy; networks appear very resistant to change in the field of welfare; hierarchies retain the ascendancy in education. Adapting these three metaphors to national policy styles, the UK appears most apt to embrace a liberal form of governance, where coordination is the role of the market, albeit a market policed by tough regulatory agencies. The traditional German social-market economy (challenged of late) was one that relied on fairly tight cooperation between social partners and the state that together comprised neo-corporatism, relying on coordination by networks. The French model was the one where traditionally most emphasis was placed on state mechanisms of coordination, though this varied according to sector and period. Of these three leading EU countries, the case of France is the one where the strongest argument for governance misfit can be made. Whether in terms of participatory democracy, the regulatory state, multi-level governance, state capacity or adaptation to the global economy, the above cases and comparisons reveal difficulties for governance to enter the realm of legitimate discourse, hence becoming part of the domestic *acquis*. The result is a form of contingent governance that refuses to bear the name.

France's contingent governance

The French polity has mutated under the combined impact of internal and external pressures for change. This book has embraced a critical version of the governance paradigm. France's governance is predicated upon the loosening of older forms of vertical statist regulation and weakening state capacity. Complex legal orders and interdependent relationships lay bare traditional beliefs about the supremacy of the state. Some interest groups have begun to shift the focus of their lobbying away from central government. The state itself now empha-sises its own productivity as the key to future prosperity. Multi-level dynamics and the requirements of multi-actor coordination create new challenges for actors vested with public authority. The operation of the international political economy has produced metaphors of a hollow state that go to the very heart of the French statist model. Understanding governing as governance in France is no different in many respects from observing interactions in comparable European countries.

What is *not* governance? The second half of the book has presented much evidence of institutions, interests and ideas resisting the pressures for change that have been collectively labelled governance. The trade unions have been engaged in a rearguard action to defend working conditions against the perceived threats of unbridled liberalism, invisible globalisation and individualisation. The mass strikes against Premier Raffarin's pension reforms in 2003 demonstrated that the unions still had the capacity to mobilise employees for strike action. Since the 1995 strike movement, the activity of the public sector unions has become almost entirely defensive, namely to resist any changes in codes, rules or working practices, and to defend the corporate ethos against any attempt to introduce individual incentives or more flexible working practices.

Other forces of resistance to governance are rather subtler. While it would be misleading to set the law *against* governance, legal pathways and traditions help to shape its precise contours. Though contractual procedures and partnerships have become embedded as routine features of inter-organisational politics, governments have not hesitated to use the law to impose solutions (as over the thirty-five-hour week), and administrative tribunals have been reluctant to consider partnerships and 'soft' contracts as having binding legal force. Embedded ideas and discursive frames can also offer stiff resistance to change. Political cultures can be extremely resistant to change, because new ideas are more easily filtered out if they are not compatible with pre-existing identity assumptions. As the case of globalisation demonstrated in Chapter 5, national elites, in France and elsewhere, will select those ideas most likely to be consistent with their interests and with pre-existing identity constructions.

In Chapter 1, it was argued that governance was best understood as a middle-range concept, something to be explained rather than an over-arching explanatory framework for analysis. French-style governance is an untidy reality, rather than a neatly ordered and organised hierarchy. The framework of analysis developed in Chapter 1 identified four key axes to comprehend French-style governance. These axes, in order of their presentation, were those of new modes of participation and regulation; multi-level and multi-actor dynamics; the hollow state and state capacity; and sector-specific versus cross-sectoral dynamics. In our discussion we presented evidence from the empirical work to justify positioning the French polity at given points along these axes. Organising the available evidence is not the same as determining the significance of these four axes for understanding the process of governing contemporary France. The most pertinent axes, in order of importance, are the hollow state versus state capacity, participation versus regulation, sector-specific versus cross-sectoral and multi-level/ multi-actor dynamics.

Making sense of the state and of public activity is all the more important in that state capacity has been weakened, taking the range of its activities as a whole. Politicians have to make sense of public activity, to propose choices between social groups or, within the limits of their resources, to enact redistributive policies. The state remains the key driver of distributional politics in France and influences the form of regulatory politics as well. The underlying political discourse, very well articulated by President Sarkozy, refers to values, choices, aggregation and leadership. Politics and government remain wedded to the idea of making fundamental choices – Muller's *hyperchoix* – even if processes of automatic government and the emergence of new arenas lessen the impact of these choices.

Taken as a whole, the trends described throughout the book place France closer to the regulatory than to the pluralist mode of governance, though this depends somewhat upon sector and level. Pluralism and participation both have a slightly artificial ring. On the part of France's governors and representative mediators, there remains an underlying suspicion of direct forms of democracy, of civic associations that escape the orbit of public authority, of new social movements that depart from the norm. Even the left has marked its distance from the democratic heritage of May '68. Neither are French governments particularly at ease with the new form of the regulatory state, the French version of which is shaped by features that set it apart.

In relation to policy sectors, we rejected in part the functional dynamics hypothesis. Governance appears as much more than a form of functionalism embedded within policy sectors that are highly resistant to political oversight and change. The argument clearly does not hold for the economy, where a powerful argument can be made for a paradigm shift from neo-Keynesianism to global market norms, whether or not this is mediated by the survival of neo-mercantilist tendencies (Clift 2008). In the field of education and welfare, the underlying continuities appear more powerful, with the welfare sector the best for sustaining a path-dependency argument. In all these examples, the policy sector is a useful heuristic. By constructing policy dynamics in terms of regular relationships, policy communities and technical expertise, however, it tends to underplay change and the power of external and internal drivers of change to reshape sectoral boundaries. Finally, multi-level and multi-actor dynamics are part of EU politics and policy-making, but, in the case of France, they must contend with a state-centric mode of coordination (or at least the attempt to impose one).

In the case of France, the overall conclusion is one of contingent governance. In those domains where a distinctive form of governance has evolved it has navigated a difficult path, littered with obstacles represented by ingrained institutions, ideas and interests. Countries faced with comparable pressures are likely to process responses in manners consistent with their own political traditions. Historical and institutional traditions are important in understanding the available pathways of governance, which operate within distinctive ideational and institutional environments and interest structures. Nationally or sectorally distinctive positions are not static, however. They evolve and transmute. Endogenous and exogenous influences gradually infiltrate the most tightly bound institutions and policy communities, as demonstrated by Palier (2006) in the field of welfare. If change in French politics and policy-making is processed in accordance with recognised codes and by identifiable institutions and interests, change itself has gradually reshaped the nature of these codes and the policy province of these established institutions and interests.

The future direction of French-style governance is not predetermined. Governments can influence the form of governance in more or less instrumental or procedural ways. Governments can accommodate or encourage participatory pluralistic tendencies, but they can also promote techniques of central steering and automatic government that minimise transaction costs and remove areas of policy from public debate and lobbying. Whether interpreted as the emasculation of the state or as its adaptation to new circumstances, the metaphor of governance is appropriate. The model of government as the sole legitimate source of power and authority and as the core of a state-centric polity cannot, by itself, make sense of the complexity described throughout this book.

Bibliography

Agence Nationale pour la Rénovation Urbaine, 2004. *Rapport d'Activité 2004*. Paris: ANRU.

Agrikoliansky, E., Fillieule, O. and Mayer, N. (eds.) 2005. *L'Alter-mondialisme en France: la longue histoire d'une nouvelle cause*. Paris: Flammarion.

Almond, G. and Verba, N. 1963. *The Civic Culture: Attitudes and Democracy in Five Nations*. Princeton: Princeton University Press.

Ambler, J. 1985. 'Neo-corporatism and the politics of French education', *West European Politics* 8, 3: 23–42.

2001. 'Politics and policy in education', in Guyomarch, Hayward, Hall and Machin (eds.), 227–43.

Andolfatto, D. and Labbé, D. 2006. 'La transformation des syndicats français. Vers un nouveau modèle social?', *Revue Française de Science Politique* 56, 2: 281–97.

Andréani, J. L. 2007. 'Les Quidproquos de la décentralisation', *Le Monde*, 16 January.

Archer, M. S. 1979. *Social Origins of Educational Systems*. London: Sage.

Ascher, F. 1998. *La République contre la ville: Essai sur l'avenir de la France urbaine*. Paris: Éditions de l'Aube.

Ashford, D. 1982. *British Dogmatism and French Pragmatism: Central–Local Policy Making in the Welfare State*. London: Allen & Unwin.

Ba, A. 2004. 'L'Autonomie financière des collectivités locales et la réforme de la décentralisation', *Revue de la Recherche Juridique* 29, 104: 1851–60.

Bache, I. and Flinders, M. (eds.) 2004. *Multi-Level Governance*. Oxford: Oxford University Press.

Balme, R. (1999). *Les Politiques de néo-régionalisme*. Paris: Economica.

Balme, R. and Woll, C. 2005. 'France: between integration and national sovereignty', in Bulmer, S. and Lequesne, C. (eds.) *The Member States of the European Union*. Oxford: Oxford University Press, 97–118.

Baraizé, F. 1996. 'L'entrée de l'enseignement supérieur dans les contrats de plan Etat-régions. La mise en réseau de la décision universitaire', in Gaudin, J. P. (ed.) *La négociation des politiques contractuelles*. Paris: L'Harmattan, pp. 136–67.

Barthélemy, M. 2000. *Associations: un nouvel âge de participation*. Paris: Presses de Sciences Po.

Baumgartner, F. 1998. 'Public interest groups in France and the United States', *Governance* 9, 1: 1–22.

Baumgartner, F. and Jones, B. D. 1993. *Agendas and Instablility in American Politics*. Chicago: Chicago University Press.

(eds.) 2002. *Policy Dynamics*. Chicago: Chicago University Press.

Baverez, N. 2003. *La France qui Tombe*. Paris: Perrin.

Beech, D. 2005. *The Dynamics of European Integration*. Basingstoke: Palgrave.

Belloubet-Frier, N. 2005. 'Les implications du processus de Bologne dans le paysage universitaire francais', *Revue Française d'Administration Publique* 114: 241–52.

Bennett, C. 1991. 'What is policy convergence and what causes it?', *British Journal of Political Science* 21: 215–33.

Benoit, K. 2006. 'Duverger's Law and the study of electoral systems', *French Politics* 4, 1: 69–83.

Benson, J. K. 1982. 'A framework for policy analysis', in Rogers, D. (ed.) *Interorganizational Coordination*. Iowa City: Iowa University Press, 137–76.

Bernard, P. (1992) 'La fonction préfectorale au cœur de la mutation de notre société', *Revue Administrative* 45, 2: 101–6.

Berstein, S. (ed.) 1999. *Les Cultures politiques en France*. Paris: Seuil.

Berthet, T. and Merle, V. 1999. *Les Régions et la formation professionnelle*. Paris: LGDJ.

Bézès, P. 2000. 'Les hauts fonctionnaires croient-ils à leurs mythes?', *Revue Française de Science Politique* 50, 2: 307–22.

2006. 'Concurrence ministérielles et différenciation: la fabrique de la réforme de l' État en France dans les années 1990', in Dreyfus and Eymeri (eds.), 236–52.

Biarez, S. 1989. *Le Pouvoir local*. Paris: Economica.

Bœuf, J.-L. 2004a. *Les Collectivités Territoriales et la Décentralisation*. Paris: Documentation française.

2004b. 'L'Intercommunalité depuis 1999: la révolution tranquille', *Les Cahiers Français* 1–2, 318: 35–43.

Boguenard, J. 2004. *La Décentralisation*. Paris: PUF.

Borraz, O. 1998. *Gouverner une Ville*. Rennes: Presses universitaires de Rennes.

2007. 'Governing standards: the Rise of standardisation processes in France and the EU', *Governance* 20, 1: 57–84.

Börzel, T. 2002. *State and Regions in the European Union*. Cambridge: Cambridge University Press.

Bouvier, M. 2003. 'Le budget 2006 en régime LOLF', *Revue Française de Finances Publiques* 91: 3–148.

Brouard, S. and Tiberj, V. 2006. 'Déclin, modèle français et mondialisation', in *Baromètre Politique Français (2006–2007)*. Paris: CEVIPOF-Ministère de l'Intérieur, 1–16.

Brown, P., Green, A. and Lauder, H. 2001. *High Skills. Globalisation, Competitiveness and Skill Formation*. Oxford: Oxford University Press.

Bulmer, S. and Lequesne, C. (eds.) 2005. *The Member-States of the European Union*. Oxford: Oxford University Press.

Bureau, D. and Mougeot, M. 2007. *Performances, incitations et gestion publique*. Paris: Documentation française.

Burnham, P., Gilland, K., Grant, W. and Layton-Henry, Z. 2004. *Research Methods in Politics*. Basingstoke: Palgrave.

Butzbach, O. and Grossman, E. 2004. 'Une instrumentation ambigue. La Réforme de la politique bancaire en France et en Italie', in Lascoumbes and Le Galès (eds.), 301–30.

Cabanes, P. and Bouygard, F. 1997. *La Loi quinquennale relative au travail, à l'emploi et à la formation professionnelle: rapport d'évaluation*. Paris: Documentation française.

Cadiou, S. 2007. 'Jeux et enjeux de connaissances', in Pasquier, Simoulin and Weisbein (eds.), 171–89.

Caillose, J. 2007. 'Questions sur l'Identité juridique de la gouvernance', in Pasquier, Simoulin and Weisbein (eds.), 25–64.

Cameron, D. R. 1996. 'Exchange rate politics in France, 1981–1983: the regime-defining choices of the Mitterrand presidency', in Daley, A. (ed.) *The Mitterrand Era. Policy Alternatives and Political Mobilization in France*. Basingstoke: Macmillan, 56–82.

Catlla, M. 2007. 'De la genèse d'une régulation territorialisée à l'émergence d'une gouvernance territoriale', in Pasquier, Simoulin and Weisbein (eds.), 89–107.

Cautrès, B. and Dennis, B. 2002. 'Les Attitudes des Français à l'égard de l'Union européenne: les logiques de refus', in Brechon, P., Laurent, A. and Perrineau, P. (eds.) *Les Cultures Politiques des Français*. Paris: Presses de Sciences Po, 323–54.

Charette, E. 2005. 'Sub-state Nationalist Movements: Brittany and Wales Compared', PhD dissertation, University of Wales, Aberystwyth.

Chartier, E. and Larvor, R. 2004. *La France Eclatée?* Spézet: Coop Breizh.

Chauvel, L. 2006. 'Générations sociales, perspectives de vie et soutenabilité du régime de protection sociale', in Culpepper, Hall and Palier (eds.), 157–96.

Chavrier, G. 2004. 'L'expérimentation locale: vers un État subsidiaire?', paper presented to the GRALE colloquium on 'Réforme de la

Décentralisation, Réforme de l'Etat', National Assembly, Paris, 22–23 January.

Checkel, J. 2001. 'Social construction and European integration', in Christiansen, Jorgensen and Wiener (eds.), 50–64.

Chenot, B. 1986. *Le Secrétariat Général du Gouvernement*. Paris: Economica.

Chevallier, J. 2003a. 'La gouvernance, un nouveau paradigme Etatique?', *Revue française d'administration publique* 105/106: 203–17.

2003b. *Le Service Public*. Paris: PUF.

Chevallier, Y. 2006. 'La gestion des ressources humaines dans le contexte de la LOLF', *Les Cahiers de la Fonction Publique et de l'Administration* 255: 8–12.

Christiansen, T. 2001, 'Introduction', in Christiansen, Jorgensen and Wiener (eds.), 1–19.

Christiansen, T., Jorgensen, K. E., and Wiener, A. (eds.) 2001. *The Social Construction of Europe*. London: Sage.

Claisse, A. 1993. 'La Modernisation Administrative en France – Au delà des réformes, le changement?', Discussion Paper no. 26. Oxford: Centre for European Studies, Nuffield College.

Clark, D. 1998. 'The modernisation of the French civil service: crisis, change and continuity', *Public Administration* 76, 1: 97–115.

2000. 'Public service reform: a comparative West European perspective', *West European Politics* 23, 3: 25–44.

Clift, B. 2003. *French Socialism in a Global Era*. London: Continuum.

2008. 'Economic policy', in Cole, A., Le Galès, P. and Levy, J. (eds.) *Developments in French Politics 4*. Basingstoke: Palgrave.

2004. 'Debating the restructuring of French capitalism and Anglo-Saxon institutional investors: Trojan horses or sleeping partners?', *French Politics* 2, 2: 333–46.

Cohen, E. 1988. 'Formation, modèle d'action et performance de l'élite industrielle: l'exemple des dirigeants issus des corps des mines', *Sociologie du Travail*, 30, 1: 587–614.

1996. *La Tentation Hexagonale. La Souveraineté à l'épreuve de la mondialisation*. Paris: Fayard.

Cole, A. 1994. *François Mitterrand: A Study in Political Leadership*. London: Routledge.

1997. 'Governing the academies: sub-central educational policy-making in France', *West European Politics* 20, 2: 137–56.

1999. 'The *service public* under stress', *West European Politics* 22, 4: 166–84.

2001a. 'The new governance of French education, *Public Administration* 79, 3: 707–24.

Cole, A. 2001b. *Franco-German Relations*. Harlow: Longman.

2001c. 'National and partisan contexts of Europeanisation: the case of the French socialists', *Journal of Common Market Studies* 39, 1: 15–32.

2002a. 'A strange affair. The French presidential and parliamentary elections of 2002', *Government and Opposition* 37, 3: 65–91.

2002b. 'The Jospin government, 1997–2002', *Modern and Contemporary France* 10, 3: 1–4.

2004. 'Devolution and decentralisation in Wales and Brittany, 2001–2002', UK Data Archive (www.data-archive.ac.uk), study number 4802.

2005. 'Education and educational governance', In Cole, A. Le Galès, P. and Levy, J. (eds.) *Developments in French Politics 3*. Basingstoke: Palgrave, 195–211.

2006. 'Decentralization in France: central steering, capacity building and identity construction', *French Politics* 4, 1: 31–57.

Cole, A., and Drake, H. 2000. 'The Europeanisation of French polity? Continuity, change and adaptation', *Journal of European Public Policy* 7, 1: 26–43.

Cole, A. and Evans, J. forthcoming. 'Utilisation de l'échelle de Moreno en France et dans le Royaume uni', *Revue Internationale de Politique Comparée*.

Cole, A. and John, P. 1995. 'Local policy networks in Britain and France: policy coordination in fragmented political sub-systems', *West European Politics* 18, 4: 88–108.

2001. *Local Governance in England and France*. London: Routledge.

Cole, A. and Jones, G. 2005. 'Reshaping the state: administrative reform and new public management in France', *Governance* 18, 4: 567–88.

Cole, A. and Loughlin, J. 2003. 'Beyond the unitary state? Public opinion, political institutions and public policy in Brittany', *Regional Studies* 37, 3: 265–76.

Cole, A. and Raymond, G. (eds.) 2006. *Redefining the Republic*. Manchester: Manchester University Press.

Cole, A. and Williams, C. 2004. 'Institutions, identities and lesser-used languages in Wales and Brittany', *Regional and Federal Studies* 14, 4: 554–79.

Commaille, J. and Jobert, B. (eds.) 1999. *Les Métamorphoses de la régulation politique*. Paris: LGDJ.

Connétable, F. 2004. 'Acte II de la décentralisation, scène 3 (1): le référendum local', *Revue de la recherche juridique* 29, 104: 1861–75.

Conseil d'État, 2006. Avis no. 373306, 29 August.

2007. *L'Administration francaise et l'Union européenne: Quelles influences? Quelles strategies?* Paris: Documentation française.

Corbett, A. and Moon, B. (eds.) 1996. *Education in France: Continuity and Change in the Mitterrand Years, 1981–95*. London: Routledge.

Cornilleau, G., Heyer, E. and Timbeau, X. 1998. 'Le temps et l'argent: les 35 heures en douceur', *Revue de l'OFCE* 64: 17–41.

Costa, O. 2001. 'La Cour de justice et le contrôle démocratique de l'Union européenne', *Revue Française de Science Politique* 51, 6: 881–902.

Coutrot, T. 1999. '35 Heures, marchés transitionnels, droits de tirage sociaux. Du mauvais usage des bonnes idées', *Droit Social* 7–8: 659–68.

Crozier, M. 1963. *Le Phénomène bureaucratique*. Paris: Seuil.

1970. *La Société bloquée*. Paris: Seuil.

1974. *Où va l'administration française?* Paris: Editions de l'Organisation.

1992. 'La Décentralisation est-elle une réforme de l'Etat?', *Pouvoirs locaux* 12: 130–4.

Crozier, M. and Friedberg, E. 1977. *L'Acteur et le système*. Paris: Seuil.

Crozier, M. and Thœnig, J.-C. 1975. 'La Régulation des systèmes organisés complexes', *Revue française de Sociologie* 16, 1: 3–32.

Crozier, M. and Tilliette, B. 2000. *Quand la France s'ouvrira*. Paris: Fayard.

Culpepper, P. 2006. 'Le système politico-économique français depuis 1985', in Culpepper, Hall and Palier (eds.), 39–70.

Culpepper, P., Hall, P. and Palier, B. (eds.) 2006. *La France en Mutation, 1980–2005*. Paris: Presses de Sciences Po.

D'Arcy, F. and Rouban, L. (eds.) 1996. *De la Ve République à l'Europe*. Paris: Presses de Sciences Po.

Darnault, N. 1997. *Reform of the Social Security System in France: Challenges and Prospects*. Brussels: European Commission.

de Montricher, N. 2006. L'Administration territoriale de la République: une idée en quête de réalité', in Dreyfus and Eymeri (eds.), 135–52.

de Winter, L. and Türsan, H. (eds.) 1998. *Regionalist Parties in Western Europe*. London: Routledge.

Deer, C. 2002. *Higher Education in England and France since the 1980s*. Oxford: Symposium Books.

Dehousse, R. 2004. 'La Méthode ouverte de coordination. Quand l'Instrument tient lieu de politique', in Lascoumes and Le Galès, 331–56.

Del Prete, D. 2004. 'La Fonction consultative du Conseil d'Etat dans la procédure d'adoption des lois', *Revue de la Recherche Juridique, Droit Prospectif* 29, 3: 1779–887.

Derouet, J.-L. 1991. 'Décentralisation et droits des usagers', *Savoir* 3, 4: 619–41.

Diart-Boucher, S. 2007. 'La Réglementation Vitivinicole Champenoise', unpublished PhD thesis, Reims University.

Dogan, M. and Pelassy, D. 1990. *How to Compare Nations: Strategies in Comparative Politics*. Chatham, NJ: Chatham House.

Drake, H. (ed.) 2005. *France and the European Union*. London: Routledge.

Drake, H. and Milner, S. 1999. 'Change and resistance to change: the political management of Europeanisation in France', *Modern and Contemporary France* 7, 2: 165–78.

Dreyfus, F. 1993. *Les institutions politiques et administratives de la France*. Paris: Economica.

Dreyfus, F., and Eymeri, J.-M. (eds.) 2006. *Science Politique de l'Administration*. Paris: Economica.

Duchesne, S. 2005. 'Identities, nationalism, citizenship and republican ideology', in Cole, A. Le Galès, P. and Levy, J. (eds.) *Developments in French Politics 3*. Basingstoke: Palgrave, 230–44.

Duclaud-Williams, R. 1993. 'The governance of education in Britain and France', in Kooiman, J. (ed.), 235–48.

    1994. 'The challenge to the state: the case of decentralisation in French education', *Manchester Papers in Politics* 4, 2–41.

Dulhpy, A. and Manigand, C. 2006. *La France au risque de l'Europe*. Paris: Armand Colin.

Dumez, H. and Jeunemaitre, A. 1993. 'Les Privatisations en France, 1986–1992', in Wright, V. (ed.) *Les Privatisations en Europe*. Paris: Actes Sud, 105–32.

Dumont, G.-F. 2005. *Les Régions et la régionalisation en France*. Paris: Ellipses.

Duperon, O. 2003. 'Le Régime des services publics en droit communautaire', *Petites Affiches* 392, 229: 6–11.

Dupuy, F. and Thœnig, J.-C. 1985. *L'Administration en Miettes*. Paris: Fayard.

Duran, P. 1993. 'Moderniser l'État ou le service public? Les chantiers de l'Équipement', *Revue Politiques et Management Public* 11, 1: 69–86.

Duran, P. and Thœnig, J.-C. 1996. 'L'Etat et la gestion publique territoriale', *Revue Française de Science Politique* 45, 4: 580–622.

Durand-Prinborgne, C. 1990. 'De l'instruction au système éducatif', *Les Cahiers Français* 249: 1–8.

    2003. 'A propos de la politique de décentralisation: vers de nouveaux transferts de compétences en éducation et formation?', *Actualité Juridique-Droit Administratif* 2: 65–71.

Dutercq, Y. 2003. 'La Politique française de décentralisation en éducation: bilan et perspectives', *Regards sur l'Actualité* 293: 17–28.

Duverger, M. 1964. *Political Parties*. London: Methuen.

    1986. *Les régimes semi-présidentiels*. Paris: PUF.

Dyson, K. 1980. *The State Tradition in Western Europe*. Oxford: Martin Robertson.

    (ed.) 2002. *European States and the Euro*. Oxford: Oxford University Press.

Dyson, K. and Featherstone, K. 1999. *The Road to Maastricht*. Oxford: Oxford University Press.

Eatwell, R. (ed.) 1997. *European Political Cultures*. London: Routledge.

Elgie, R. 1993. *The French Prime Minister*. Basingstoke: Macmillan.

(ed.) 1999. *Semi-Presidentialism in Europe*. Oxford: Oxford University Press.

(ed.) 2000. *The Changing French Political System*. London: Frank Cass.

Elgie, R. and Griggs, S. 2000. *Debates in French Politics*. London: Routledge.

Enfert, C. 2005. 'La France et la transposition des directives', *Revue Trimestrielle de droit européen* 41, 3: 671–86.

Epstein, R. 2005. 'Gouverner à distance. Quand l'État se retire des territoires', *Esprit* 11: 96–111.

2006. 'Des contractualisations territoriales aux appels à projets', in Nemery, J.-C. (ed.) *Les Pôles de compétitivité dans le système français et européen*. Paris: L'Harmattan, 81–90.

Esping Anderson, G. 1990. *The Three Worlds of Welfare Capitalism*. Cambridge: Polity Press.

Evans, J. (ed.) 2003. *The French Party System*. Manchester: Manchester University Press.

Eymeri, J.-M. 2003. 'Définir la position de la France dans l'Union européenne. La Médiation interministérielle des généralistes du SGCI', in Smith, A. and Nay, O. (eds.) *Le Gouvernement du compromis: courtiers et généralistes dans l'action politique*. Paris: Economica, 149–75.

Faure, A., Pollet, G. and Warin, P. (eds.) 1995. *La construction du sens dans les politiques publiques. Débats autour de la notion de référentiel*. Paris: L'Harmattan.

Featherstone, K. and Radaelli, C. (eds.) 2004. *The Politics of Europeanization*. Oxford: Oxford University Press.

Feller, V. 2006. 'De l'ordonnance du 2 janvier 1959 à la loi organique relative aux lois de finances', *Les Cahiers de la Fonction Publique et de l'Administration* 255: 4–7.

Filaire, J. 1992. 'L'Evolution récente des compétences décisionnels du recteur d'académie', *Savoir* 4, 1: 55–78.

Finance Ministry, 2005. 'Guide Pratique de la déclinaison des programmes. Les budgets opérationnels du programme', January. Paris: Ministère du budget, des comptes publics et de la fonction public.

Fixari, D. and Kletz, F. 1996. 'Pilotage d' établissement scolaire: auto-évaluation et évaluation', *Politiques et Management Public* 14, 2: 71–103.

Flora, P., Kuhnle, S. and Urwin, D. 1999. *State Formation, Nation-Building and Mass Politics in Europe*. Oxford: Oxford University Press.

Fonrojet, S. 2004. 'L'Organisation territoriale: quelle répartition des compétences?', *Les Cahiers Français* 1–2, 318: 22–9.

Font, J. 2007. 'Citizen juries and political parties: the Spanish experience', paper presented at the conference on 'Les partis politiques à l' épreuve des procedures délibératives', LaSSP, Toulouse, 15 June.

Fontaine, J. 1996. 'Public policy analysis in France: transformation and theory', *Journal of European Public Policy* 3, 3: 481–98.

Fontaine, J. and Warin, P. 2000. 'Retour des évaluations: les politiques publiques territorialisées entre affichage et incertitude de leur région-alisation', *Pole-Sud* 12: 1–12.

Forrester, V. 1996. *L'Horreur économique*. Paris: Fayard.

Fouilleux, E. 2003. *La Politique agricole commune et ses réformes: une politique européenne à l'épreuve de la globalisation*. Paris: L'Harmattan.

Fourastié, J. 1980. *Les Trente glorieuses ou la révolution invisible de 1946–1975*. Paris: Fayard.

François, B. 1999. *Le régime politique de la Ve République*. Paris: La Découverte.

François, B. and Neveu, E. (eds.) 1999. *Espaces Publics Mosaïques: Acteurs, arènes et rhétoriques des débats publics contemporains*. Rennes: Presses Universitaires de Rennes.

Friedberg, E. 1974. 'Administration et entreprises', in Crozier, M. (ed.) *Où va l'administration française?* Paris: Editions de l'Organisation, 20–44.

  1993. *Le Pouvoir et le règle*. Paris: Seuil.

Furet, F., Julliard, J. and Rosanvallon, P. 1988. *La République du Centre. La fin de l'exception française*. Paris: Calmann-Lévy.

Gaffney, J. 1996 (ed.) *Political Parties in the European Union*. London: Routledge.

  2003. 'The French Fifth Republic as an opportunity structure: a neo-institutional and cultural approach to the study of leadership politics', *Political Studies* 51, 4: 686–705.

Garton Ash, T. 2007. 'Présidentielle: La Victoire de Blair', *Le Monde*, 21 April.

Gatto, D. and Thœnig, J.-C. 1993. *La sécurité publique à l'épreuve du terrain: le policier, le magistrat et le préfet*. Paris: Harmattan.

Gaudemet, Y. and Gohin, O. 2004. *La République Décentralisée*. Paris: Editions Panthéon-Assas.

Gaudin, J.-P. 1995. 'Politiques urbaines et négociations territoriales. Quelle légitimité pour les réseaux de politiques publiques?', *Revue Française de Science Politique* 45, 1: 31–56.

  1999. *Gouverner par Contrat. L'Action publique en question*. Paris: Presses de Sciences Po.

2002. *Pourquoi la Gouvernance?* Paris: Presses de Sciences Po.

2004. 'Contractualisation, gouvernance et régulation politique', *Admini-stration et Education* 4: 15–20.

Gavroy, J. 2002. 'Le projet de loi constitutionnel relatif à l'organisation décentralisée de la République', *Regards sur l'Actualité* 282: 5–15.

Gordon, P. and Meunier, S. 2001. *The French Challenge: Adapting to Globalisation*. Washington: Brookings Institution Press.

Grémion, P. 1976. *Le Pouvoir péripherique: bureaucrates et notables dans le régime politique français*. Paris: Seuil.

Grémion, C. 1979. *Profession Décideurs: pouvoirs des hauts fonctionnaires et réformes de l'état*. Paris: Gauthier-Villars.

Griggs, S. 1999. 'Restructuring health policy networks: a French polity style?', *West European Politics* 22, 4: 184–204.

Grossman, E. 2003. 'Les groupes d'intérêt économiques face à l'intégration européenne: le cas du secteur bancaire', *Revue française de Science Politique* 53, 5: 737–60.

2007. 'Les groupes d'intérêt en France et en Europe', in Perrineau, P. and Rouban, L. (eds.) *La Politique en France et en Europe*. Paris: Presses de Sciences Po, 155–84.

Grossman, E. and Sauger, N. 2007. 'Political institutions under stress? Assessing the impact of European integration on French political insti-tutions', *Journal of European Public Policy* 14, 7: 1117–34.

Grossman, E. and Saurugger, S. 2004. 'Les groupes d'intérêt français: entre exception française, l'Europe et le monde', *Revue Internationale de Politique Comparée* 11, 4: 507–29.

Groud, H. 2006. 'La notion de partenariat public-privé à la française', in Nemery, J.-C. (ed.) *Les Pôles de compétitivité dans le système français et européen*. Paris: L'Harmattan, 39–62.

Gueland, C. 2007. 'L'Etat… Et pourtant il bouge', *Le Monde*, 10 January.

Gueldry, M. R. 2001. *France and European Integration. Toward a Trans-national Polity*. Westport: Praeger.

Guettier, C. 2006. 'Les agences administratives en France', *Les Cahiers de la Fonction Publique et de l'Administration* 351: 3–10.

Gugliemi, G. J. 1994. *Introduction au Droit des Services Publics*. Paris: LGDJ.

Guiliani, J.-D. 1991. *Marchands d'influence: les lobbies en France*. Paris: Seuil.

Guyomarch, A., Hayward, J., Hall, P. and Machin, H. (eds.) 2001. *Developments in French Politics?*. Basingstoke: Palgrave.

Guyomarch, A., Machin, H., and Ritchie, E. (eds.) 1996. *France in the European Union*. Basingstoke: Macmillan.

Guy-Peters, B. 1998. *Comparative Politics*. Basingstoke: Palgrave.

1999. *The New Institutionalism*. London: Sage.

Habermas, J. 1993. *L'Espace public*. Paris: Payot.

Haegel, F. (ed.) 2007. *Partis Politiques et système partisan en France*. Paris: Presses de Science Po.

Hainsworth, P. 2006. 'France says no: the 29 May 2005 referendum on the European constitution', *Parliamentary Affairs* 59: 98–117.

Hall, P. 1986. *Governing the Economy. The Politics of State Intervention in Britain and France*. Oxford: Polity Press.

    1993. 'Policy paradigms, social learning and the state', *Comparative Politics* 25, 3: 275–96.

    2001. 'The evolution of economic policy-making', in Guyomarch, Hayward, Hall and Machin (eds.), 172–90.

Hall, P. and Soskice, D. (eds.) 2001. *Varieties of Capitalism: The Institutional Foundations of Competitiveness*. Oxford: Oxford University Press.

Hall, P. and Taylor, R. 1996. 'La Science politique et les trois neo-institutionalismes', *Revue Française de Science Politique* 47, 3–4: 469–96.

Hancke, B. 2001. 'Revisiting the French model. Coordination and restructuring in French industry in the 1980s', in Hall and Soskice (eds.), 307–34.

Harmsen, R. 1999. 'The Europeanisation of national administrations: a comparative study of France and the Netherlands', *Governance* 12, 1: 81–113.

Hassenteufel, P. and Smith, A. 2005. 'Essoufflement ou second souffle? L'analyse des politiques publiques "à la française"', *Revue Française de Science Politique* 52, 1: 53–73.

Hay, C. and Rosamond, B. 2002. 'Globalisation, European integration and the discursive construction of economic imperatives', *Journal of European Public Policy* 9, 2: 147–67.

Hayward, J. 1986. *The State and the Market Economy*. Brighton: Harvester Wheatsheaf.

    (ed.) 1993. *De Gaulle to Mitterrand: Presidential Power in France*. London: Hurst.

    1997. 'Changing partnerships: firms and the French state', *Modern and Contemporary France* 5, 2: 155–65.

    (ed.) 2008. *A Leaderless Europe?* Oxford: Oxford University Press.

Hayward, J. and Wright, V. (eds.) 2002. *Governing from the Centre: Core Executive Coordination in France*. Oxford: Oxford University Press.

Hazareesingh, S. 1994. *Political Traditions in Modern France*. Oxford: Oxford University Press.

Heinz, W. 1994. *Partenariats public-privé dans l'aménagement urbain*. Paris: L'Harmattan.

Hendriks, G. and Morgan, A. 2001. *The Franco-German Axis in European Integration*. Cheltenham: Edward Elgar.

Hérard, A. and Maurin, A. 2000. *Institutions Judiciaires*. Paris: Editions Sirey.

Hertzog, R. 2004. 'La loi organique relative à l'autonomie financière des collectivités territoriales: précisions et complications', *Actualité Juridique-Droit Administratif*, 25 October, 2003–12.

Hix, S. 2005. *The Political System of the European Union*. Basingstoke: Palgrave.

Hix, S. and Lord, C. 1997. *Political Parties in the European Union*. Basingstoke: Macmillan.

Hoare, R. 2000. 'Linguistic competence and regional identity in Brittany: attitudes and perceptions of identity', *Journal of Multilingual and Multicultural Development* 21, 4: 324–46.

Hoffmann, S. 1965. *In Search of France*. New York: Harper Torchbooks.

Holliday, I., Marcou, G., and Vickerman, R. 1991. *The Channel Tunnel*. London: Pinter.

Hood, C. 1995. 'The new public management in the 1980s: variations on a theme', *Accounting, Organizations and Society* 20, 2/3: 93–109.

2007. 'Understanding public policy through its instruments', *Governance* 20, 1: 1–144.

Hooghe, L. (ed.) 1996. *Cohesion and European Integration: Building Multi-Level Governance*. Oxford: Clarendon Press.

Hooghe, L. and Marks, G. 2001. *Multi-Level Governance and European Integration*. Lanham: Rowman and Littlefield.

Howarth, D. 2001. *The French Road to European Monetary Union*. Basingstoke: Palgrave.

Howarth, J. 1993. 'The president's special role in foreign and defence policy', in Hayward, J. (ed.) *De Gaulle to Mitterrand. Presidential Power in France*. London: Hurst, 150–89.

Howarth, J. and Cerny, P. (eds.) 1981. *Elites in France*. London: Pinter.

Howell, C. 2008. 'Between state and market: crisis and transformation in French industrial relations', in Cole, A., Le Galès, P. and Levy, J. *Developments in French Politics 4*. Basingstoke: Palgrave.

Irondelle, B. 2005. 'French political science and European integration: the state of the art', *French Politics* 4, 2: 188–208.

Jabko, N. 2004. 'The importance of being nice: an institutionalist analysis of French preferences on the future of Europe', *Comparative European Politics* 2, 3: 282–301.

Jeffery, C. 2000. 'Sub-national mobilisations and European Integration', *Journal of Common Market Studies* 38, 1: 1–23.

Jessop, R. 1998. 'L'Essor de la gouvernance et ses risques d'échec: le cas du développement économique', *Revue Internationale des Sciences Sociales* 155: 19–30.

    2000. 'Governance failure?', in Stoker, G. (ed.) *The New Politics of British Local Governance*. Basingstoke: Macmillan, 11–32.

    2007. 'L'imaginaire économique et l' économie politique des échelles', in Pasquier, Simoulin and Weisbein (eds.), 65–85.

Jobert, B. (ed.) 1994. *Le Tournant néo-libéral en Europe*. Paris: L'Harmattan.

Jobert, B. and Muller, P. 1987. *L'État en Action: politiques publiques et corporatisme*. Paris: PUF.

John, P. 2001. *Local Governance in Western Europe*. London: Sage.

John, P. 1998. 'Urban economic policy networks in Britain and France: a sociometric approach', *Environment and Planning C: Government and Policy* 16, 307–22.

John, P. and Cole, A. 2000. 'When do countries, sectors and localities matter?', *Comparative Political Studies* 33, 2: 248–68.

Jones, G. W. 2003. 'The Effects of the 1989–1997 Administrative Reforms on the Ministerial Field Services', PhD thesis, Southampton Institute/ Nottingham Trent University.

Jouve, B. 1995. 'Réseaux et Communautés Politiques', in Le Galès and Thatcher (eds.), 121–40.

Jouve, B. and Léfèvre, C. 1999. 'De la gouvernance urbaine au gouvernement des villes? Permanence ou recomposition des cadres de l'action publique en Europe', *Revue Française de Science Politique* 49, 6: 835–54.

Kassim, H. 1997. 'French autonomy and the European Union', *Modern and Contemporary France* 5, 2: 167–80.

Keating, M. 1998. *The New Regionalism in Western Europe: Territorial Restructuring and Political Change*. Cheltenham: Edward Elgar.

Keeler, J. 1987. *The Politics of Neocorporatism in France: Farmers, the State and Agricultural Policy-Making in the Fifth Republic*. Oxford: Oxford University Press.

Keiger, J. 2005. 'Foreign and defense policy: constraints and continuity', in Cole, A., Le Galès, P. and Levy, J. (eds.) *Developments in French Politics 4*. Basingstoke: Palgrave, 138–53.

Kessler, M.-C. 1986. *Les grands corps de l'Etat*. Paris: Presses de la FNSP.

Kickert, W. (ed.) 1997. *Public Management and Administrative Reform in Western Europe*. Cheltenham: Edward Elgar.

Kiwan, N. 2006. 'The citizen and the subject', in Cole, A. and Raymond, G. (eds.) *Redefining the Republic*. Manchester: Manchester University Press, 97–116.

Kjaer, A. 2004. *Governance*. London: Sage.

Klom, A. 1996. 'Liberalisation of regulated markets and its consequences for trade: the internal market for electricity as a case study', *Journal of Energy and Natural Resources Law* 14, 1: 1–13.

Knapp, A. and Wright, V. 2001. *The Government and Politics of France.* London: Routledge.

Kohler-Koch, B. and Eising, R. (eds.) 1999. *The Transformation of Governance in the European Union.* London: Routledge.

Kooiman, J. (ed.) 1993. *Modern Governance.* London: Sage.

2003. *Governing as Governance.* London: Sage.

Kresl P. and Gallais, S. 2002. *France Encounters Globalization.* Cheltenham: Edward Elgar.

Labayle, H. and Sudre, F. 2004. 'Droit administratif et Convention Européenne des Droits de l'Homme', *Revue Française de Droit Administratif* 20, 5: 981–90.

Laborier, P. 2003. 'Historicité et sociologie de l'action publique', in Laborier, P. and Trom, D. (eds.) *Historicités de l'action publique.* Paris: PUF, 419–62.

Ladrech, R. 1994. 'Europeanization of domestic politics and institutions: the case of France', *Journal of Common Market Studies* 32, 1: 69–88.

2000. *Social Democracy and the Challenge of the European Union.* London: Lynne Rienner.

Lafaye, C. 1996. *La Sociologie des Organisations.* Paris: Nathan.

Lagroye, J. 1973. *Société et Politique. Jacques Chaban-Delmas à Bordeaux.* Paris: Pédone.

Lalliement, M. 2006. 'Transformation des relations du travail et nouvelles formes d'action publique', in Culpepper, Hall and Palier (eds.), 109–54.

Lamarque, D. 2004. 'La Contractualisation dans le secteur de la Santé', *Administration et Education* 4: 37–45.

Lascoumes, P. and Le Galès, P. (eds.) 2004. *Gouverner par les Instruments.* Paris: Presses de Sciences Po.

Latour, B. 2004. *La fabrique du droit: une ethnographie du Conseil d'État.* Paris: La Découverte.

Lavabre, M.-C. and Platone, F. 2003. *Que reste-t-il du PCF?* Paris: Editions Autrement.

Lazega, E. 1994. 'Analyse des réseaux et sociologie des organisations', *Revue Française de Sociologie* 35, 2: 293–320.

Le Coadic, R. 1998. *L'Identité bretonne.* Rennes: Presses universitaires de Rennes.

Le Galès, P. 1993. *Politique urbaine et developpement local.* Paris: L'Harmattan.

1995. 'Du gouvernement local à la gouvernance urbaine', *Revue Française de Science Politique* 45, 1: 57–95.

Le Galès, P. 1999. 'Crise de Gouvernance et Globalisation', *Revue Inter-nationale de Politique Comparée*, 6, 3: 627–52.

2002. *European Cities: Social Conflicts and Governance*. Oxford: Oxford University Press.

2005. 'Reshaping the state? Administrative and decentralization reforms', in Cole, A., Le Galès, P. and Levy, J. (eds.) *Developments in French Politics 3*. Basingstoke: Palgrave, 122–37.

2006. '*Les deux moteurs de la décentralisation. Concurrences Politiques et restructuration dès l'Etat Jacobin*', in Culpepper, Hall and Palier (eds.), 303–41.

2008. 'Territorial politics in France: *le calme avant la tempête?*', in Cole, A., Le Galès, P. and Levy, J. (eds.) *Developments in French Politics 4*. Basingstoke: Palgrave.

Le Galès, P. and Lequesne, C. (eds.) 1998. *Regions in Europe*. London: Routledge.

Le Galès, P. and Thatcher, M. (eds.) 1995. *Les Réseaux de politique publique, débats autour des 'policy networks'*. Paris: L'Harmattan.

Le Lidec, P. 2007. 'Le jeu du compromis: L'État et les collectivités terri-toriales dans le décentralisation en France', *Revue française d'admini-stration publique* 121–2: 111–30.

Leca, J. 1996. 'La Gouvernance de la France sous la Cinquième Répub-lique', in Quermonne, J. L. (ed.) *De la Vème République à l'Europe*. Paris: Presses de Sciences Po, 329–65.

Lequesne, C. 1993. *Paris-Bruxelles*. Paris: Presses de la FNSP.

1996. 'French central government and the European political system', in Meny, Y., Muller P. and Quermonne J.-L., (eds.) *Adjusting to Europe*. London: Routledge, 110–20.

Lequesne, C. and Surel, Y. (eds.) 2004. *L'intégration européenne: entre dynamique institutionnelle et recomposition de l'État*. Paris: Presses de Sciences Po.

Levy, J. 1999. *Tocqueville's Revenge: State, Society and Economy in Con-temporary France*. Cambridge, MA: Harvard University Press.

2001. 'Territorial politics after decentralisation,' in Guyomarch, Hayward, Hall and Machin (eds.), 92–115.

2005. 'Economic policy and policy-making,' in Cole, A., Le Galès, P. and Levy, J. (eds.) *Developments in French Politics 3*. Basingstoke: Palgrave, 170–94.

(ed.) 2006. *The State after Statism*. Cambridge, MA: Harvard University Press.

Levy, J., Cole, A. and Le Galès, P. 2005. 'The shifting politics of the Fifth Republic', in Cole, A., Le Galès, P. and Levy, J. (eds.) *Developments in French Politics 3*. Basingstoke: Palgrave, 1–18.

Lijphart, A. 1999. *Patterns of Democracy: Government Forms and Performance in Thirty-Six Countries*. New Haven: Yale University Press.

Lorrain, D. 1991. 'De l'Administration républicaine au gouvernement urbain', *Sociologie du Travail* 33: 4, 461–84.

  1993. 'Après la décentralisation: l'action publique flexible', *Sociologie du Travail* 35, 3: 285–307.

  2004. 'Les pilotes invisibles de l'action publique. Le désarroi du politique?', in Lascoumes and Le Galès (eds.) 163–97.

Loughlin, J. (ed.) 2001. *Subnational Democracy in the European Union: Challenges and Opportunities*. Oxford: Oxford University Press.

  2004. 'The transformation of governance: new directions in policy and politics', *Australian Journal of Politics and History* 50, 1: 8–22.

Lovecy, J. 2000. 'End of French exceptionalism?', in Elgie (ed.), 205–24.

Lowi, T. 1964. 'American business, public policy, case studies and political theory', *World Politics* 16, 4: 677–715.

Lowndes, V. 1996. 'Varieties of new institutionalism: a critical approach', *Public Administration*, 74, 2: 181–97.

Mabileau, A. 1991. *Le système local en France*. Paris: Montchrestien.

  1997. 'Les Génies invisibles du local. Faux-semblants et dynamiques de la décentralisation', *Revue Française de Science Politique* 47, 3–4: 340–76.

McAna, M. 2003. 'The Front National in Municipal Power in Toulon and Orange', PhD thesis, University of Bradford.

McClean, M. 2006. 'The interventionist state: demise or transformation?', in Cole, A. and Raymond, G. (eds.) *Redefining the Republic*. Manchester: Manchester University Press, 134–55.

McClean, M. and Milner, S. 2001. (eds.) *France and Globalisation*. Special issue of *Modern and Contemporary France* 9, 3.

McEwen, N. and Moreno, L. (eds.) 2005. *The Territorial Politics of Welfare*. London: Routledge.

McGrew, A. 2002. 'Between two worlds: Europe in a globalizing era', *Government and Opposition* 37, 3: 343–58.

Machin, H. 1976. *The Prefect in the French Administration*. London: Croom Helm.

McMillan, J. F. 1997. 'France', in Eatwell, R. (ed.) *European Political Cultures*. London: Routledge, 67–87.

Maia, J. 2005. 'La contrainte européenne sur la loi', *Pouvoirs* 114: 53–7.

Majone, G. 1996. *La Communauté européenne: un état régulateur*. Paris: Montchrestien.

Majone, J. (ed.) 2003. *Regional Institutions and Governance in the European Union*. London: Praeger.

Mandin, C. and Palier, B. 2004. 'L'Europe et les politiques sociales: vers une harmonisation cognitive des réponses nationales', in Lequesne and Surel (eds.), 255–85.

Mangenot, M. 2005. 'Le Conseil d'Etat and Europe', in Drake, *France and the European Union*, 86–104.

March, J. and Olsen, J. 1989. *Rediscovering Institutions*. New York: The Free Press.

Marcou, G. 1992. 'Les collectivités territoriales et l'Education nationale' *Savoir* 4, 2: 189–215.

     2004. 'Décentralisation: approfondissement ou nouveau cycle?', *Les Cahiers français* 318: 8–14.

Marcussen, M., Risse, T., Engel-Martin, D., Knopf, H.-J. and Roscher, K. 2001. 'Constructing Europe? The evolution of nation-state identities', in Christiansen, Jorgensen and Wiener (eds.), 101–19.

Marin, B. and Mayntz, R. (eds.) 1991. *Policy Networks*. Frankfurt: Campus.

Marks, G. 1993. 'Structural policy and multilevel governance in the EC', in Cafruny, A. and Rosenthal, G. (eds.) *The State of the EC. Vol. 2: The Maastricht Debates and Beyond*, Boulder, CO: Lynne Rienner, 391–410.

Marks, G. and Wilson, C. 2000. 'National parties and the consolidation of Europe', in Banchoff, T. and Smith, M. P. (eds.) *Legitimacy and the European Union. The Contested Polity*. London: Routledge, 113–33.

Marsh, D. and Rhodes, R. A. W. (eds.) 1992. *Policy Networks in British Government*. Oxford: Clarendon Press.

Marsh, D. and Smith, M. 2000. 'Understanding policy networks: towards a dialectical approach', *Political Studies* 48, 1: 4–21.

Marsh, S. and Mackenstein, H. 2005. *The International Relations of the European Union*. London: Longman.

Martinaud, C. (ed.) 1993. *L'Expérience française du financement privé des investissements publics*. Paris: Economica.

Massot, J. and Fouquet, O. 1993. *Le Conseil d'état: juge de cassation*. Paris: Berger-Levrault.

Mauroy, P. 2000. *Refonder l'action publique locale: rapport au Premier ministre*. Paris: Documentation française.

Maus, D. 1996. *Le Parlement sous la cinquieme République*. Paris: PUF.

Mayntz, R. 1991. *Policy Networks*. Boulder, CO: Westview.

     1993. 'Governing failures and the problem of governability: some comments on a theoretical paradigm', in Kooiman (ed.), 9–20.

Mazey, S. and Richardson, J. 2006. 'Interest groups and EU policy-making: organisational logic and venue shopping', in Richardson, J. (ed.) *European Union Power and Policy Making*. London: Routledge, 247–68.

Mazur, A. 2005. 'Gendering the Fifth Republic'. in Cole, A., Le Galès, P. and Levy, J., (eds.) *Developments in French Politics 3*, pp. 212–29.

Mendras, H. 1989. *La Séconde révolution française*. Paris: Gallimard.

Menon, A. 2001. 'L'Administration française à Bruxelles', *Revue Française de Science Politique* 51, 5: 763–86.

Mény, Y. 1986. 'La légitimation des groupes d'intérêt par l'administration française', *Revue Française d'Administration Publique* 39: 99–110.

(ed.) 1993. *Le mimétisme institutionnel*. Paris: L'Harmattan.

Mény, Y. and Thœnig, J.-C. 1989. *Politiques Publiques*. Paris: PUF.

Merrien, F.-X. 1998. 'De la gouvernance et des Etats-providence contemporains', *Revue Internationale des Sciences Sociales* 155: 61–72.

Meunier, S. 2004. 'Globalisation and Europeanisation: a challenge to French politics', *French Politics* 2, 2: 125–50.

Meynaud, J. 1958. *Les groupes de pression en France*. Paris: Colin.

Michel, H. 2002. 'Le droit comme registre d'Européisation d'un groupe d'intérêt. La défense des propriétaires et la Charte des droits fondamentaux de l'UE', *Politique Européenne* 7, 1–10.

Milner, S. 2006. 'Urban governance and local democracy in France', in Cole, A. and Raymond, G. (eds.) *Redefining the French Republic*. Manchester: Manchester University Press, 65–81.

Moravcsik, A. 1991. 'Negotiating the Single European Act: national interests and conventional statecraft in the European Community', *International Organization* 45, 1: 19–56.

1998. *The Choice for Europe. Social Purpose and State Power from Messina to Maastricht*. Ithaca and London: Cornell University Press.

2001. 'Constructivism and European integration: a critique', in Christiansen, Jorgensen and Wiener (eds.), 176–87.

Moreno, L. forthcoming. 'La question Moreno', *Revue Internationale de Politique Comparée*.

Muller, P. 1989. *Airbus, l'ambition européenne. Logique de l'Etat, logique de marché*. Paris: L'Harmattan.

1990a. *Les politiques publiques*. Paris: PUF.

1990b. 'Les politiques publiques entre secteurs et territoires', *Politiques et Management Public* 8, 3: 19–33.

1992. 'Entre le local et l'Europe. La crise du modèle français des politiques publiques', *Revue Française de Science Politique* 42, 2: 275–97.

1999. 'Gouvernance Européenne et globalisation', *Revue Internationale de Politique Comparée* 6, 3: 707–17.

2000. 'L'analyse cognitive des politiques publiques: vers une sociologie politique de l'action publique', *Revue Française de Science Politique* 50, 2: 189–208.

Muller, P. 2005. 'Esquisse d'une théorie du changement dans l'action publique. Structures, acteurs et cadres cognitifs', *Revue Française de Science Politique* 55, 1: 155–87.

Muller, P. and Surel, Y. 2002. *L'Analyse des politiques publiques*. Paris: Montchrestien.

Musselin, C. 2003. 'L'Evolution des universités depuis vingt ans', *Regards sur l'Actualité* 293, 49–61.

National Education Ministry 1999. 'Circulaire de rentrée, 1999', *Bulletin Official de l'Education Nationale* 1, 7 January. Paris: Ministère éducation nationale.

Nay, O. 1997. *La Région, une Institution. La représentation, le pouvoir et la règle dans l'espace régional*. Paris: L'Harmattan.

Nemery, J. C. (ed.) 2003. *Intercommunalités*. Paris: L'Harmattan.

Nemery, J., Bricault, J.-M. and Thuriot, F. 2005. *Aménagement du Territorie*. Paris: Gridauh.

Neveu, E. 2002. *Sociologie des mouvements sociaux*. Paris: La Découverte.

Oberdorff, H. 1998. *Les institutions administratives*. Paris: Armand Colin.

Offerlé, M. 1999. *Sociologie des groupes d'intérêt*. Paris: Montchrestien.

Ohnet, J.-M. 1996. *Histoire de la Décentralisation française*. Paris: Hachette.

Osborne, D. and Gaebler, T. 1992. *Reinventing Government*. Reading, MA: Addison-Wesley.

Padioleau, J.-G. 1982. *L'Etat au concret*. Paris: PUF.

1991. 'L'Action publique moderniste', *Politiques et Management Public* 9, 3: 133–43.

1999. 'L'Action publique post-moderne. Le gouvernement politique des risques', *Politiques et Management Public* 17, 4: 85–127.

Page, E. 1991. *Localism and Centralism in Europe*. Oxford: Oxford University Press.

Palier, B. 2000. 'Defrosting the French welfare state', *West European Politics* 23, 2: 113–36.

2004. 'Les instruments, traceurs du changement. La politique des retraites en France', in Lascoumes and Le Galès (eds.), 273–300.

2006. 'Un long adieu à Bismarck', in Culpepper, Hall and Palier (eds.), 197–228.

Palier, B. and Surel, Y. 2005. 'Les "trois L" et analyse de l'Etat en action', *Revue Française de Science Politique* 55, 1: 7–32.

Parsons, N. 2005. *Industrial Relations in France*. London: Continuum.

Pasquier, R. 2004. *La Capacité politique des régions. Une comparaison France/Espagne*. Rennes: Presses universitaires de Rennes.

Pasquier, R., Simoulin, V. and Weisbein, J. (eds.) 2007. *La Gouvernance territoriale. Pratiques, discours et théories*. Paris: LGDJ.

Pasquier, R. and Weisbein, J. 2007. 'La gouvernance territoriale: une perspective pragmatique', in Pasquier, Simoulin and Weisbein (eds.), 211–22.

Pavé, P. 1992. 'La gestion à l'assaut de l'État: la modernisation des Directions départementales de l'Équipement', in Muller, P. (ed.) *L'administration française est-elle en crise?* Paris: L'Harmattan, 239–49.

Paxton, R. 1972. *Vichy France: Old Guard and New Order*. New York: Columbia University Press.

Perrineau, P. 2005. (ed.) *Le Vote européen, 2004–2005*. Paris: Presses de Sciences Po.

Perrineau, P. and Rouban, L. (eds.) 2007. *La Politique en France et en Europe*. Paris: Presses de Sciences Po.

Perucca, B. 2000. 'Réforme de la formation: le "oui mais" du Medef à la validation des acquis', *Les Echos*, 22 February.

Philpponneau, M. 1977. *Changer la vie, changer la ville*. Rennes: Breiz.

Pierre, J. (ed.) 2000. *Debating Governance*. Oxford: Oxford University Press.

Pierson, P. 1996. 'The path to European integration: a historical institutionalist analysis', *Comparative Political Studies* 29, 2: 123–63.

2000. 'Increasing returns, path dependence and the study of politics', *American Political Science Review* 9, 2: 251–67.

Pontier, J.-M. 1998. *Les Contrats de plan entre l'État et les régions*. Paris: PUF.

Portier, N. 2003. *Les pays*. Paris: Documentation française.

Pouvoirs, 2003. *Le Conseil Constitutionnel*. Paris: Seuil.

Powell, W. and Di Maggio, P. 1991. *The New Institutionalism in Organisational Analysis*. Chicago: Chicago University Press.

Putnam, R. 1993. *Making Democracy Work. Civic Traditions in Modern Italy*. Princeton, Princeton University Press.

1998. 'Diplomacy and domestic politics: the logic of two-level games', *International Organization* 42, 3: 427–60.

Quittkat, C. 2002. 'Les organisations professionnelles françaises: l'européanisation de l'intermédiation des intérêts', *Politique Européenne* 7: 66–95.

Raab, C. 1992. 'Taking networks seriously: education policy in Britain', *European Journal of Political Research* 21, 69–90.

Radaelli, C. 1997. *The Politics of Corporate Taxation. Knowledge and International Policy Agendas*. London: Routledge.

2000. 'Logiques de pouvoirs et "récits" dans les politiques publiques de l'Union européenne', *Revue Française de Science Politique* 50, 2: 255–75.

Rangeon, F. (1996) 'Le Gouvernement local', in CURAPP *La Gouvernabilité*. Paris: PUF, 160–72.

Raymond, G. 2006. 'The republican ideal and the reality of the Republic', in Cole, A. and Raymond, G. (eds.) *Redefining the French Republic*. Manchester: Manchester University Press, 1–13.

Revauger, J.-P. 2006. 'Social policy and the challenge to the "republican model"', in Cole, A. and Raymond, G. (eds.) *Redefining the French Republic*. Manchester: Manchester University Press, 117–33.

Reverchon, A. 2003. 'La Formation professionnelle toujours en quête de cohérence', *Le Monde*, 17 June.

    2005. 'Un trou énorme dans la statistique nationale', *Le Monde*, 15 November.

Rhodes, R. A. W. 1988. *Beyond Westminster and Whitehall*. London: Unwin Hyman.

    1996. 'The new governance: governing without government', *Political Studies* 44, 4: 652–67.

    1997. *Understanding Governance: Policy Networks, Governance, Reflexivity and Accountability*. Buckingham: Open University Press.

Richardson, J. (ed.) 1982. *Policy Styles in Western Europe*. London: Allen & Unwin.

Richardson, J. and Jordan, G. 1979. *Governing under Pressure*. Oxford: Martin Robertson.

Richter, L. 2004. 'La Contractualisation comme technique de gestion des affaires publiques', *Administration et Education* 4: 21–6.

Roger, A. 2007. 'Introduction', paper presented to the conference on '*Les partis politiques à l'épreuve des procédures délibératives*', LaSSP, Toulouse, 15 June.

Rokkan, S. and Urwin, D. 1982. *The Politics of Territorial Identity*. London: Sage.

Rosamond, B. 2001. 'Discourses of globalisation and European identities', in Christiansen, Jorgensen and Wiener (eds.), 158–73.

Rosanvallon, P. 1976. *L'Age de l'autogestion*. Paris: Seuil.

    2004. *Le modèle politique français*. Paris: Seuil.

Rose, R. 1993. *Lesson-drawing in Public Policy: A Guide to Learning across Time and Space*. Chatham, NJ: Chatham House.

Rosenau, J. N. (ed.) 1992. *Governance without Government: Order and Change in World Politics*. Cambridge: Cambridge University Press.

Ross, G. 1997. 'Jospin so far', *French Politics and Society* 15, 3: 9–19.

Rouban, L. 1994. *Le pouvoir anonyme. Les mutations de l'Etat à la française*. Paris: Presses de la FNSP.

    1995. 'Public administration at the crossroads: the end of French specificity?', in Pierre, J. (ed.) *Bureaucracy in the Modern State*. Cheltenham: Edward Elgar, 43–63.

Rouban, L. 1997. *La Fin des technocrates?* Paris: Presses de Sciences Po.

2003. 'Reformer ou Recomposer l'Etat? Les enjeux sociopolitiques d'une mutation annoncée', *Revue Française d'Administration Publique* 105/106: 153–66.

Rozenberg, O. 2007. 'Résister à l'Europe au nom du national, de la souveraineté, du local ou de l'antilibéralisme. Les conditions d'activation de quatre idéologies critiques de la construction européenne en France', in Lacroix, J. and Coman, R. (eds.) *Resister à l'Europe. Figures des oppositions au modèle européen.* Brussels: Editions de l'Université de Bruxelles.

Rozenberg, O. and Surel, Y. 2003. 'Parlements et Union européenne', *Politique Européenne* 9: 5–29.

Ruane, J., Todd, J. and Mandeville, A. (eds.) 2003. *Europe's Old States in the New World Order: The Politics of Transition in Britain, France and Spain.* Dublin: University of Dublin Press.

Rui, S. 2004. *La Démocratie en débat. Les citoyens face à l'action publique.* Paris: Armand Colin.

Sabatier, P. (ed.) 1999. *Theories of the Policy Process.* Boulder, CO: Westview Press.

Sabatier, P. and Jenkins-Smith, H. C. 1993. *Policy Learning and Change.* Boulder, CO: Westview Press.

Sabatier, P. and Schlager, E. 2000. 'Les Approches cognitives des politiques publiques: perspectives américaines', *Revue Française de Science Politique* 50, 2: 209–34.

Sadran, P. 1992. *Le système administratif français.* Paris: Montchrestien.

2002. 'Le référendum local', *Regards sur l'Actualité* 286: 29–36.

Sales, E. 2005. 'La transposition de directives communautaires: une exigence de valeur constitutionnelle sous réserve de constitutionalité', *Revue Trimestrielle de droit européen* 41, 3: 597–620.

Sarkozy, N. 2006. *Témoignages.* Paris: XO Editions.

Sauger, N., Brouard, S. and Grossmann, E. 2007. *Les Français contre l'Europe? Le sens du referendum du 29 mai 2005.* Paris: Presses de Sciences Po.

Sauger, N. and Laurent, A. (2005) 'Le référendum de ratification du Traité constitutionnel européen: comprendre le Non français', *Les Cahiers du CEVIPOF* 42, 1–173.

Sauron, J.-L. and Asseraf, G. 1999. 'Le Conseil européen de Cologne des 3 et 4 juin 1999', *Revue du Marché commun et de l'Union européenne* 430, 7–8: 441–7.

Saurugger, S. 2002. 'L'expertise: un mode de participation des groupes d'intérêt au processus décisionnel communautaire', *Revue Française de Science Politique* 52, 4: 375–401.

Saurugger, S. 2003. (ed.) *Les Modes de représentation dans l'Union eur-opéenne*. Paris: L'Harmattan.

2007. 'Differential impact: Europeanising French non-state actors', *Journal of European Public Policy* 14, 4: 1079–97.

Saurugger, S. and Grossman, E. 2006. 'Les Groupes d'intérêt français. Transformation des rôles et des enjeux politiques', *Revue Française de Science Politique*, 56, 2: 197–203.

Schmidt, V. 1996. *From State to Market? The Transformation of French Business and Government*. Cambridge: Cambridge University Press.

1997. 'Economic policy, political discourse, and democracy in France', *French Politics and Society* 15, 2: 37–48.

2002. *The Futures of European Capitalism*. Oxford: Oxford University Press.

Schmitter, P. and Lehmbruch, G. (eds.) 1979. *Trends toward Corporatism*. London: Sage.

Schnapper, D. 1994. *La Communauté des citoyens: sur l'idée moderne des nations*. Paris: Gallimard.

Scott, J. 1991. *Social Network Analysis*. London: Sage.

Selck, T. J. and Kaeding, M. 2004. 'Divergent interests and different success rates: France, Germany, Italy and the United Kingdom in EU legislative negotiations', *French Politics* 2: 81–94.

Shackleton, J. R. 1995. *Training for Employment in Western Europe and the United States*. Cheltenham: Edward Elgar.

Sharpe, L. J. 1993. *The Rise of Meso Government in Europe*. London: Sage.

Sharpf, F. W. 1997. *Games Real Actors Play: Actor-centered Institution-alism in Policy Research*. Boulder, CO: Westview Press.

Siné, A. 2006. *L'ordre budgétaire: l'économie politique des dépenses de l'État*. Paris: Economica.

Sintomer, Y. 2007. *Le Pouvoir au peuple. Jurys citoyens, tirage au sort et démocratie participative*. Paris: La Découverte.

Siwek-Pouydesseau, J. 1996. 'Les syndicats de fonctionnaires', *Revue Française d'Administration Publique* 80: 609–20.

Smith, A. 1999. 'Public-policy analysis in contemporary France: academic approaches, questions and debates', *Public Administration* 77, 1: 111–31.

2005. 'The Europeanisation of the French state', in Cole, A., Le Galès, P. and Levy, J. (eds.) *Developments in French Politics 3*. Basingstoke: Palgrave, 105–21.

2006. 'Le Gouvernement de l'Union européenne et une France qui change', in Culpepper, Hall and Palier (eds.), 343–72.

Smith, P. 2006. *The French Senate*. Basingstoke: Palgrave.

Smith, T. 2004. *France in Crisis*. Cambridge: Cambridge University Press.

Steinmo, S. and Thelen, K. 1992. *Structuring Politics: Historical Institutionalism in Comparative Analysis*. Cambridge: Cambridge University Press.

Stevens, A. 2003. *The Government and Politics of France*. Basingstoke: Palgrave.

Stirn, B. and Oberdorff, H. 2004. 'Le juge administratif français dans un environnement européen', in Lukaszewicz, B. and Oberdorff, H. (eds.) *Le Juge administratif et l'Europe: le dialogue des juges*. Grenoble: Presses Universitaires de Grenoble.

Stone, A. 1992. *The Birth of Judicial Politics in France: The Constitutional Council in Comparative Perspective*. Oxford: Oxford University Press.

Stone, C. 1989. *Regime Politics, Governing Atlanta, 1946–1988*. Lawrence: University Press of Kansas.

Strudel, S. 2007. 'Nicolas Sarkozy: Rupture tranquille ou syncrétisme tourmenté?', *Revue Française de Science Politique* 57, 3–4: 459–74.

Suleiman, E. N. 1974. *Politics, Power and Bureaucracy in France*. Princeton: Princeton University Press.

1978. *Elites in French Society: The Politics of Survival*. Princeton: Princeton University Press.

Surel, Y. 2000a. 'The role of cognitive and normative frames in policymaking', *Journal of European Public Policy* 7, 4: 495–512.

2000b. 'L'intégration européenne vue par l'approche cognitive et normative des politiques publiques', *Revue Française de Science Politique* 50, 2: 235–55.

Taiclet, A. F. 2007. 'Le développement économique territorial au regard des hypothèses de la gouvernance territoriale', in Pasquier, Simoulin and Weisbein (eds.), 109–27.

Taylor-Goodby, R. 1999. 'Policy change at a time of retrenchment: recent pension reform in France, Germany, Italy and the UK', *Social Policy and Administration* 33, 1: 1–18.

Thatcher, M. 1997. 'L'Impact de la Communauté européenne sur la règlementation nationale: les services publiques en France et en Grande-Bretagne', *Politiques et Management Public* 15, 3: 141–68.

1999. *The Politics of Telecommunications. National Institutions, Convergence, and Change in Britain and France*. Oxford: Oxford University Press.

Thœnig, J.-C. 1973. *L'Ere des technocrates*. Paris: Editions de l'Organisation.

Thuriot, F. 2004. *L'Offre artisitique et patrimoniale en Région. Proximité et rayonnement culturels*. Paris: L'Harmattan.

Todd, E. 1988. *La Nouvelle France*. Paris: Seuil.

1995. 'Aux origines du malaise politique française. Les classes sociales et leur représentation', *Le Débat*, 83: 98–120.

Touraine, A. 1994. 'On the frontier of social movements', *Current Sociology* 52, 4: 717–25.

Vallement, S. 2004. 'L'Expérience du ministère de l'Équipement', *Administration et Education* 4: 29–36.

Van Zanten, A. 2004. *Les Politiques de l'Education*. Paris: PUF.

2006. 'La Construction des politiques de l'éducation. De la centralisation à la délégation au local', in Culpepper, Hall and Palier (eds.), 229–63.

Wasserman, S. and Faust, K. 1994. *Social Network Analysis*. Cambridge: Cambridge University Press.

Wasserman, S. and Galaskiewicz, J. 1994. *Advances in Social Network Analysis*. London: Sage.

Waters, S. 2003. *New Social Movements in France*. Basingstoke: Palgrave.

Weaver, R. K. 1988. *Automatic Government: The Politics of Indexation*. Washington: Brookings Institution Press.

Webber, D. (ed.) 1999. *The Franco-German Relationship in the European Union*. London: Routledge.

Wieviorka, M. (ed.) 1997. *Une société fragmentée? Le multiculturalisme en débat*. Paris: La Découverte.

Williams, P. M. 1964. *Crisis and Compromise: Politics in the Fourth Republic*. London: Longman.

1969. *The French Parliament*. London: Longman.

Wolfreys, J. 2003. 'Beyond the mainstream; *la gauche de la gauche*', in Evans, J. (ed.) *The French Party System*. Manchester: Manchester University Press, 91–104.

Woll, C. 2006. 'La réforme du MEDEF: chronique des difficultés de l'action collective patronale', *Revue Française de Science Politique* 56, 2: 255–79.

Worms, J.-P. 1966. 'Le Prefet et ses notables', *Sociologie du Travail*, 8, 3: 20–44.

Wright, V. 1978. *The Government and Politics of France*. London: Unwin Hyman.

1996. 'The national co-ordination of European policy-making: negotiating the quagmire', in Richardson, J. (ed.) *European Union: Power and Policy-Making*. London: Routledge, 148–69.

2000. 'The Fifth Republic: from the *Droit de l'État* to the *État de droit?*', in Elgie (ed.), 92–119.

Wright, V. and Cassese, S. (eds.) 1996. *La recomposition de l'Etat en Europe*. Paris: La Découverte.

Zeller, A. and Stussi, P. 2002. *La France enfin forte de ses Régions*. Paris: Gualino.

Index

academic inspectorates 58
acquis communautaire 93
action sociology school 168
action system 54, 148
adaptation (to Europe) 87, 97
adjoints 71
adjusting (to Europe) 97
administrative corps 142
administrative law 4, 37, 99, 106
administrative tribunals 98, 211
advisory committees 69
advocacy coalition framework
    174, 204
AERES 34, 37
aerospace 171
AFFSA 33
AFIFT 33
AFPA 154
agencies 3, 20, 32, 33, 36, 50, 51, 106,
    136, 167, 197, 198, 201, 207
agency 2
AGF 117
Agir Chômage 161
Agricultural ministry 181, 182, 183
agriculture 96, 103, 164, 171, 172
AII 33
Air France–KLM 117
air transport 106
Airbus 192
Alcan 119
Allègre, Claude 40, 41
Alsace 59, 74, 77, 91, 198
Alstom 118, 188
altermondialisme, 160, 161
aménagement du territoire 62, 118
Americanisation 177
Amiens 72
Amsterdam summit (1997) 94
Amsterdam treaty (1997) 92, 102, 107
ANCS 33

Anglo-Saxon neo-liberalism 125, 177
Anglo-Saxon pension funds 118
annual budgets 51
annual list of operations 156
ANR 33
ANRU 33, 65, 66
anti-globalisation movements, 160
anti-nuclear movements 160
anti-racism 160
appellation d'origine 142
apprenticeships 154, 157
appropriate behaviour 2, 31, 178,
    180, 193
Arcelor 188
Archer, Mary 129, 131
architects 69
ARF 67
ARH 34, 37, 38
Armées 2000 179
army 48, 49, 163
ART 33, 106
article 1 (1958 Constitution) 59
article 72 (1958 Constitution) 59
associations 6, 13, 37, 130, 140, 152,
    153, 158, 159, 160, 162, 163,
    199, 202, 204, 212
associations law (1901) 139
ATTAC 109, 110, 111, 160, 177
Aubry, Martine 126
Audit Commission 50
audits 32, 34
Austria 140, 206
automatic government 35
autonomists 77, 78

Balladur, Edouard 43, 125
Bank of France 115
banking 164
banking sector 164
Barcelona summit (2002) 106

Basque country, 77
Basque language 77
Baumgartner, Frank 140
Belgium, 76, 208
beliefs 128, 178
benchmarking 15, 30
Berlusconi, Silvio 187
best practice 15, 107, 189
Beveridge model 123, 203
Bézès, Philip 6
Bismarckian model 123, 203
Blair, Tony 94, 184, 185, 187, 188,
    189, 191
blame avoidance 88
blocks of competencies 56
BNP 119
Bolkestein services directive 107,
    109, 166
Bologna process 135
Bonduelle, Bruno 72
BOP 45
Bordeaux 69
Borloo, Jean-Louis 66
bouclier fiscal 187
Bouygues 117
Bové, José 160, 161, 177
Breton cultural movements 83
Breton Democratic Union 83
Breton identities 78, 83
Breton language 77, 81
Britain 90, 92, 105, 131
British policy networks tradition 153
Brittany 38, 39, 59, 70, 77, 78, 79, 80,
    84, 101, 146, 153
Brussels 29, 73, 74, 91, 94, 104, 164,
    166, 197, 198
Brussels summit (2007) 188
budget division 43, 44
budgetary autonomy 50
budgetary policy instruments 44
budgetary reform, 26, 43,
    46, 197
bureaucracy 3, 10, 30, 178
bureaucratic inertia 130
bureaucratic networks 148
business community 130, 151, 152,
    167, 185, 199

cabinets 6, 42
CAC 40 118

CADA 32
Caisse des dépôts et de consignations
    63, 66
caisses 37, 122
CAP 90, 91, 93, 94
capitalism without capital 115
CAR 63
Carrefour 117
Catholic Church 2
Catholic schools 162
CCF 117
central government 55, 64, 151
central steering, 41, 52
centralisation 27, 28, 64, 128, 129
Centre for the Sociology of
    Organisations 145
centre-periphery relations 53, 54
centres de responsabilité 30
CFDT 141
CFTC 141
CGC 141
CGPME 146
CGT 141, 162
Chambers of Commerce 71, 152,
    155, 199
Channel tunnel rail link 72, 152
Charter for Public Services 30
Charter of Fundamental Rights 107
chartes culturels 38
chef d'état major (chief of staff) 49
Chevènement, Jean-Pierre 193
Chevènement law (1999) 58
China 120
Chirac, Jacques 92, 97, 120, 193
church 143, 158
CIACT 65
CIC 117
cities 91, 149, 152, 167, 199
citizens' juries 19, 186, 197
citizenship 55, 159, 160, 162,
    166, 184
city communities 58
city contract 132, 133, 207
CIVC 142
civic forums 19
civil servants 3, 26, 30, 124, 148,
    178, 200
civil service 29, 121
civil service code 180
classical liberalism 116

CMU 124, 200
CNE 34, 126
CNIL 32
CNPF 121
COB 32
cognitive and normative matrix 175
cognitive and normative school 168, 169, 173
collective bargaining 21, 141, 207
collèges 58, 129, 131, 155
Cologne summit (1999) 95
co-management 164, 169
comitology 91
Commission (European) 74
  see also European Commission
common foreign and security policy 61, 93
communes 9, 39, 53, 55, 56, 59, 61, 68, 69
Communist Party 54
  see also PCF
communities of communes 58
compensation state 21
compulsory membership (of groups) 140
concession 37
conseils de quartiers 75, 197
constitution (1958) 50, 98
  article 1 58
  article 72 59
Constitutional council 5, 7, 8, 9, 44, 77, 92, 98, 102
constructivist school 168, 177, 206
consultants 69
contingent governance 213
contract of objectives 38
contracts 51, 65
contractualisation 26, 30, 36, 38, 39, 40, 41, 42, 50, 51, 181, 198, 211
contrats d'agglomeration 38
contrats de pays 38
coordination 1, 12, 90
Copé, Jean-François 32
corporatism (neo-) 124, 128, 140, 144
corporatist model 139, 140, 144
corporatist welfare states 123, 128
corps 27, 53, 148, 178, 180
corps des mines 148
corps intermediaries 28
Corsica 8, 59, 77, 84

Corsican assembly 77
Council of Europe 13
Council of Ministers 6, 18, 66
Council of State 5, 7, 8, 32, 37, 60, 67, 77, 91, 92, 97, 98, 99, 100, 101, 107, 110, 118, 138
Court of Accounts 6, 32, 33, 37, 50
CPE 127
CPNT 104, 110
cross-regulation 53, 54, 62
Crozier, Michel 28, 64
CSA 32
CSG 123
CSO 53, 147
cultural services 10
culture 178
Culture ministry 42, 45, 46
cumul des mandats 54, 108, 110
customs division 49

Danone 118
DATAR 63, 65
Dati, Rachida 192
DDE 39, 40, 63, 66
de Gaulle, Charles 92, 93, 189
Debré law (1959) 161
decentralisation 18, 23, 27, 31, 52, 55, 62, 64, 70, 71, 74, 84, 85, 132, 135, 153, 167, 186, 196, 205
decentralisation reforms (1982−3) 55, 74, 83
decentralisation reforms (2003−4)
  constitutional reform, 17 March 2003 58, 59
  law of 2 March 2003 (local referendums) 58
  law of 29 July 2004 (local government finances) 58, 67
  law of 13 August 2004 (transfer of competencies) 58, 59, 207
defence 13
Defence ministry 46, 48, 49, 177
Delanoë, Bertrand 70
delegated administrative powers 129
democracy 19, 75, 160, 173, 186, 212
democratic deficit 102, 166
democratic deliberation 19, 20
democratic fora 186
democratic institutions 194
Denmark 92

départements 39, 42, 53, 55, 56, 57,
    58, 59, 60, 61, 68, 155
departmentalists 55, 60
deregulation 21
Désirs d'avenir 185
DGCP 49, 179
DGI 49, 179
DIACT 63, 65, 74
directives 1, 100, 101, 164
dirigisme/dirigiste 28, 115, 116, 118,
    119, 122, 163, 204, 210
discursive coalitions 114
divisions 180
D-Mark 104, 105
doctors 143
Doha round of WTO talks 120, 166
Durkheim, E. 28, 172
Duverger, Maurice 4

EADS 188
ECB 20, 95, 105, 112, 198, 209
ECOFIN 96
economic and monetary union *see*
    EMU
economic development 18, 56, 60, 149,
    151, 202
economic government 95, 114, 136,
    204, 209
economic liberalisation 122
economic patriotism 118, 119, 202
economic policy 174, 202, 204, 205
economists 69, 174
economy 13, 136, 180, 204, 209
EDF 125
EDF-GDF 106
education 9, 18, 32, 57, 60, 85, 114,
    122, 128, 136, 143, 153, 154,
    167, 200, 201, 202, 204, 205, 213
education ministers 40
Education ministry 32, 34, 39, 40, 41,
    42, 45, 46, 48, 51, 58, 129, 130,
    132, 143, 144, 145, 155, 179,
    181, 182, 183
education officials 129
Education Priority Zones *see zones
    d'éducation prioritaires*
electronic democracy 19
Elf-Aquitaine 117
elites 5, 26, 28, 121
Élysée palace 7, 100, 190

employers 140, 144, 145, 146, 153
employers' associations 38, 58, 71,
    145, 203
employment policy 94, 125, 126, 153
EMU 93, 95, 104, 105, 107, 116,
    122, 209
ENA 28
energy policy 142
enlargement 90
environment 56
EPCI 56, 58, 61, 69, 75
EPIC 66
EPR 63
EPSC 133
Epstein, Renaud 65
ERASMUS 135
Esping-Andersen, Gosta 123
état civil 30
ethnic identity 2, 76
EU competition policy 9, 33, 99,
    105, 106
EU Constitutional treaty (draft)
    see Lisbon treaty (2008)
EU law 100, 102
Euralille 72, 73, 152
euro 36, 95, 116
eurobarometer 89
European Central Bank *see* ECB
European Charter of Fundamental
    Rights 165
European Charter of Minority
    Languages 99
european civil service 17
European Commission 17, 20, 94,
    96, 101, 108, 116, 118,
    165, 198
European Council 91, 92, 93
European Court of Human Rights 9,
    13, 98
European Court of Justice 9, 20, 97,
    98, 101, 112, 198
European integration 51, 87, 88, 89,
    92, 104, 136, 167, 170, 176, 177,
    184, 185, 196
European parliament 92, 93, 103,
    104, 108
European political parties 103
European social forum 110
European social model 94
European sociology 172

European structural funds 17, 59, 91
European Union 17, 18, 22, 87, 89,
    90, 105
Europeanisation 23, 27, 51, 87, 88, 91,
    104, 110, 111, 120, 134, 165,
    166, 205
Eurosceptical movements 110, 111
eurozone 105
evaluation 30, 37
expertise 39, 69, 76, 166, 203,
    204, 213

Fabius, Laurent 186
family allowances 122
family policy 122
FCPE 131
federalism 56, 89, 208
FEEP 131
field services 10, 30, 31, 38, 39, 41, 42,
    43, 66, 68, 153, 181, 182, 183
Fifth Republic 4, 36, 44, 102
Fillon, François 191
Finance committee (National
    Assembly) 44
Finance ministers 96, 105
Finance ministry 32, 43, 46, 47, 48,
    117, 156, 204
financial inspectorate 6
firefighting 9
firms 37, 103, 115, 117, 119, 121, 145,
    155, 167, 199
first employment contract *see* CPE
Flanders 77
FNSEA 141
Force Ouvrière 122, 141, 179
Forrester, V. 177
Foucault, Michel 35, 169
France Télécom 118, 180
Franco-German relationship 89, 93, 94
French administration 32
French business 116
French capitalism 116, 117
French Catalonia 77
French culture 177
French economy 28, 43, 115
French left 177, 184, 185
French legal system 3
French model 139, 177, 193, 206, 210
French National Assembly 44
French political culture 29

French polity 210
French public law tradition 22
French regulation school 16
French Revolution 53, 138
French social model 109, 111, 122,
    125, 128, 203, 204
French socialists 89, 184
    see also PS
French state tradition 58, 128
French-style corporatism 154
Friedberg, Erhard 54, 145, 147, 148
Front national 109, 110
functionalism 202
funeral parlours 9

GAN 117
Garton Ash, Timothy 188
GATT 120
Gaullism 177, 189
GDF 117, 125, 188
gendarmerie 49
gender 161
general interest 138
general practitioners 143
General Secretariat of the Government
    (SGG) 7, 101
General Secretary of the Elysée 7, 190
German *Länder* 208
German unification 89
Germany 12, 17, 90, 93, 94, 95, 96,
    105, 108, 112, 113, 140, 174,
    175, 198, 199, 206, 207, 208, 209
Giscard d'Estaing, Valéry 92
global capitalism 116
global economy, 27, 54, 136, 204, 212
global governance 176
globalisation 21, 23, 27, 51, 112,
    116, 117, 119, 120, 126, 136,
    176, 177, 205, 209, 211
good governance 11
Gordon, Philip 119
governance misfit 207, 208
government departments 31, 47
Gramsci, Antonio 172, 175
grands corps 31, 142, 146, 167,
    202, 204
grands projets 121, 171
Greater Lille committee 72
Greece 96, 201
Griggs, Steven 173

Grossman, Emiliano 164
groups 138, 167
Growth and Stability Pact 95, 96, 201
Guéant, Claude 7, 190
Guiano, Henri 190

Habermas, Jürgen 19
Hall, Peter, 35
headscarf affair 159
health 56, 60, 122, 124, 143, 144
health insurance 122
Hegel, G. W. F. 28
hierarchies 16, 137
higher education 40, 64, 130, 157
Highways and Bridges *corps* 31, 144, 173
   see also Ponts et Chaussées
historical institutionalism 203
hollow state 24, 136, 137, 196, 200, 206, 208, 212
honeycomb state 54
housing 10
human rights 160
hyperchoix 193, 212
hypotheses 50, 52, 212

ideas 24, 211
identity 52, 172
IGAEN 32, 130
IGAS 32
IGEN 32, 130
IGPN 32
immigrants 161, 163
INAO 142
independent administrative authorities 32
industrial groups 145, 146
industrial patriotism 118
industrial policy 27, 105
industrial relations 21, 144
industry ministry 148
inertia (Europeanisation) 87, 110
Infrastructure ministry 31, 39, 40, 42, 62, 69, 181, 182, 183
inspectorates 32
inspectors 131
institutions 128, 165, 167, 178, 194, 195, 211, 213
instrumentalised governance 23

instruments 30, 35, 37
intellectual property 120
inter-communal bodies 56, 68, 70
interest groups 53, 210
interests 24, 35, 128, 129, 138, 139, 175, 195, 202, 206, 211, 213
Interior ministry 31, 46, 49
International Monetary Fund 13
international political economy 110, 112, 136, 200, 210
international relations 13
interviews 41, 42, 46
Ireland 92
Islam 159
issue networks 147
Italy 76, 96, 107, 112, 120, 174, 175, 198, 201, 208, 209

Jacobins 28
Jessop, Robert 14, 200
Jeunesse agricole chrétienne 173
Jobert, Bruno 62, 143, 169, 173, 209
Jospin, Lionel 30, 40, 43, 75, 94, 96, 117, 120, 162, 179, 184, 185, 193
Juppé, Alain 30, 43, 124, 125, 178
Justice ministry 45, 48

Keynesian welfare state 14, 176, 198, 200
Keynesianism 174, 212
Kouchner, Bernard 191

labour flexibility 94, 126
Labour ministry 154
labour movement 160
laïcité 184
language rights 78
large cities 54
Lascoumes, Pierre 35
lawyers 69
Le Galès, Patrick 1, 35
Leca, Jean 1
levels 16, 50, 55
Levy, Jonah 29, 118, 122
lifelong learning 154, 157
Lille 62, 69, 72, 73, 151, 152, 199
Lille Academy 41
Lisbon summit (2000) 95
Lisbon treaty (2008) 102

local authorities 6, 29, 36, 51, 53, 55, 56, 60, 62, 68, 69, 71, 72, 85, 132, 136, 153, 159, 162, 164, 167, 183, 198
local authority spending 21
local governance 23, 69, 182
local government 5, 9, 10, 23, 68, 182
local plans 39
local politicians 54, 70
local referenda 19, 186, 197
local security contracts 132
local taxation 61
localities 64, 68
loi le Chapelier 138
LOLF 44, 45, 46, 47, 48, 49, 50, 51, 183, 201
L'Oréal 117
Luxembourg summit (1997) 94
lycées 58, 129, 130, 131, 155, 156
Lyons 69

Maastricht referendum (1992) 108, 111
Maastricht treaty 89, 92, 95, 102
maisons des services publics 30
managed globalisation 120
March, James 178
markets 14, 16, 137, 184, 210
Marseilles 69
Martinon, David 190
Marxism 184
Masstricht convergence criteria 43
Matginon process (2001) 77
Mauroy report 75
May '68 55, 130, 134, 212
mayors 54, 70, 75, 163, 199
MEDEF 119, 141, 145, 146, 153, 162, 164
médiateurs 169, 172, 173
medical profession 143
Mediterranean welfare states 123
Meny, Yves 138
meso-level of public administration 63
metropolitanisation 68
Meunier, Sophie 119
minimal welfare states 123
ministries 45, 180
minority nationalists 76
missions (LOLF) 45, 49
Mittal 119, 188

Mitterrand, François 89, 92, 161
mixed economy societies 71, 73, 199
model of territorial administration 27, 53, 196
mondialisation maîtrisée 119, 120
monetary policy 35
monetary union 104
   see also EMU
monitoring 189, 197, 201
Montesquieu, Charles de Secondat, baron de 28
Moreno scale 79
Mouvement pour la France (MPF) 104
Mouvement Républicain et Citoyen (MRC) 104
Muller, Pierre 62, 143, 168, 169, 172, 173, 175, 212
multi-actor coordination/ multi-actorness 16, 24, 50, 52, 68, 85, 139, 167, 168, 196, 198, 199, 210, 212
multi-level analysis 17
multi-level dynamics 24, 52, 68, 73, 85, 136, 139, 168, 196, 198, 205, 210, 212
multi-level governance 17, 165, 166, 198
multi-level government 17
Municipal Reform Act (1884) 9
municipalities 55
Muslim community 159

Nantes 69
Napoleon I 3, 179
Napoleonic 3, 208
Napoleonic model 53
National Assembly 8, 47, 102, 102
National Assembly finance committee 44
national champions 106, 115, 117
national educational traditions 128
national interest 91, 93
neo-corporatist policy style 206
neo-liberal 35, 36, 44
neo-liberalism 14, 15, 177, 209
Netherlands 12
networked governance 139, 166
networks 1, 15, 16, 27, 35, 50, 114, 137, 144, 145, 146, 149, 152, 154, 163, 167, 181, 183, 199, 201, 202, 210

new employment contract (CNE)
    127
new institutionalist tradition 2,
    180, 182
new social movements 103, 159, 160,
    161, 164, 212
New Zealand 15
NHS 124
Nice treaty (2000) 120
Nissan 117
Nord/Pas-de-Calais 64, 70, 144, 153
Normandy 59, 77
norms 16, 29
notables 54, 148
Novartis 188
NPM 34, 35, 47, 50, 67
nuclear energy 166, 171
NUTS regions 205

Occitan 77
Occitania 77
Old-age pensions 122, 124
Olsen, Mancur 178
ombudsman 32
One and Indivisible Republic 53
OPCA 145, 146, 157
open method of coordination 36, 95,
    108, 176
ordonnance of 1959 44, 46, 47
Ordre des Médecins 142
Ordre des Pharmaciens 142
organisations 2, 50, 146, 153, 178

Page, Edward 208
Palier, Bruno 128, 213
paradigm shift 14
Pareto-efficient formulae 22
Paribas 117, 119
Paris red belt 163
Paris region 54
Paris stock exchange 115, 117
parliament 5
participation 19, 160, 186,
    211, 212
participatory governance 19, 52, 139,
    194, 205, 207
partnerships 65, 71, 199, 211
Party of European Socialists 104
party politics 6, 54, 90, 163
party system 76, 103, 160

path dependent 93, 152, 203, 213
pay as you go 124
PCF 109, 163
Pechiney 117
Pécresse, Valérie 134
performance indicators 20, 30, 33, 34,
    37, 40, 44, 47, 48, 50, 51, 197,
    201, 207
permanent representation 91, 98
Picq report (1994) 26, 44
Pierson, Paul 209
planning 115
planning commissariat 170
pluralist model 139, 147, 159, 196
Poitiers 69
Poitou-Charentes 60, 185, 186
police 49, 163
policy communities/policy community
    19, 62, 129, 144, 147, 154, 155,
    171, 174, 203, 209, 213
policy fora 174
policy implementation 140
policy instruments 12, 20, 33, 35, 175,
    197, 201, 205
policy networks 12, 91, 145, 146,
    147, 148, 149, 173,
    174, 182
policy sectors 15, 18, 114, 136, 147,
    171, 174, 175, 200, 202, 203,
    204, 212
policy transfer 88
policy-orientated learning 181
political culture 171, 211
political economy 14, 24, 50, 200
political institutions 2, 24,
    46, 195
political leadership 4, 68, 70, 88
political parties 29, 53, 103, 104, 160,
    168, 193, 194
Ponts et Chaussées 5, 62
Portugal 96
positive discrimination 189
postal services 107
PRDF 39, 154
prefectoral corps
prefects 5, 31, 53, 54, 66
president 5, 192
presidential election (2007) 104, 177
presidentialisation (under Sarkozy)
    189–92

presidents of regional councils 61
prime minister 5, 6, 7, 43, 65, 67,
    100, 191
private government 144
private interests 199
private sphere 158
privatisation 12, 13, 116
procedural governance 23
professional branches 155
professional groups 139, 140, 144
professional orders 142
professional roles 171, 188
professions 38, 123, 138, 139, 143,
    147, 153, 154, 167, 171, 176, 178
programme directors (LOLF) 45,
    48, 49
programmes (LOLF) 45, 47
projet d'établissement 131
projet socialiste (2006) 131, 186
projets de services 30
property developers 69
protectionism 116
proximity 55, 64, 74
PS 104, 109, 111, 131, 159, 161,
    186, 191
public administration 6, 13, 47, 48, 206
public corporations 142
public enquiries
public expenditure 50
public forums 69
public health 10
public law 3, 10, 16, 37
public schools 161
public sector 121, 142
public sector monopolies 106
public sector unions 180
public sector workers 179, 180
public service 36, 106, 125, 143
public service mission 14, 178
public services 4, 9, 10, 105, 141
public sphere 19, 158, 166
public–private partnerships 71
public–private sphere 72, 152, 199

QMV 97, 120

Raffarin, Jean-Pierre 30, 58, 60, 158,
    178, 211
rail service 56, 107
rational choice 20, 178

RATP 125
Reagan, Ronald 187
realm of discourse 206
rectorates 155, 182
rectors 42, 58, 156
referendum on the draft constitutional
    treaty (2005) 104, 108
référentiel 26, 121, 138, 169, 170,
    171, 172, 173, 174, 175, 176,
    204, 206
reform of the state 26, 29, 31
regional authorities 29, 31, 56, 59, 61,
    69, 71, 85, 130, 132, 136, 153,
    155, 164, 198
regional councils 38, 55, 56, 58, 60,
    63, 64, 68, 70, 153, 155,
    156, 157
regional election (2004) 60
regional hospital agencies 38, 201
regional prefectures 63, 64, 74, 151,
    153, 156
regional presidents 65, 67
regional public sphere 153, 182
regionalisation 77
regionalists 55, 60
regions 53, 64, 68, 70, 74, 77, 91, 154,
    155, 158, 167
regulation 11, 16, 27, 212
regulatory governance 22, 38, 50,
    85, 207
regulatory regime 165
regulatory state 18, 19, 35, 36, 197,
    198, 205, 207, 212
rejection (of European integration) 87
religion 2
Renault 117
Rennes 69, 70, 73, 151, 152, 199
representative democracy 19, 178
Republic 184
republican corporatism 143
republican model/tradition 28, 60, 76,
    77, 158, 159
republican political institutions
    143, 206
republicanism 10, 160
research and development 132
resistance (to European integration) 87
Revolutionary Communist League
    (LCR) 161
Richard report 61

Richter, Laurent 36
RMI/RMA 56, 60, 123, 200
Rocard programme 30, 43
Rome treaty (1957) 188
Royal, Ségolène 126, 185, 186, 190,
    193, 194, 209
rules 16

Sanofi-Aventis 188
Sarkozy, Nicolas 4, 7, 90, 92, 95, 105,
    117, 134, 177, 185, 186, 187,
    188, 189, 190, 191, 192, 193,
    194, 209, 212
Sautter, Christian 49, 179
Savoy 59, 77
Scandinavia 140, 206
Schnapper, Dominique 208
Schumpeterian workfare state 14, 200
Scotland 208
secondary education 56, 64, 132,
    154, 157
sector *see* policy sectors
sectoral corporatism 169, 203
SEM *see* mixed economy societies
Senate 60, 75, 192
services votés 44, 45, 50
SGAE 74, 91, 100, 101
SGAR 74, 151
Shanghai table 134
Single European Act 89, 92, 93, 106,
    108, 164
single market 93, 116
SIVOM 56
SIVU 56
SNCF 99, 124, 125, 179
SNECMA 117
SNES 131
Social Affairs ministry 66, 143
social anesthesia state 29
social capital 163
social expenditure 127
social market economy 15, 210
social movements 196
social partners 6, 38, 122, 123, 124,
    140, 141, 144, 145, 153, 157,
    167, 201
social partnership 122, 128, 137, 139,
    140, 144, 145, 146, 153, 166,
    167, 176
social policy 123, 125, 127, 200, 201

social protection 27, 122, 125, 128
social security 6, 9, 37, 51, 122
social state 143
social welfare 60, 122, 140, 144
social-democratic parties 185
Socialist government (1981–6) 55
Socialist Party 55, 104, 126, 160,
    184, 186
    see also French Socialists, PS
Société générale 119
sociological institutionalism 178, 183
sociometric network mapping 149
soft law 20, 99, 108
sovereignty 13, 88, 209
Spain 76, 84, 90, 91, 112, 198, 208
Spanish autonomous communities 208
special regimes (pensions) 125
special statute 59
Stability Pact 95
standard-setting 20
state 26, 29, 51
state aids 116, 118
state capacity 14, 20, 25, 29, 136, 137,
    139, 167, 185, 196, 200, 208, 212
state capacity-building 50, 85, 193
state capitalism 116
state corporatism 62, 141, 144, 166,
    167, 196
state field services
state interventionism 121
state productivity 32, 46, 189
state reform 52
state-centric model 26, 27, 28, 29, 62,
    103, 115, 163, 177, 200, 205
state–group relations 103, 208
state–region plans 36, 38, 39, 64, 65,
    132, 153
state–society relations 139, 158
steering 12, 67
Strasbourg 104
Strauss-Kahn, Dominique 186
strong state 1, 26, 28, 29
structural funds 36, 74, 91
structure 1
structure plans 39
students 134
sub-national governance 56, 61, 62,
    70, 84, 208
sub-national politics 23
subsidiarity 17, 89

SUD 179
Suez 117, 134, 188
Suleiman, Ezra 28
Sweden 208

target-setting 189, 201
targets 207
tax collection 48
taxation 9, 187
teachers 143
teaching profession 131
teaching unions 179
technical state 143, 151
territorial capacity building 52
territorial coordination 85
territorial governance 76
territorial mobilisation 84
territorial politics 51
territorial state 151
territory 2
Thatcher, Margaret 21, 187, 188
thin universalism 159
think tanks 69
Third Republic 138
thirty-five-hour week 96, 126, 185,
    186, 211
Thœnig, Jean-Claude 173
Tocqueville, Alexis de 28
TOS 154
Touraine, Alain 160
trade negotiations 120
trade unions 38, 58, 121, 123, 140,
    141, 144, 145, 146, 153, 155,
    179, 203, 211
training 56, 58, 60, 122, 144, 145, 146,
    153, 154, 155, 156, 157, 167,
    189, 201
Training Act (1971) 144
Training Act (1993) 31, 38, 156
training levy 144, 145
training plans 144
transport 56, 60, 64, 86
trésor 95
trust 152
two-level bargaining 94, 166

UK 12, 15, 76, 90, 108, 112, 174, 175,
    188, 198, 199, 207, 208, 209
UMP 67, 104, 111, 159, 189, 191
unemployment insurance 122
UNICE 164

unitary state 52, 53, 59, 76, 84
United Kingdom *see* UK
United Nations 13
universal welfare states 123
universities 133, 135
university 2000 plan 64, 132, 154
university autonomy 133, 134,
    189, 192
UNPI 165
untidy reality 161, 162
UPA 146
urban communities 69
urban governance 72
urban planners 69
urban policy 142
urban regime theory 73, 85
urban riots (November 2005) 70, 162
urban transport 9
US 15, 22, 209
US community power tradition 149
US public policy 165
u-turn (1983) 118

varieties of capitalism 15
Villeneuve d'Ascq 63
Villepin, Dominique 61, 63, 65, 118,
    119, 127, 193
vocational education 155
voluntary associations *see* associations
Voynet law (1999) 58

waste management 9
water 9
Weber, Max 3, 27, 35
welfare (general) 13, 14, 18, 114, 122,
    136, 166, 167, 200, 201, 202,
    204, 205, 209, 213
welfare benefits 189
welfare state 14, 21, 27, 86,
    123, 127
White Paper on financial services 164
White Paper on governance 17
women's rights 160
World Bank 13
world economy 116
World Trade Organization 13, 119,
    120, 166, 207

Yade, Rama 192

zones d'éducation prioritaires 133, 161